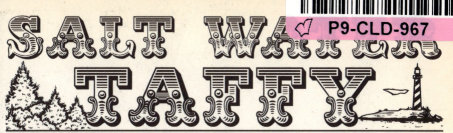

SALT WATER TAFFY

⌒ THE SEASIDE ADVENTURES OF ⌒

JACK AND BENNY

⌒ IN ⌒

THE TRUTH ABOUT DR. TRUE

Written & Illustrated by

MATTHEW LOUX

Lettered by DOUGLAS E. SHERWOOD
Design by MATTHEW LOUX, KEITH WOOD & STEVEN BIRCH
Edited by RANDAL C. JARRELL

Published by Oni Press, Inc.
JOE NOZEMACK, publisher
JAMES LUCAS JONES, editor in chief • RANDAL C. JARRELL, managing editor
CORY CASONI, sales & marketing • KEITH WOOD, art director
JILL BEATON, assistant editor • DOUGLAS E. SHERWOOD, production assistant

ONI PRESS, INC.
1305 SE MARTIN LUTHER KING JR. BLVD.
SUITE A
PORTLAND, OR 97214
USA

www.onipress.com • www.actionmatt.com

First edition: September 2009
ISBN-13: 978-1-934964-04-0

1 3 5 7 9 10 8 6 4 2

PRINTED IN CANADA.

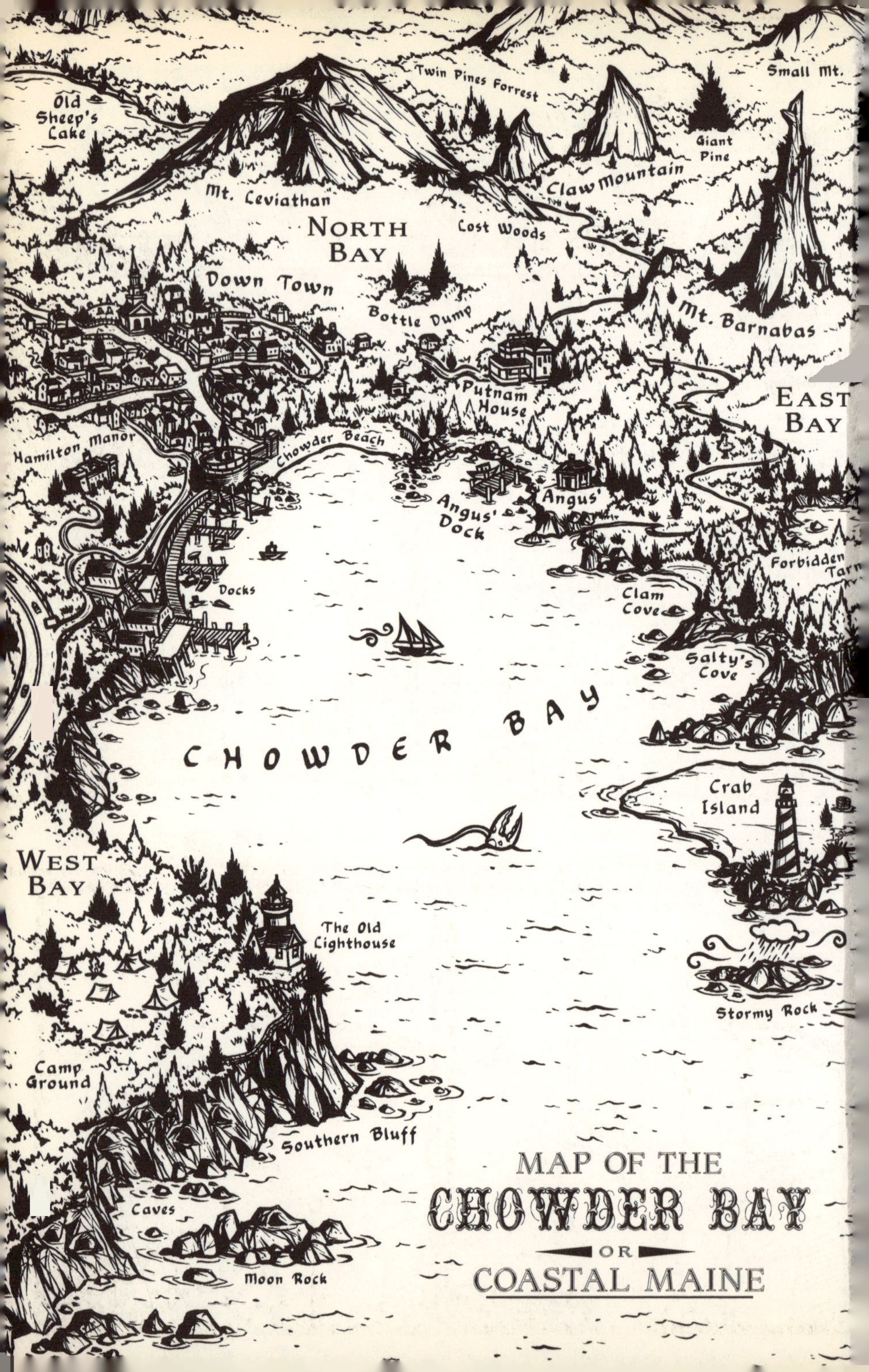
Old Sheep's Lake
Twin Pines Forrest
Small Mt.
Giant Pine
Claw Mountain
Mt. Leviathan
North Bay
Lost Woods
Down Town
Bottle Dump
Mt. Barnabas
Putnam House
East Bay
Hamilton Manor
Chowder Beach
Angus'
Angus' Dock
Docks
Forbidden Tarn
Clam Cove
Salty's Cove
CHOWDER BAY
Crab Island
West Bay
The Old Lighthouse
Stormy Rock
Camp Ground
Southern Bluff
Caves
Moon Rock

MAP OF THE CHOWDER BAY OR COASTAL MAINE

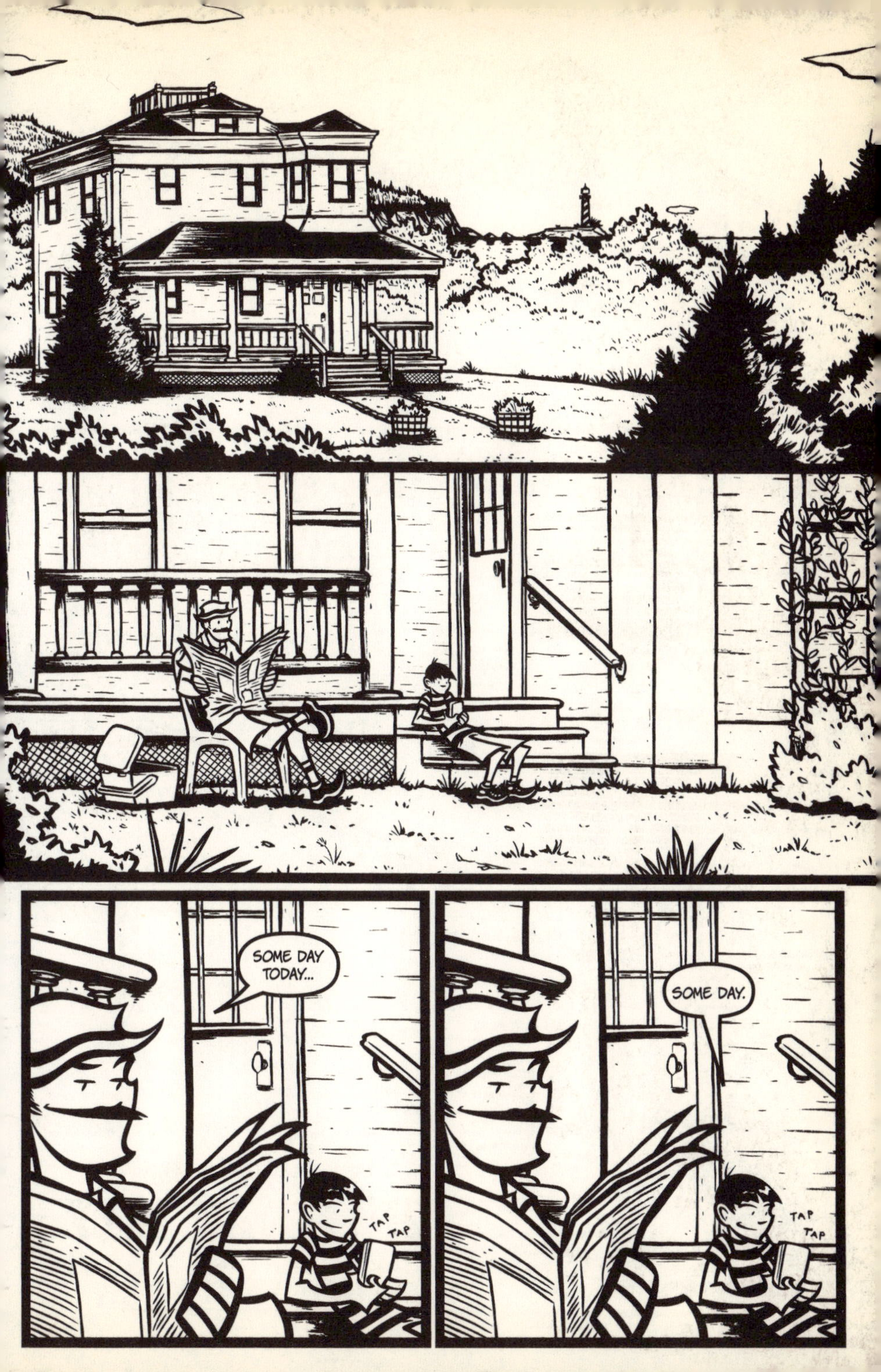
SOME DAY TODAY...
TAP TAP
SOME DAY.
TAP TAP

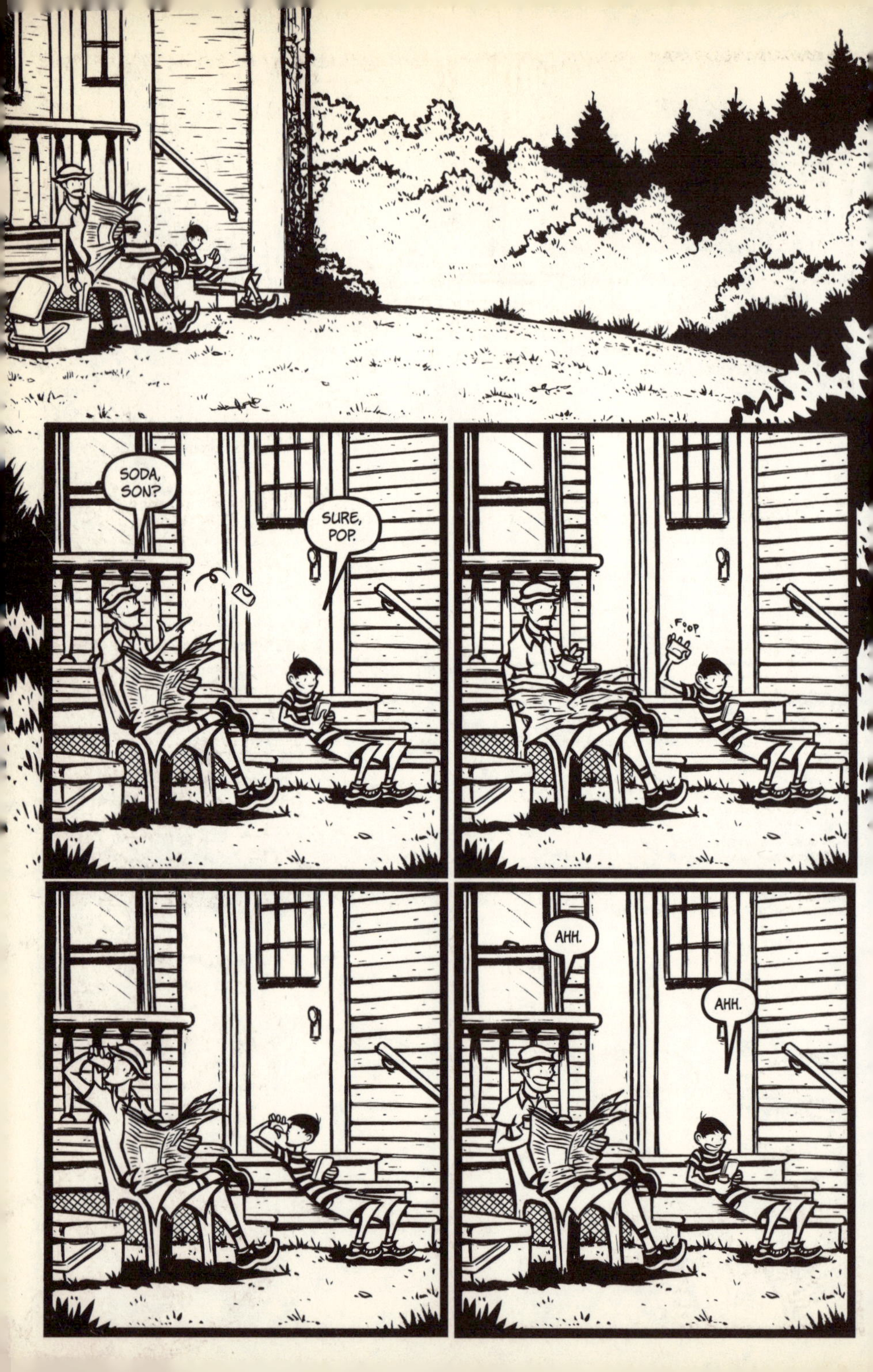
SODA, SON?
SURE, POP.
FOOP
AHH.
AHH.

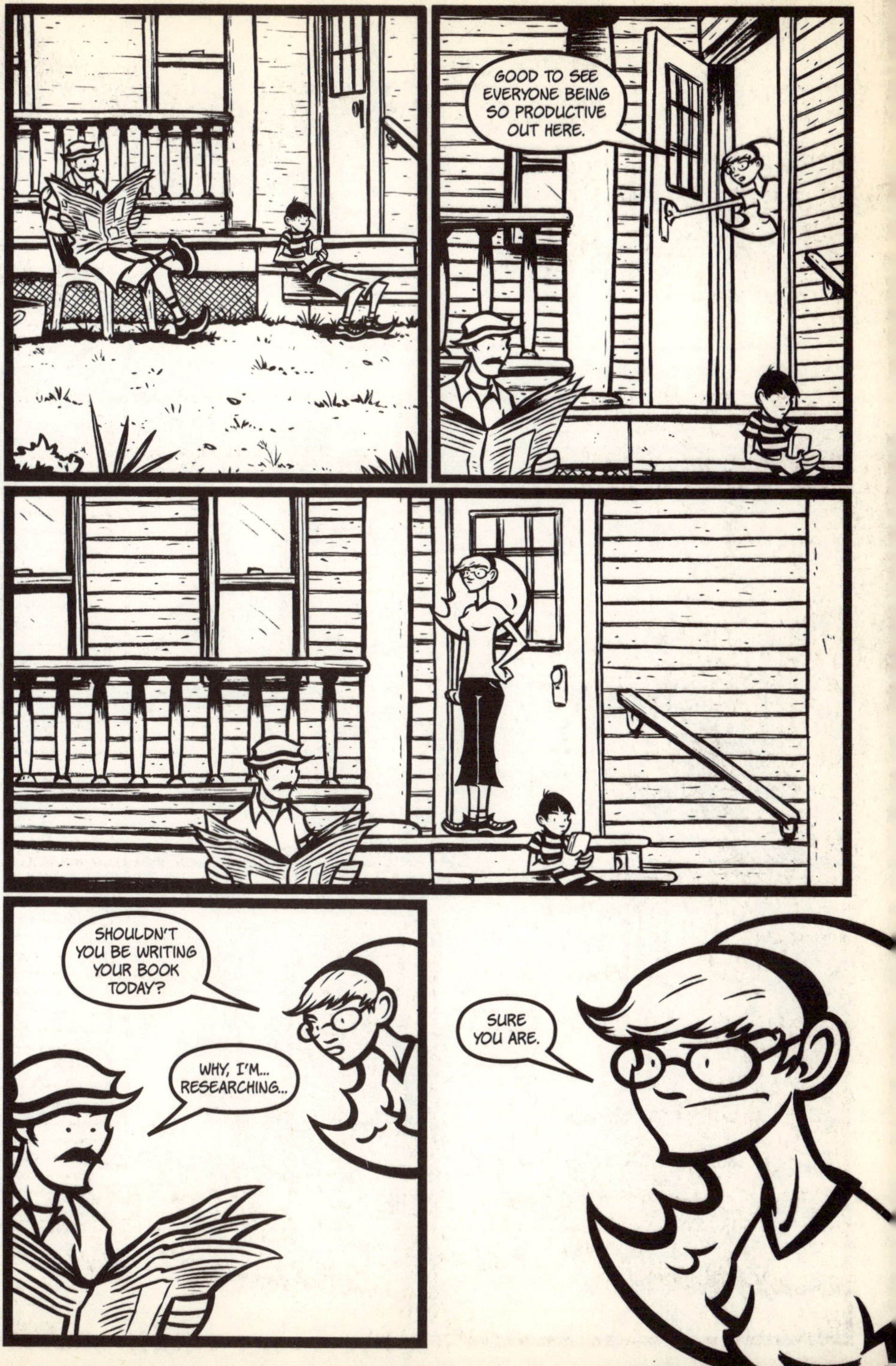
GOOD TO SEE EVERYONE BEING SO PRODUCTIVE OUT HERE.
SHOULDN'T YOU BE WRITING YOUR BOOK TODAY?
WHY, I'M... RESEARCHING...
SURE YOU ARE.

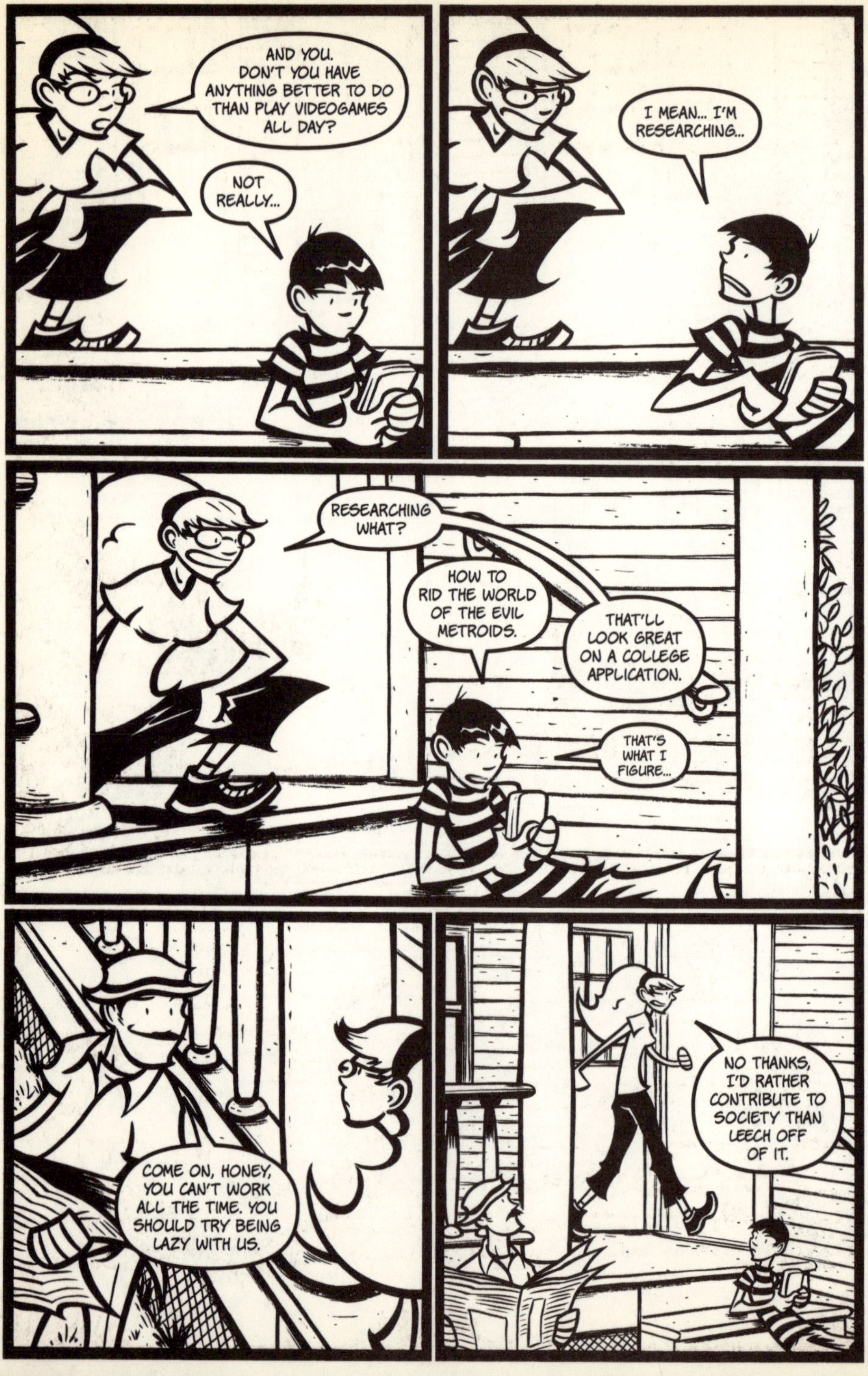
AND YOU. DON'T YOU HAVE ANYTHING BETTER TO DO THAN PLAY VIDEOGAMES ALL DAY?
NOT REALLY...
I MEAN... I'M RESEARCHING...
RESEARCHING WHAT?
HOW TO RID THE WORLD OF THE EVIL METROIDS.
THAT'LL LOOK GREAT ON A COLLEGE APPLICATION.
THAT'S WHAT I FIGURE...
COME ON, HONEY, YOU CAN'T WORK ALL THE TIME. YOU SHOULD TRY BEING LAZY WITH US.
NO THANKS, I'D RATHER CONTRIBUTE TO SOCIETY THAN LEECH OFF OF IT.

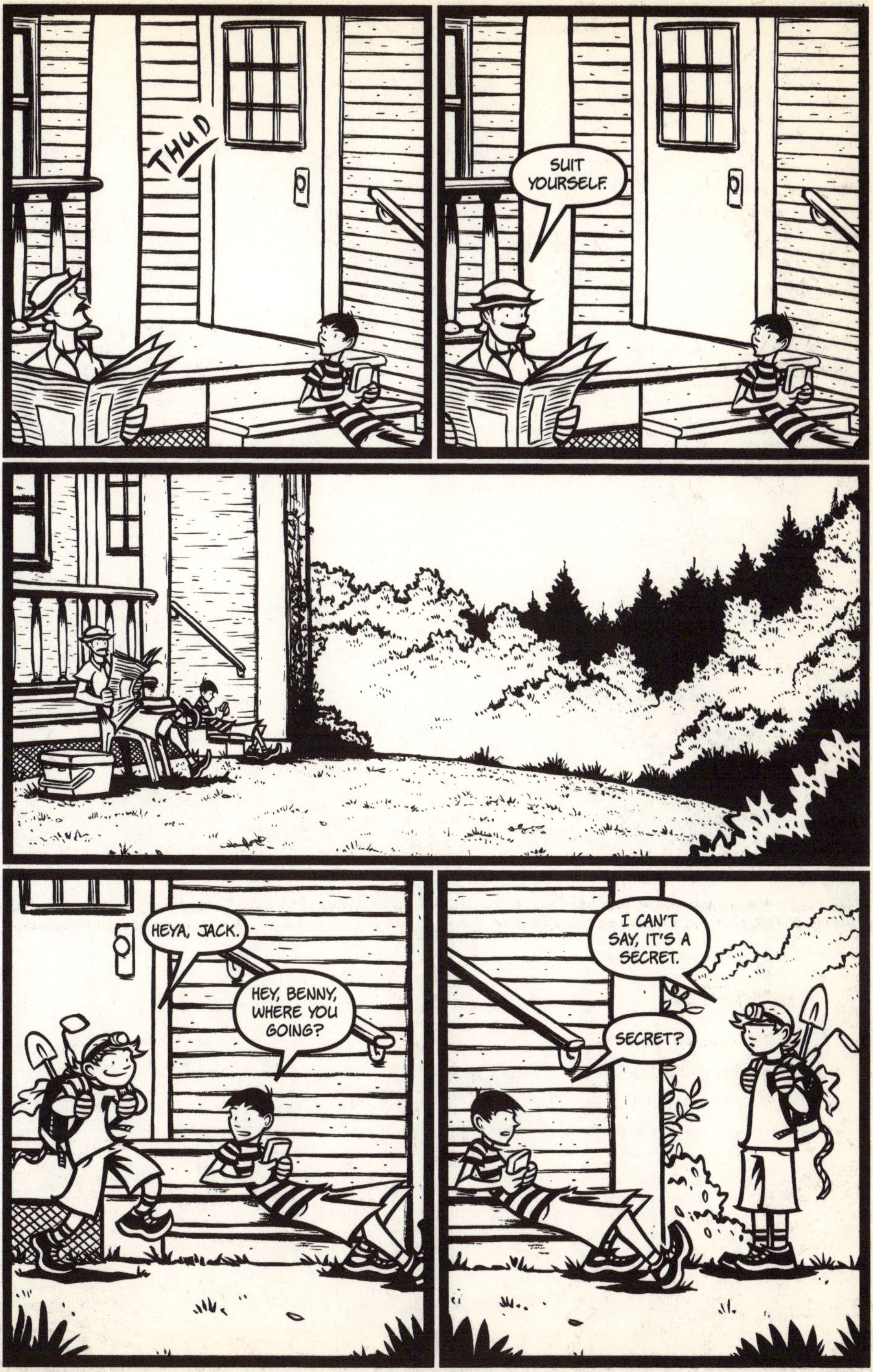
THUD
SUIT YOURSELF.
HEYA, JACK.
HEY, BENNY, WHERE YOU GOING?
I CAN'T SAY, IT'S A SECRET.
SECRET?

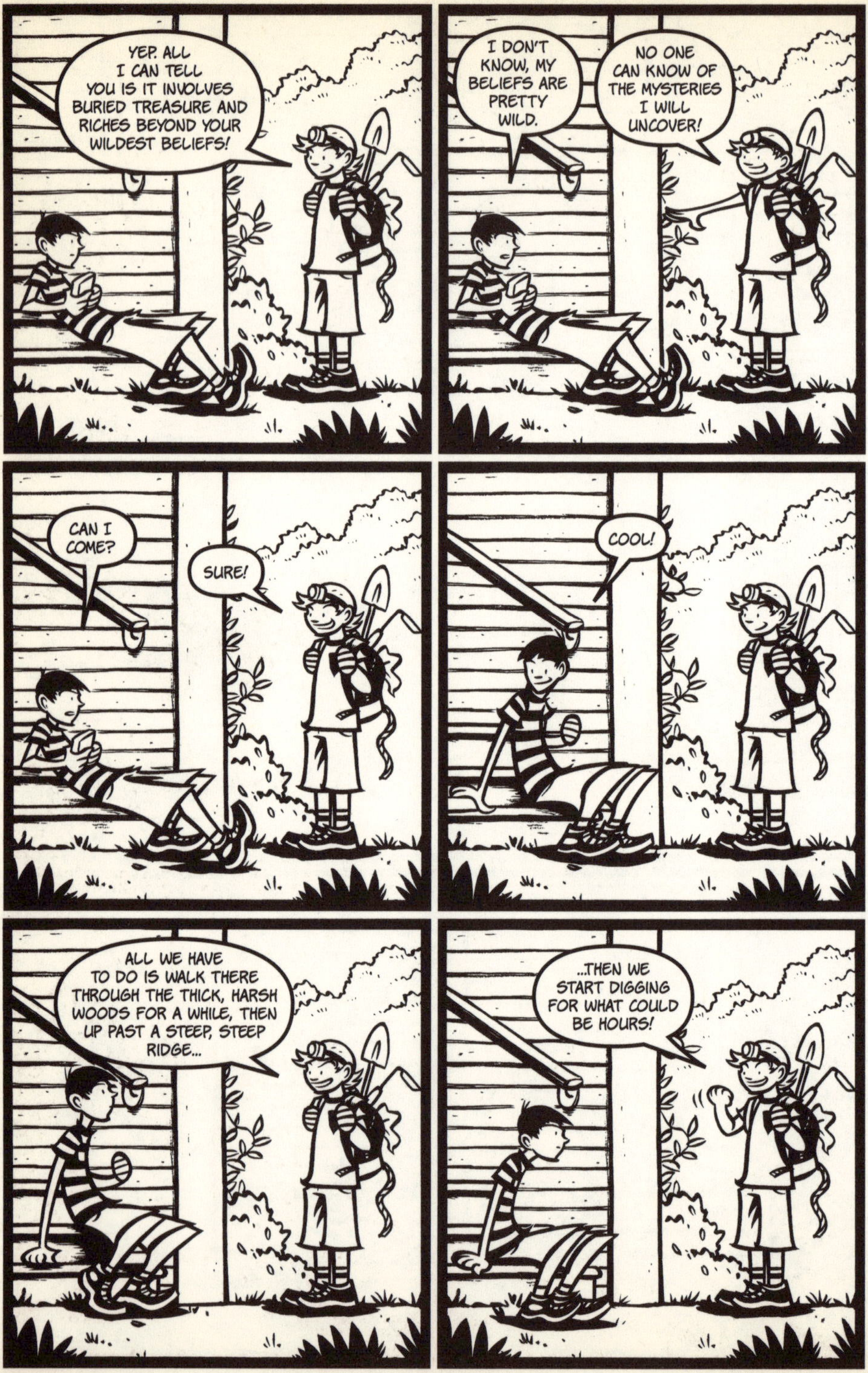
YEP. ALL I CAN TELL YOU IS IT INVOLVES BURIED TREASURE AND RICHES BEYOND YOUR WILDEST BELIEFS!
I DON'T KNOW, MY BELIEFS ARE PRETTY WILD.
NO ONE CAN KNOW OF THE MYSTERIES I WILL UNCOVER!
CAN I COME?
SURE!
COOL!
ALL WE HAVE TO DO IS WALK THERE THROUGH THE THICK, HARSH WOODS FOR A WHILE, THEN UP PAST A STEEP, STEEP RIDGE...
...THEN WE START DIGGING FOR WHAT COULD BE HOURS!

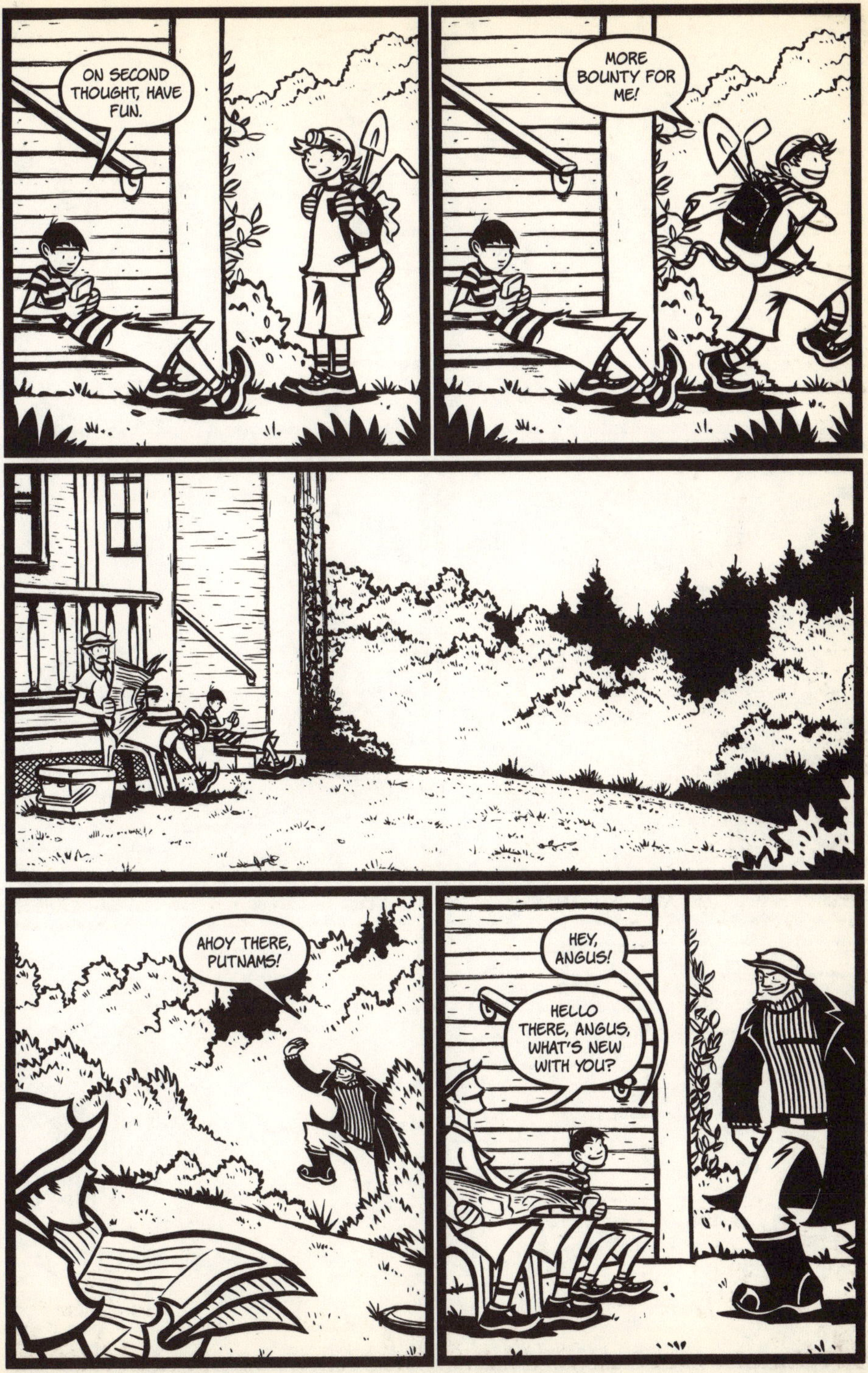
ON SECOND THOUGHT, HAVE FUN.
MORE BOUNTY FOR ME!
AHOY THERE, PUTNAMS!
HEY, ANGUS!
HELLO THERE, ANGUS, WHAT'S NEW WITH YOU?

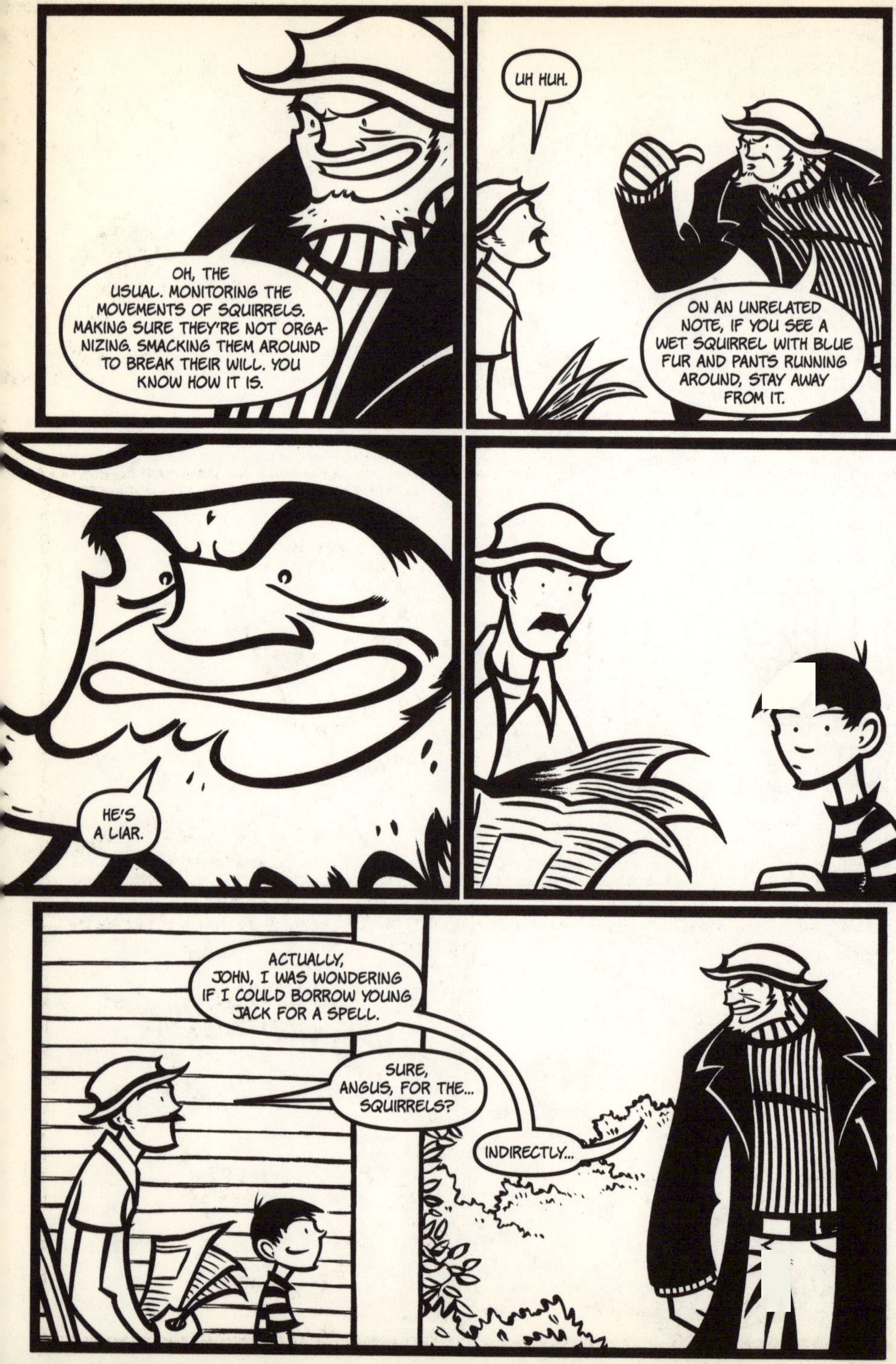
OH, THE USUAL. MONITORING THE MOVEMENTS OF SQUIRRELS. MAKING SURE THEY'RE NOT ORGA-NIZING. SMACKING THEM AROUND TO BREAK THEIR WILL. YOU KNOW HOW IT IS.
UH HUH.
ON AN UNRELATED NOTE, IF YOU SEE A WET SQUIRREL WITH BLUE FUR AND PANTS RUNNING AROUND, STAY AWAY FROM IT.
HE'S A LIAR.
ACTUALLY, JOHN, I WAS WONDERING IF I COULD BORROW YOUNG JACK FOR A SPELL.
SURE, ANGUS, FOR THE... SQUIRRELS?
INDIRECTLY...

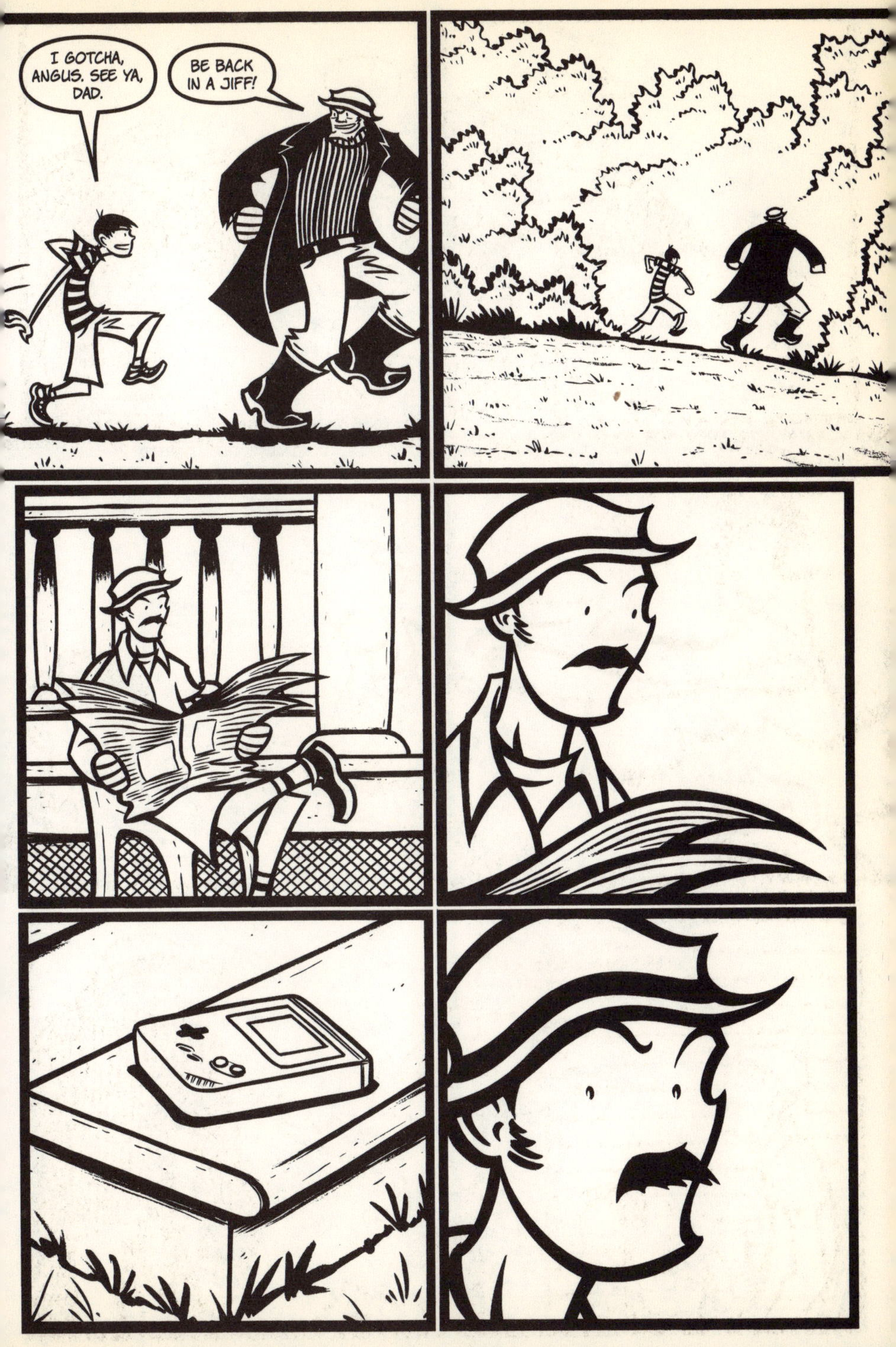
I GOTCHA, ANGUS. SEE YA, DAD.
BE BACK IN A JIFF!

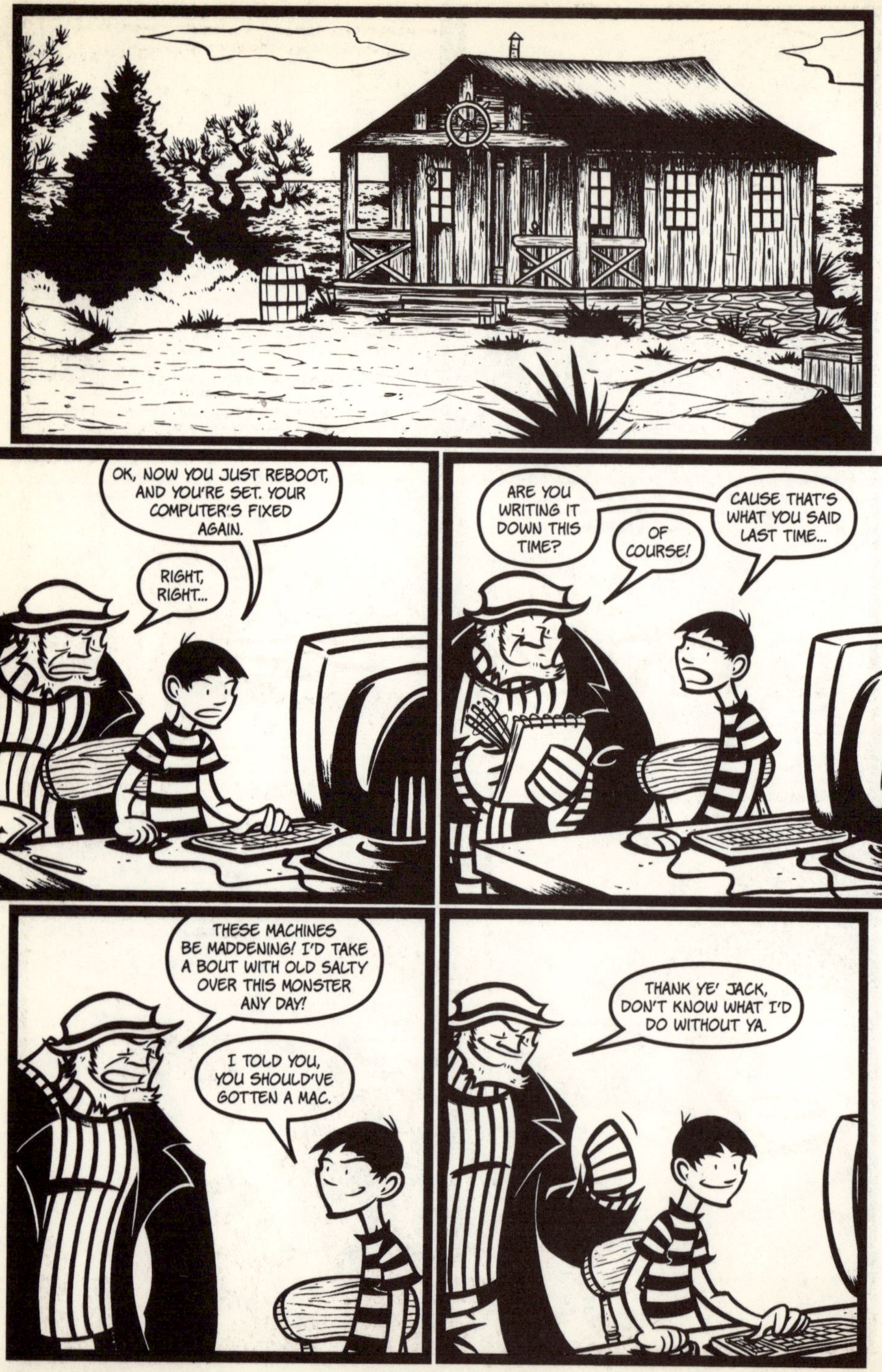
OK, NOW YOU JUST REBOOT, AND YOU'RE SET. YOUR COMPUTER'S FIXED AGAIN.
RIGHT, RIGHT...
ARE YOU WRITING IT DOWN THIS TIME?
CAUSE THAT'S WHAT YOU SAID LAST TIME...
OF COURSE!
THESE MACHINES BE MADDENING! I'D TAKE A BOUT WITH OLD SALTY OVER THIS MONSTER ANY DAY!
I TOLD YOU, YOU SHOULD'VE GOTTEN A MAC.
THANK YE' JACK, DON'T KNOW WHAT I'D DO WITHOUT YA.

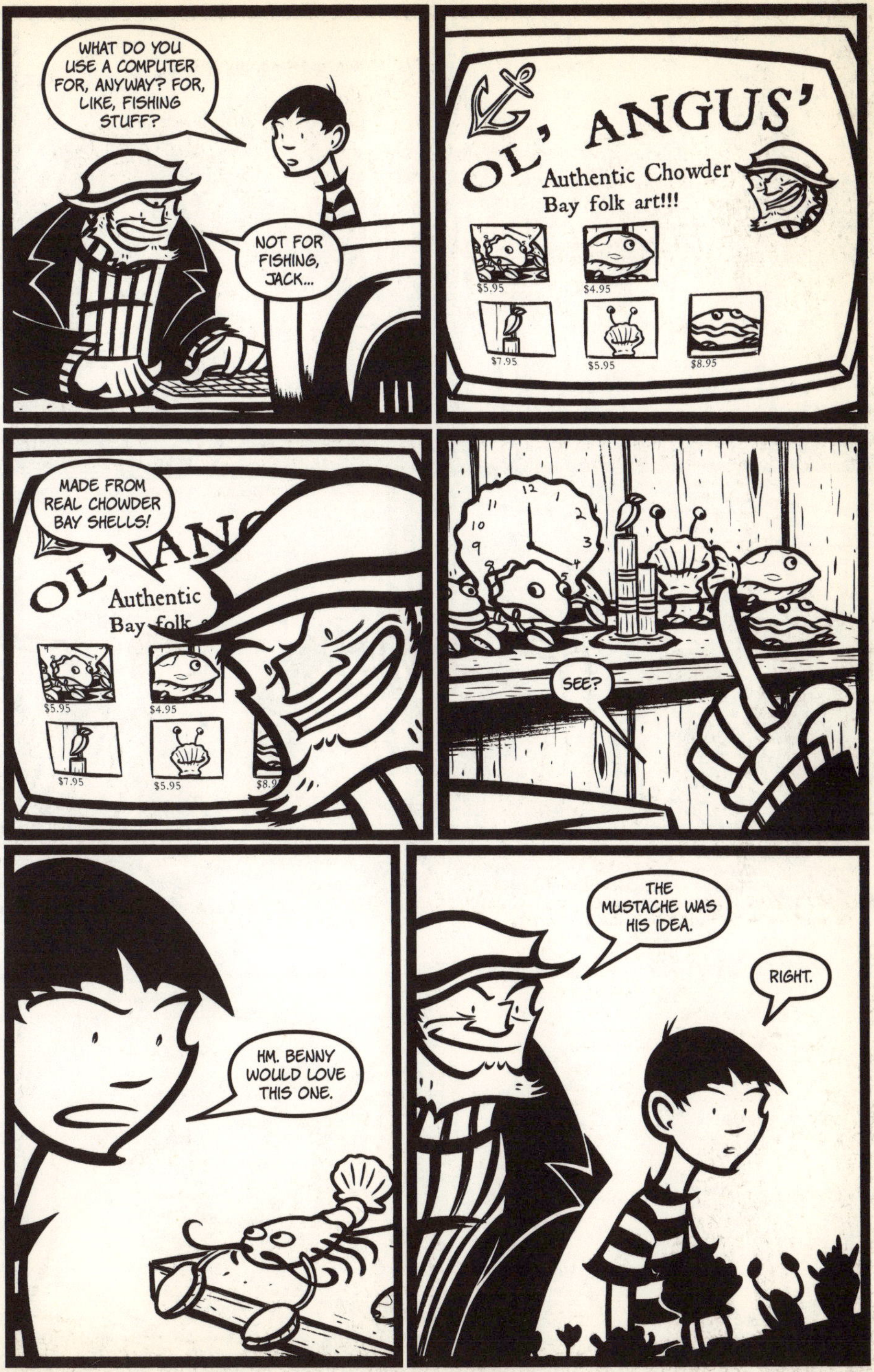
WHAT DO YOU USE A COMPUTER FOR, ANYWAY? FOR, LIKE, FISHING STUFF?
NOT FOR FISHING, JACK...
OL' ANGUS'
Authentic Chowder Bay folk art!!!
$5.95
$4.95
$7.95
$5.95
$8.95
MADE FROM REAL CHOWDER BAY SHELLS!
SEE?
HM. BENNY WOULD LOVE THIS ONE.
THE MUSTACHE WAS HIS IDEA.
RIGHT.

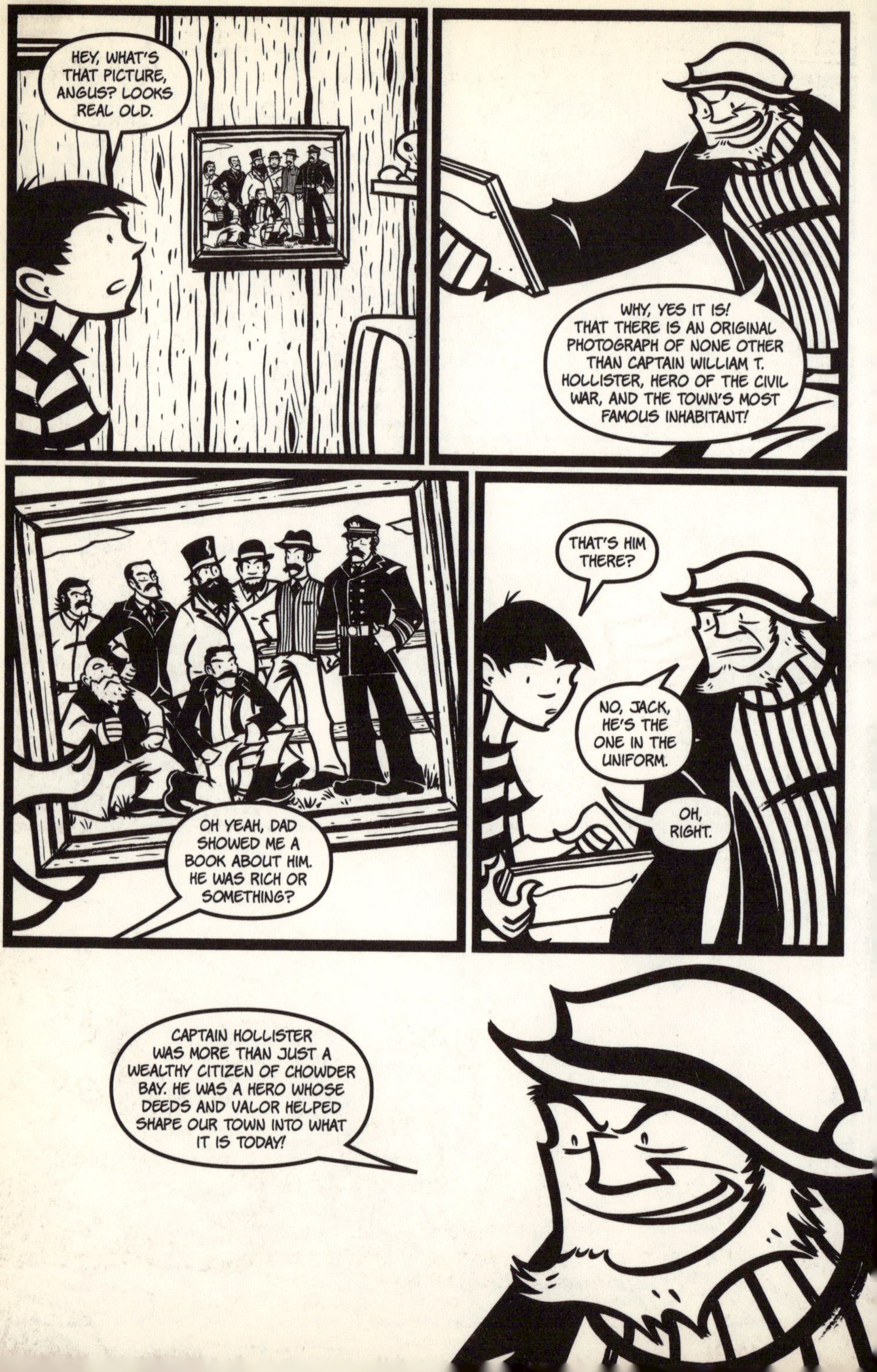
HEY, WHAT'S THAT PICTURE, ANGUS? LOOKS REAL OLD.
WHY, YES IT IS! THAT THERE IS AN ORIGINAL PHOTOGRAPH OF NONE OTHER THAN CAPTAIN WILLIAM T. HOLLISTER, HERO OF THE CIVIL WAR, AND THE TOWN'S MOST FAMOUS INHABITANT!
OH YEAH, DAD SHOWED ME A BOOK ABOUT HIM. HE WAS RICH OR SOMETHING?
THAT'S HIM THERE?
NO, JACK, HE'S THE ONE IN THE UNIFORM.
OH, RIGHT.
CAPTAIN HOLLISTER WAS MORE THAN JUST A WEALTHY CITIZEN OF CHOWDER BAY. HE WAS A HERO WHOSE DEEDS AND VALOR HELPED SHAPE OUR TOWN INTO WHAT IT IS TODAY!

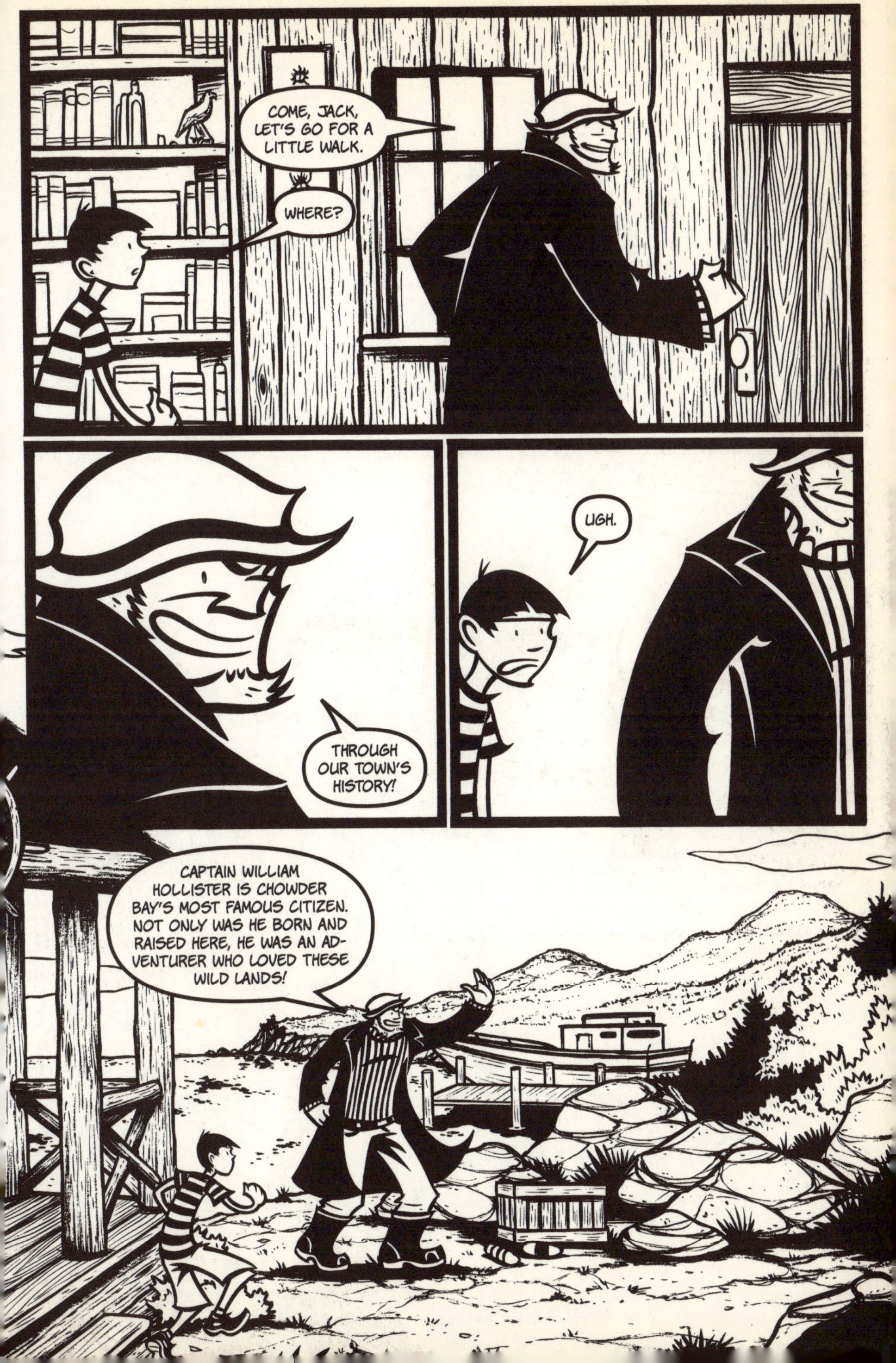
COME, JACK, LET'S GO FOR A LITTLE WALK.
WHERE?
THROUGH OUR TOWN'S HISTORY!
UGH.
CAPTAIN WILLIAM HOLLISTER IS CHOWDER BAY'S MOST FAMOUS CITIZEN. NOT ONLY WAS HE BORN AND RAISED HERE, HE WAS AN AD-VENTURER WHO LOVED THESE WILD LANDS!

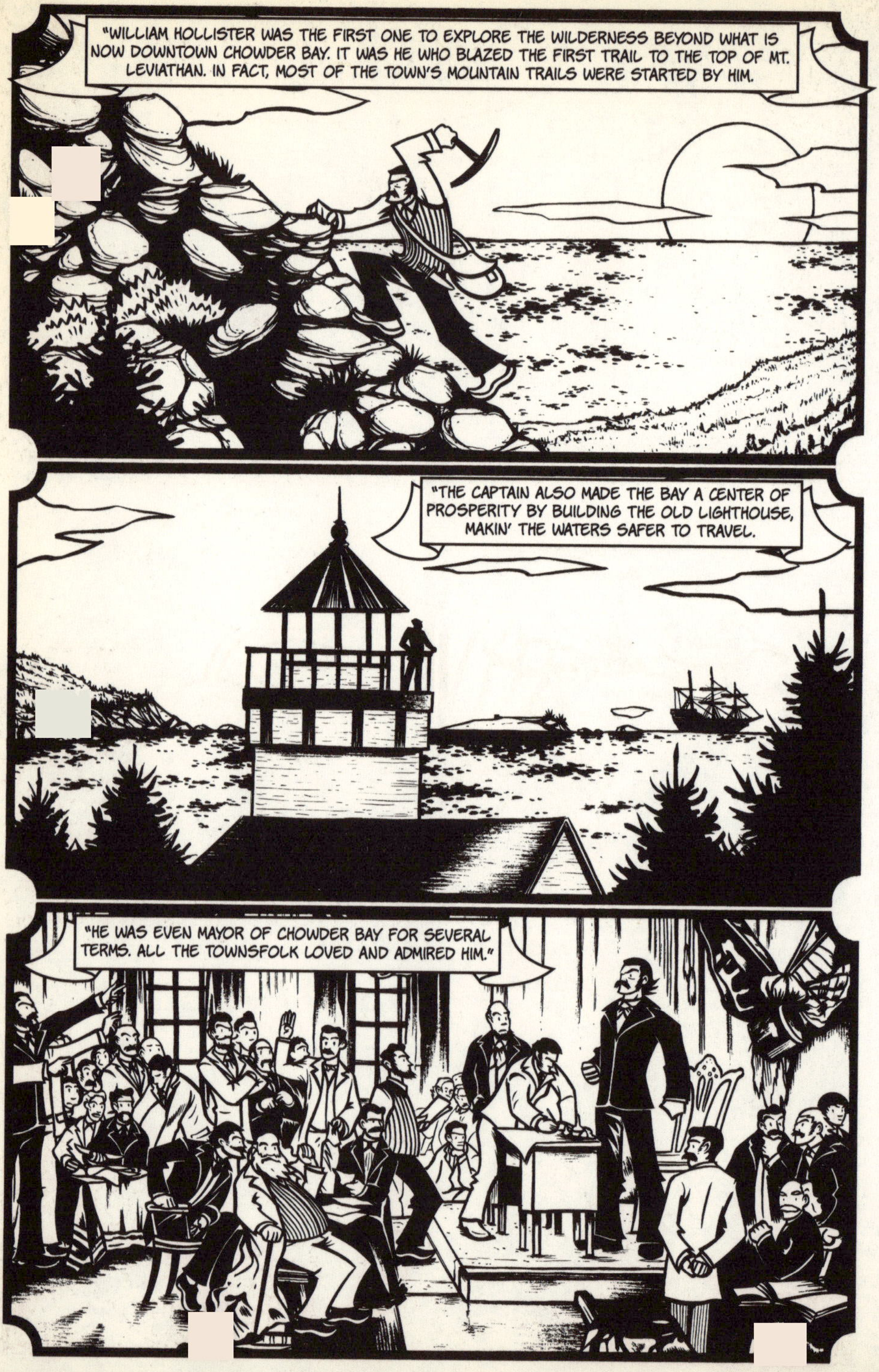
"WILLIAM HOLLISTER WAS THE FIRST ONE TO EXPLORE THE WILDERNESS BEYOND WHAT IS NOW DOWNTOWN CHOWDER BAY. IT WAS HE WHO BLAZED THE FIRST TRAIL TO THE TOP OF MT. LEVIATHAN. IN FACT, MOST OF THE TOWN'S MOUNTAIN TRAILS WERE STARTED BY HIM.
"THE CAPTAIN ALSO MADE THE BAY A CENTER OF PROSPERITY BY BUILDING THE OLD LIGHTHOUSE, MAKIN' THE WATERS SAFER TO TRAVEL.
"HE WAS EVEN MAYOR OF CHOWDER BAY FOR SEVERAL TERMS. ALL THE TOWNSFOLK LOVED AND ADMIRED HIM."

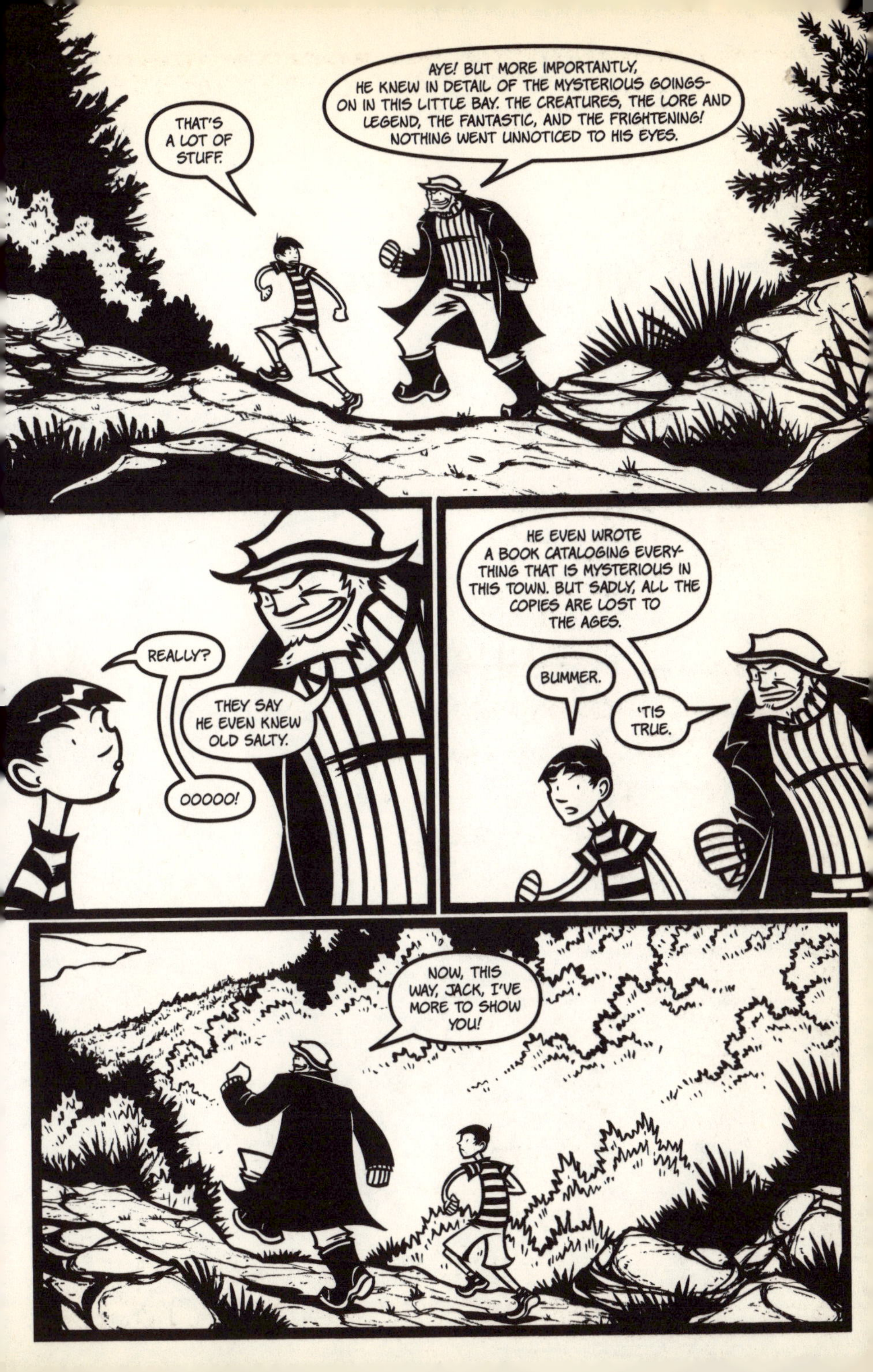
THAT'S A LOT OF STUFF.
AYE! BUT MORE IMPORTANTLY, HE KNEW IN DETAIL OF THE MYSTERIOUS GOINGS-ON IN THIS LITTLE BAY. THE CREATURES, THE LORE AND LEGEND, THE FANTASTIC, AND THE FRIGHTENING! NOTHING WENT UNNOTICED TO HIS EYES.
THEY SAY HE EVEN KNEW OLD SALTY.
REALLY?
OOOOO!
HE EVEN WROTE A BOOK CATALOGING EVERYTHING THAT IS MYSTERIOUS IN THIS TOWN. BUT SADLY, ALL THE COPIES ARE LOST TO THE AGES.
BUMMER.
'TIS TRUE.
NOW, THIS WAY, JACK, I'VE MORE TO SHOW YOU!

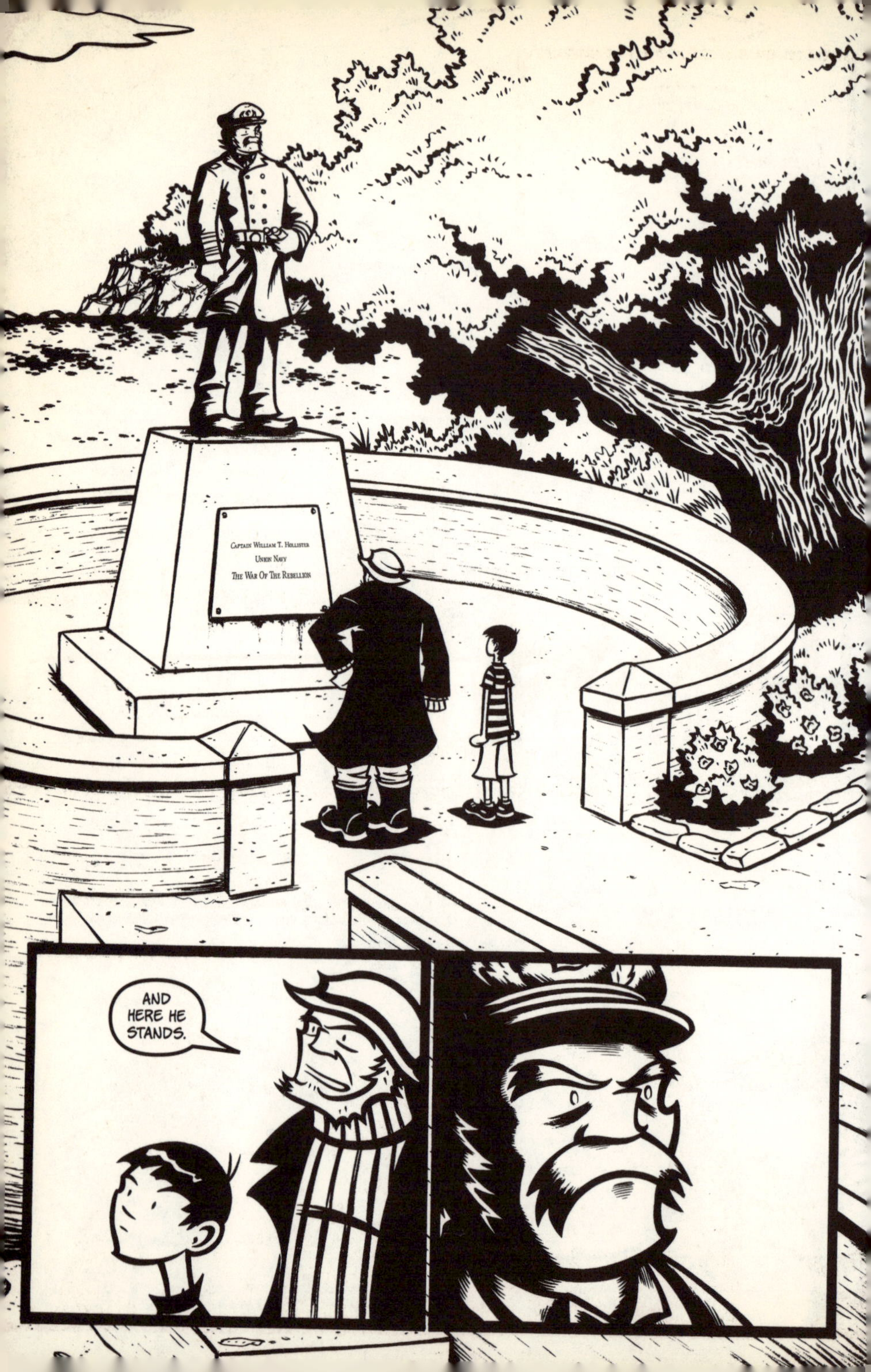
CAPTAIN WILLIAM T. HOLLISTER
UNION NAVY
THE WAR OF THE REBELLION
AND HERE HE STANDS.

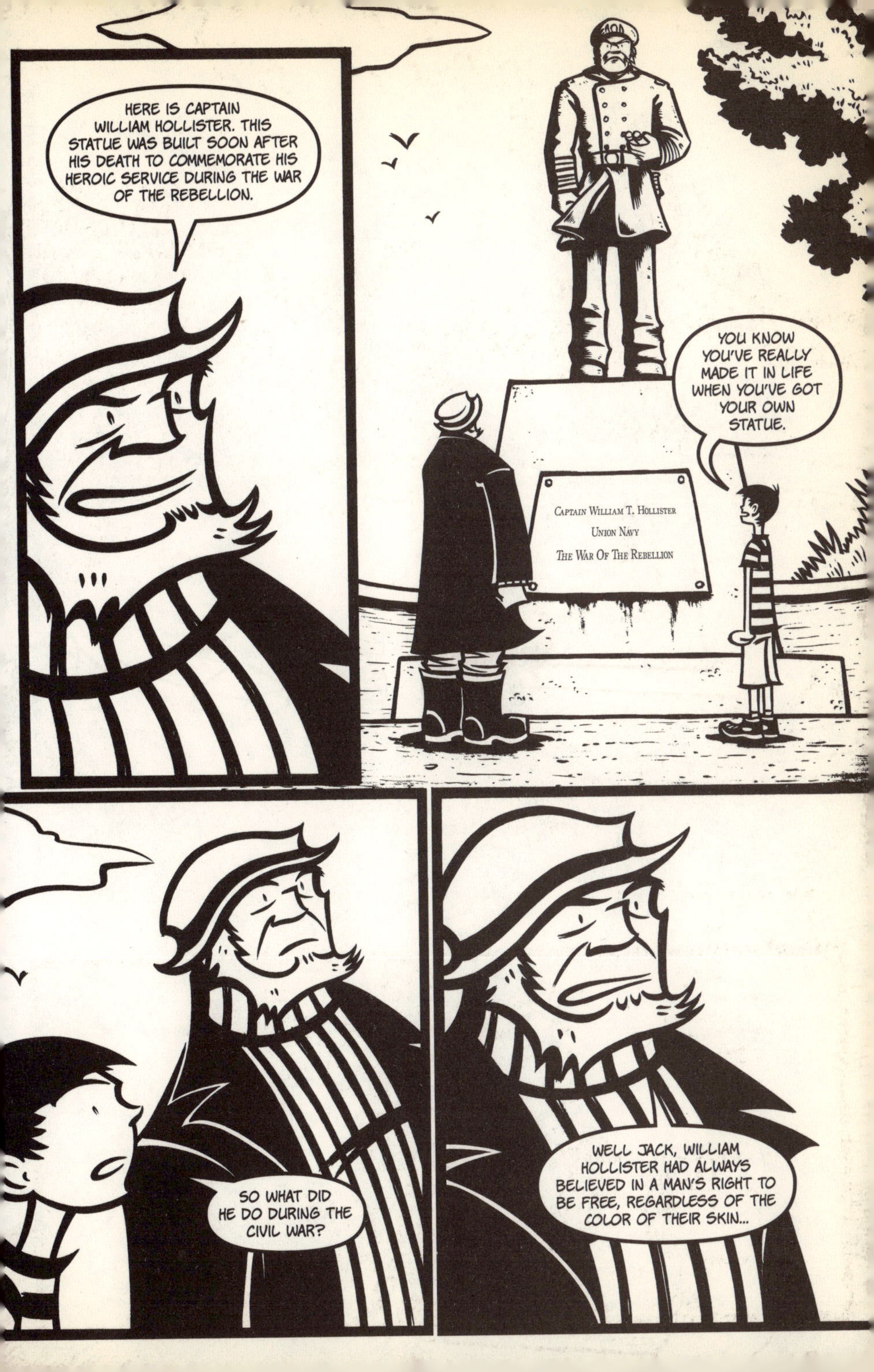
HERE IS CAPTAIN WILLIAM HOLLISTER. THIS STATUE WAS BUILT SOON AFTER HIS DEATH TO COMMEMORATE HIS HEROIC SERVICE DURING THE WAR OF THE REBELLION.
CAPTAIN WILLIAM T. HOLLISTER
UNION NAVY
THE WAR OF THE REBELLION
YOU KNOW YOU'VE REALLY MADE IT IN LIFE WHEN YOU'VE GOT YOUR OWN STATUE.
SO WHAT DID HE DO DURING THE CIVIL WAR?
WELL JACK, WILLIAM HOLLISTER HAD ALWAYS BELIEVED IN A MAN'S RIGHT TO BE FREE, REGARDLESS OF THE COLOR OF THEIR SKIN...

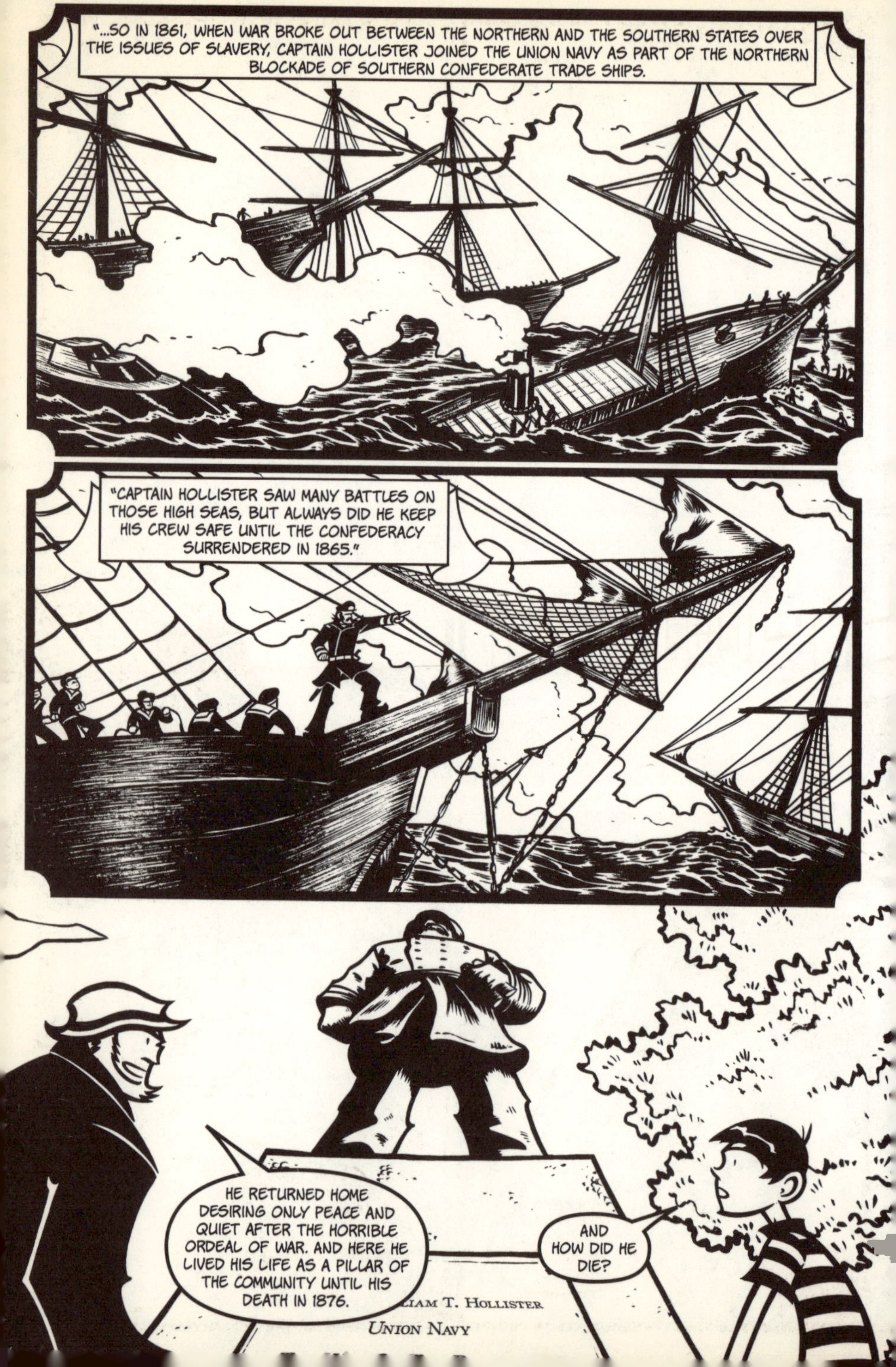
"...SO IN 1861, WHEN WAR BROKE OUT BETWEEN THE NORTHERN AND THE SOUTHERN STATES OVER THE ISSUES OF SLAVERY, CAPTAIN HOLLISTER JOINED THE UNION NAVY AS PART OF THE NORTHERN BLOCKADE OF SOUTHERN CONFEDERATE TRADE SHIPS.
"CAPTAIN HOLLISTER SAW MANY BATTLES ON THOSE HIGH SEAS, BUT ALWAYS DID HE KEEP HIS CREW SAFE UNTIL THE CONFEDERACY SURRENDERED IN 1865."
HE RETURNED HOME DESIRING ONLY PEACE AND QUIET AFTER THE HORRIBLE ORDEAL OF WAR. AND HERE HE LIVED HIS LIFE AS A PILLAR OF THE COMMUNITY UNTIL HIS DEATH IN 1876.
AND HOW DID HE DIE?
T. HOLLISTER
UNION NAVY

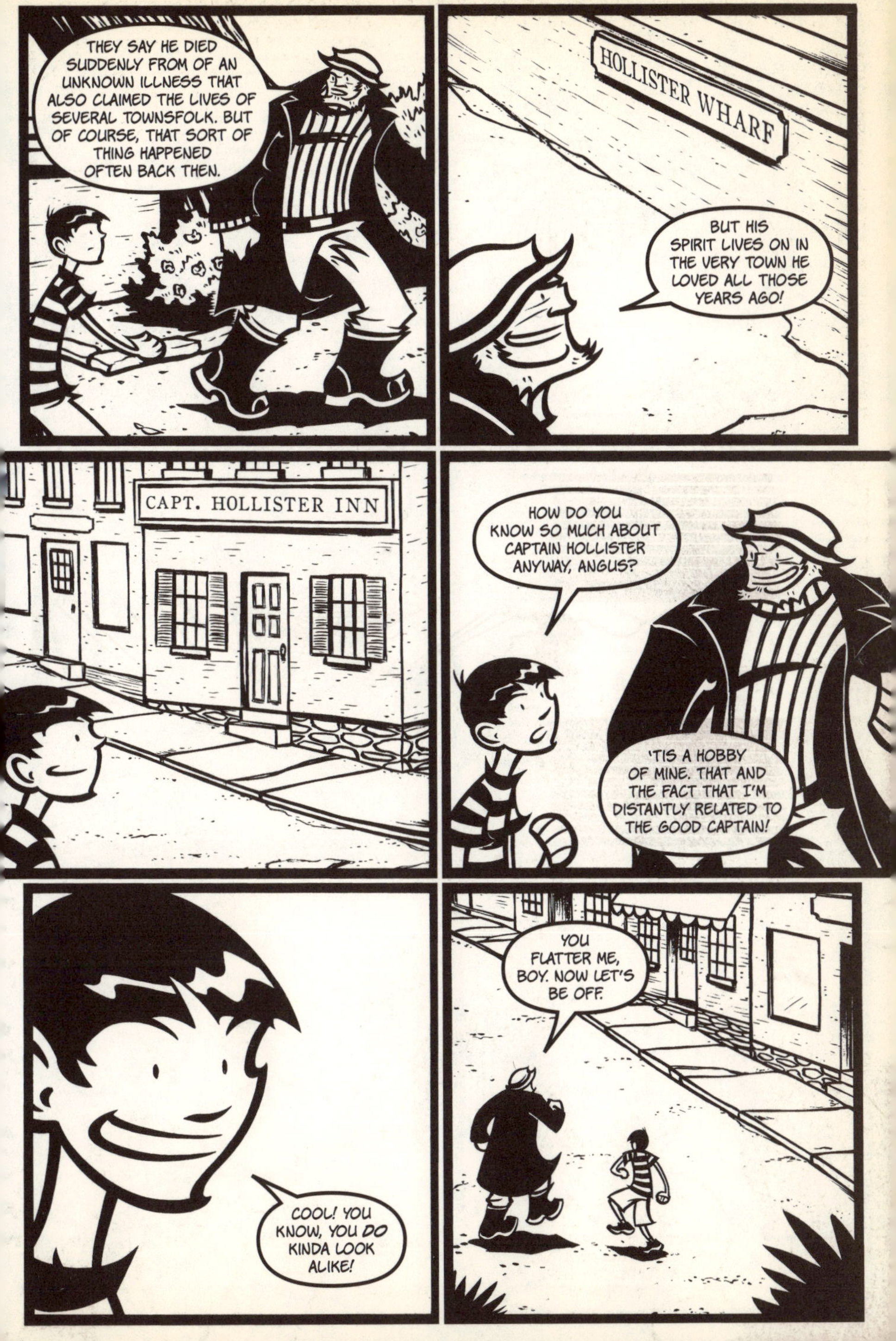
THEY SAY HE DIED SUDDENLY FROM OF AN UNKNOWN ILLNESS THAT ALSO CLAIMED THE LIVES OF SEVERAL TOWNSFOLK. BUT OF COURSE, THAT SORT OF THING HAPPENED OFTEN BACK THEN.
HOLLISTER WHARF
BUT HIS SPIRIT LIVES ON IN THE VERY TOWN HE LOVED ALL THOSE YEARS AGO!
CAPT. HOLLISTER INN
HOW DO YOU KNOW SO MUCH ABOUT CAPTAIN HOLLISTER ANYWAY, ANGUS?
'TIS A HOBBY OF MINE. THAT AND THE FACT THAT I'M DISTANTLY RELATED TO THE GOOD CAPTAIN!
COOL! YOU KNOW, YOU *DO* KINDA LOOK ALIKE!
YOU FLATTER ME, BOY. NOW LET'S BE OFF.

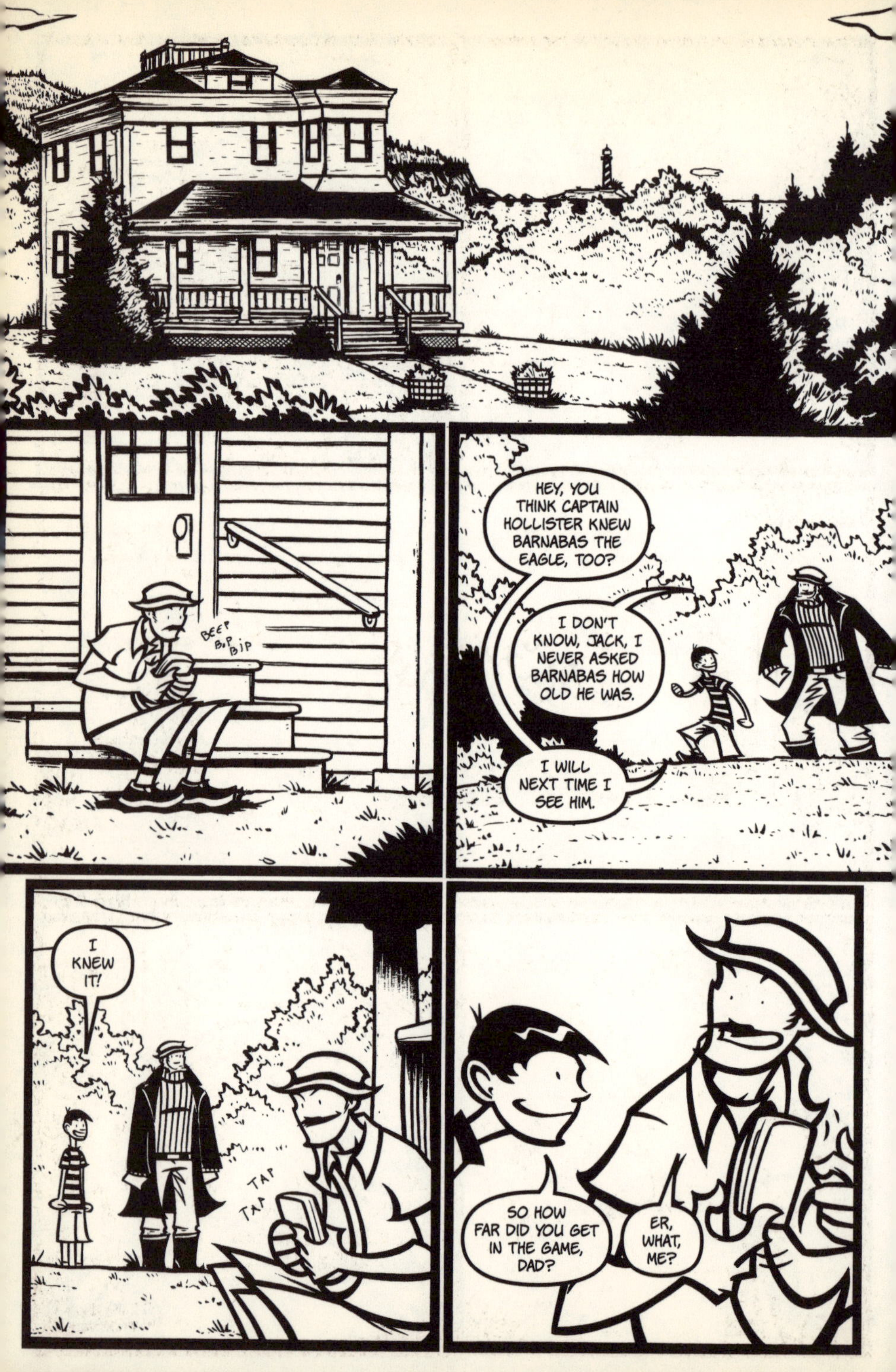
BEEP
BOP
BIP
HEY, YOU THINK CAPTAIN HOLLISTER KNEW BARNABAS THE EAGLE, TOO?
I DON'T KNOW, JACK, I NEVER ASKED BARNABAS HOW OLD HE WAS.
I WILL NEXT TIME I SEE HIM.
I KNEW IT!
TAP
TAP
SO HOW FAR DID YOU GET IN THE GAME, DAD?
ER, WHAT, ME?

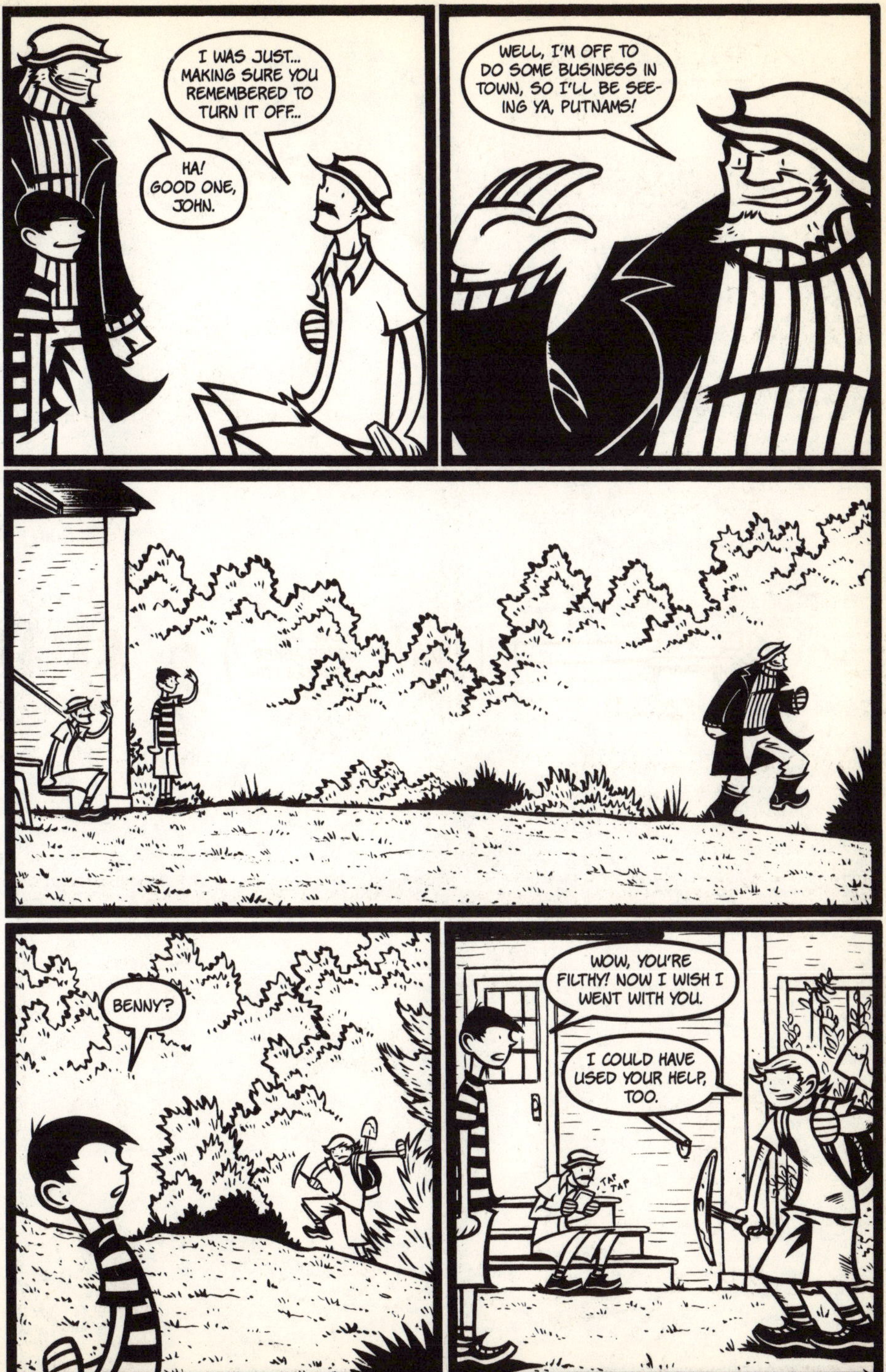
I WAS JUST... MAKING SURE YOU REMEMBERED TO TURN IT OFF...
HA! GOOD ONE, JOHN.
WELL, I'M OFF TO DO SOME BUSINESS IN TOWN, SO I'LL BE SEE-ING YA, PUTNAMS!
BENNY?
WOW, YOU'RE FILTHY! NOW I WISH I WENT WITH YOU.
I COULD HAVE USED YOUR HELP, TOO.
TAP TAP

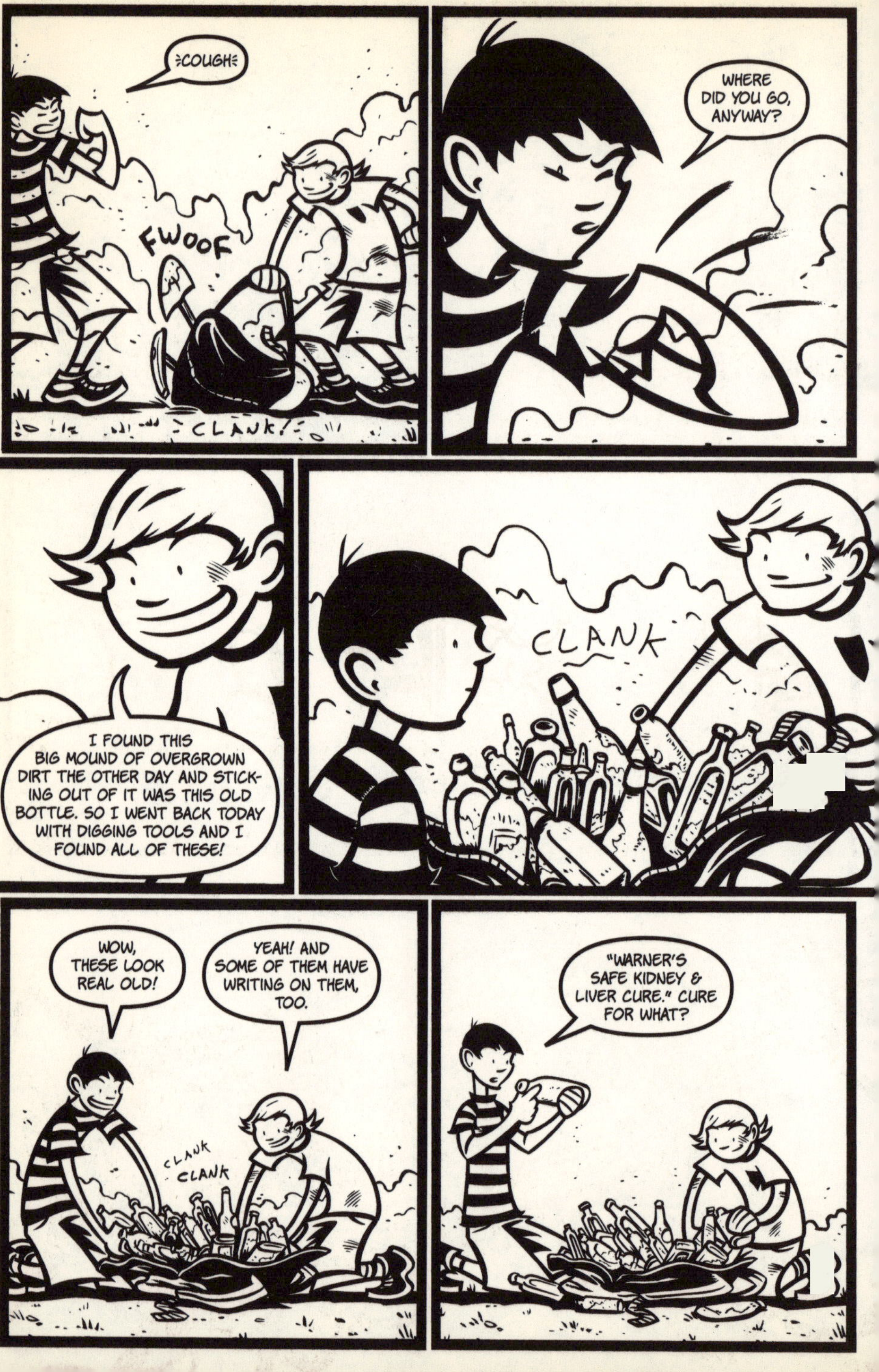
COUGH
FWOOF
CLANK!
WHERE DID YOU GO, ANYWAY?
I FOUND THIS BIG MOUND OF OVERGROWN DIRT THE OTHER DAY AND STICKING OUT OF IT WAS THIS OLD BOTTLE. SO I WENT BACK TODAY WITH DIGGING TOOLS AND I FOUND ALL OF THESE!
CLANK
WOW, THESE LOOK REAL OLD!
YEAH! AND SOME OF THEM HAVE WRITING ON THEM, TOO.
CLANK
CLANK
"WARNER'S SAFE KIDNEY & LIVER CURE." CURE FOR WHAT?

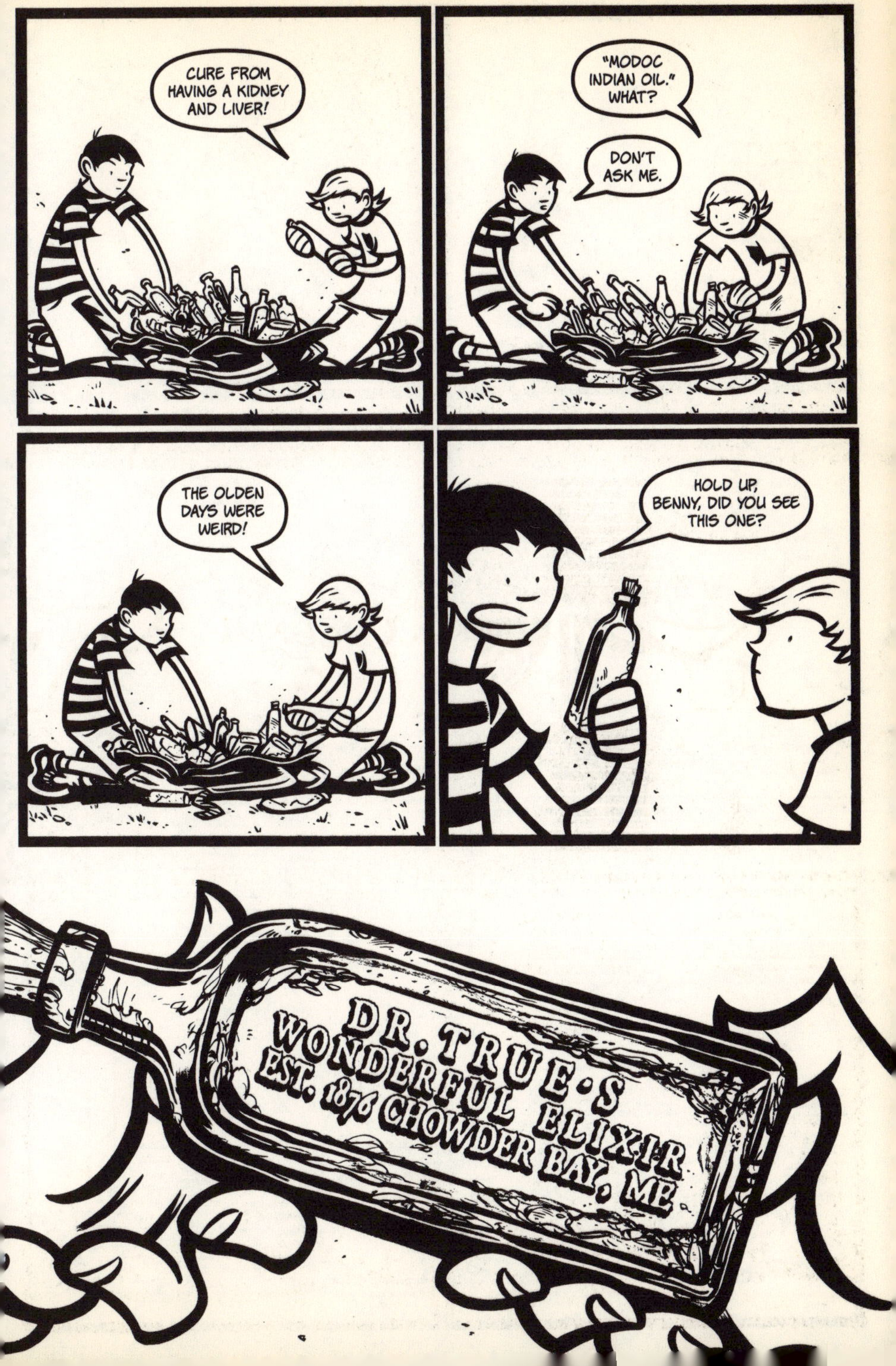
CURE FROM HAVING A KIDNEY AND LIVER!
"MODOC INDIAN OIL." WHAT?
DON'T ASK ME.
THE OLDEN DAYS WERE WEIRD!
HOLD UP, BENNY, DID YOU SEE THIS ONE?
DR. TRUE·S
WONDERFUL ELIXIR
EST. 1876 CHOWDER BAY, ME

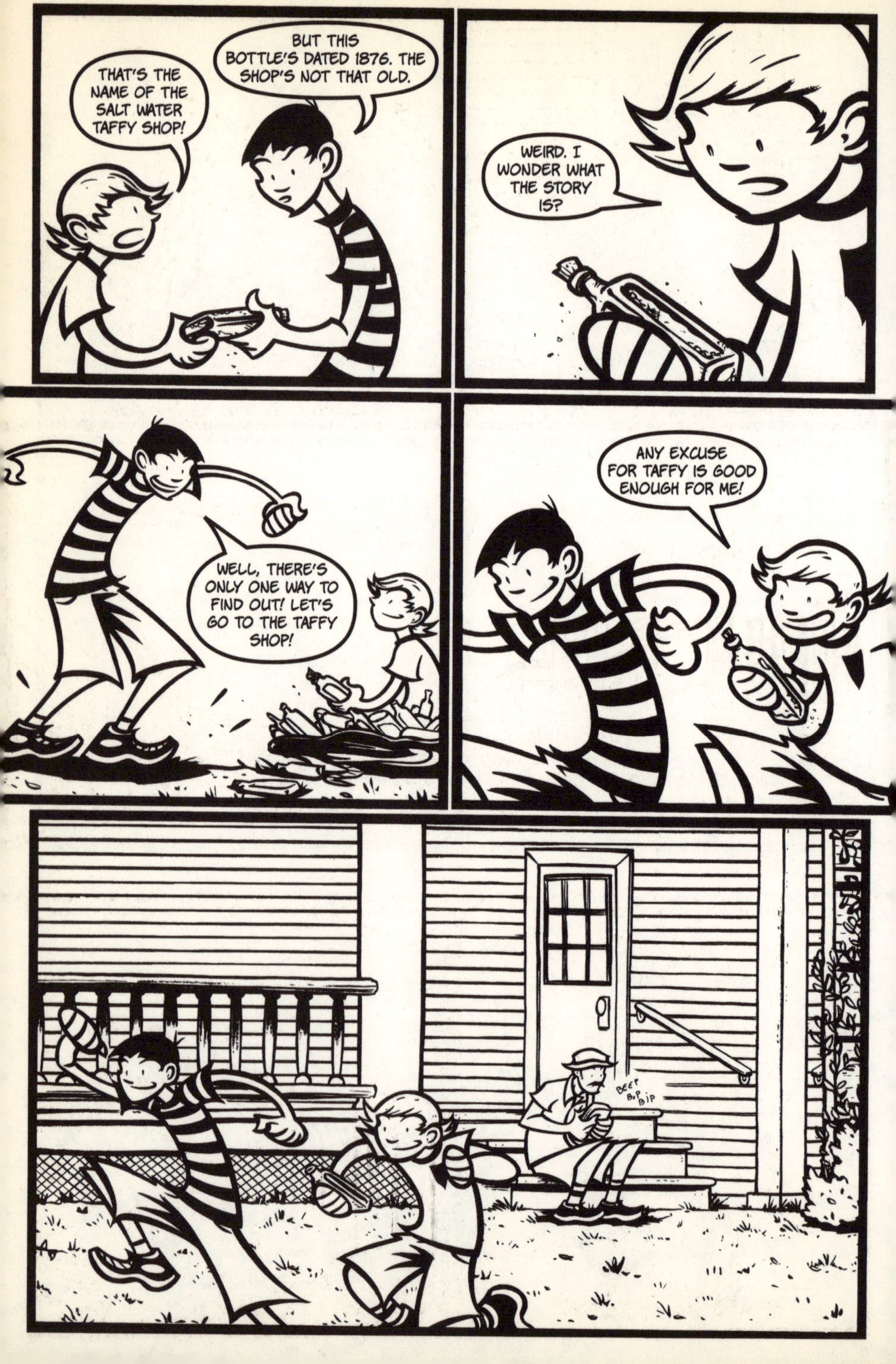
THAT'S THE NAME OF THE SALT WATER TAFFY SHOP!
BUT THIS BOTTLE'S DATED 1876. THE SHOP'S NOT THAT OLD.
WEIRD. I WONDER WHAT THE STORY IS?
WELL, THERE'S ONLY ONE WAY TO FIND OUT! LET'S GO TO THE TAFFY SHOP!
ANY EXCUSE FOR TAFFY IS GOOD ENOUGH FOR ME!
BEEP
BOP
BIP

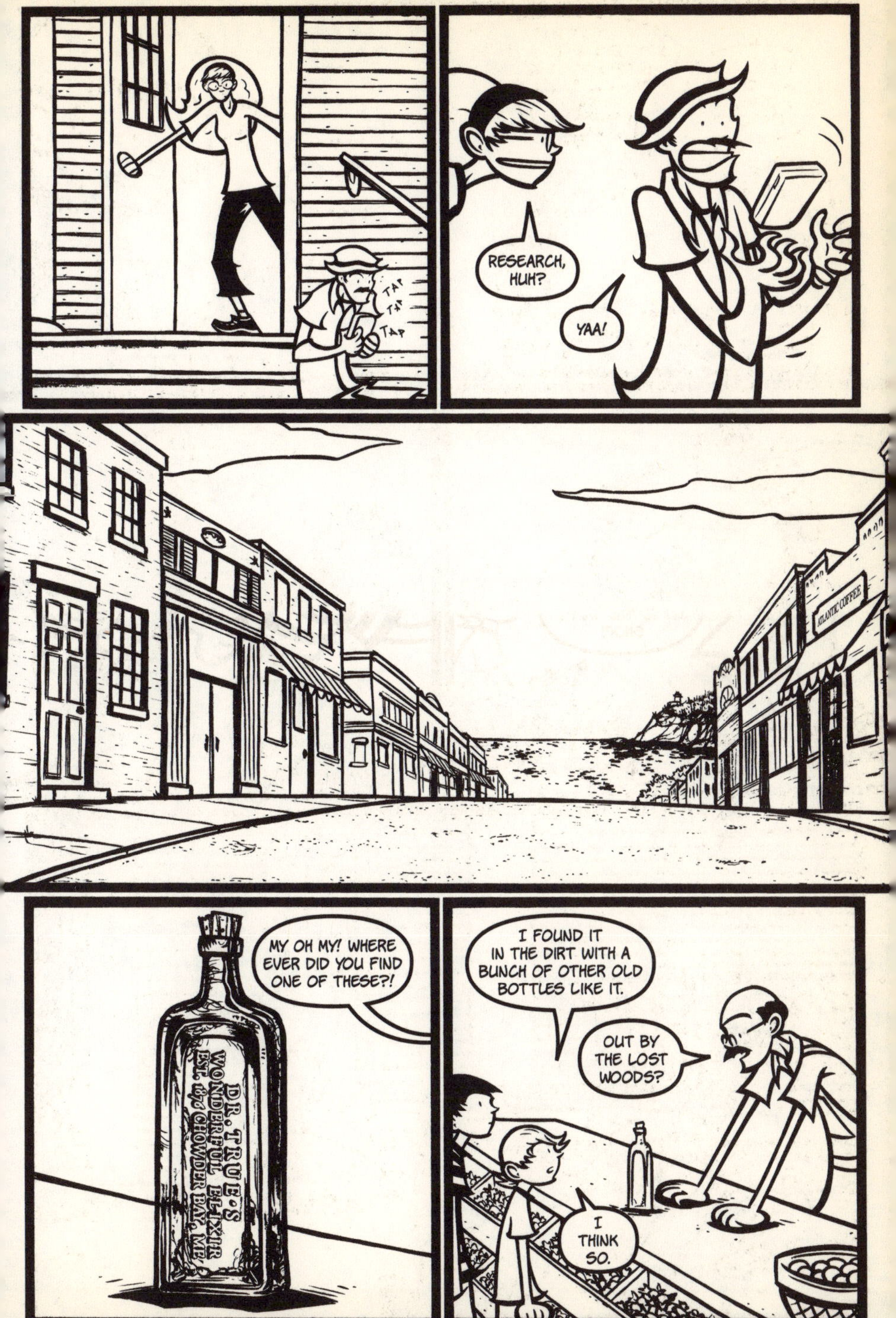
TAP
TAP
TAP
RESEARCH, HUH?
YAA!
ATLANTIC COFFEE
MY OH MY! WHERE EVER DID YOU FIND ONE OF THESE?!
DR. TRUE'S WONDERFUL ELIXIR EST. 187 CHOWDER BAY, ME
I FOUND IT IN THE DIRT WITH A BUNCH OF OTHER OLD BOTTLES LIKE IT.
OUT BY THE LOST WOODS?
I THINK SO.

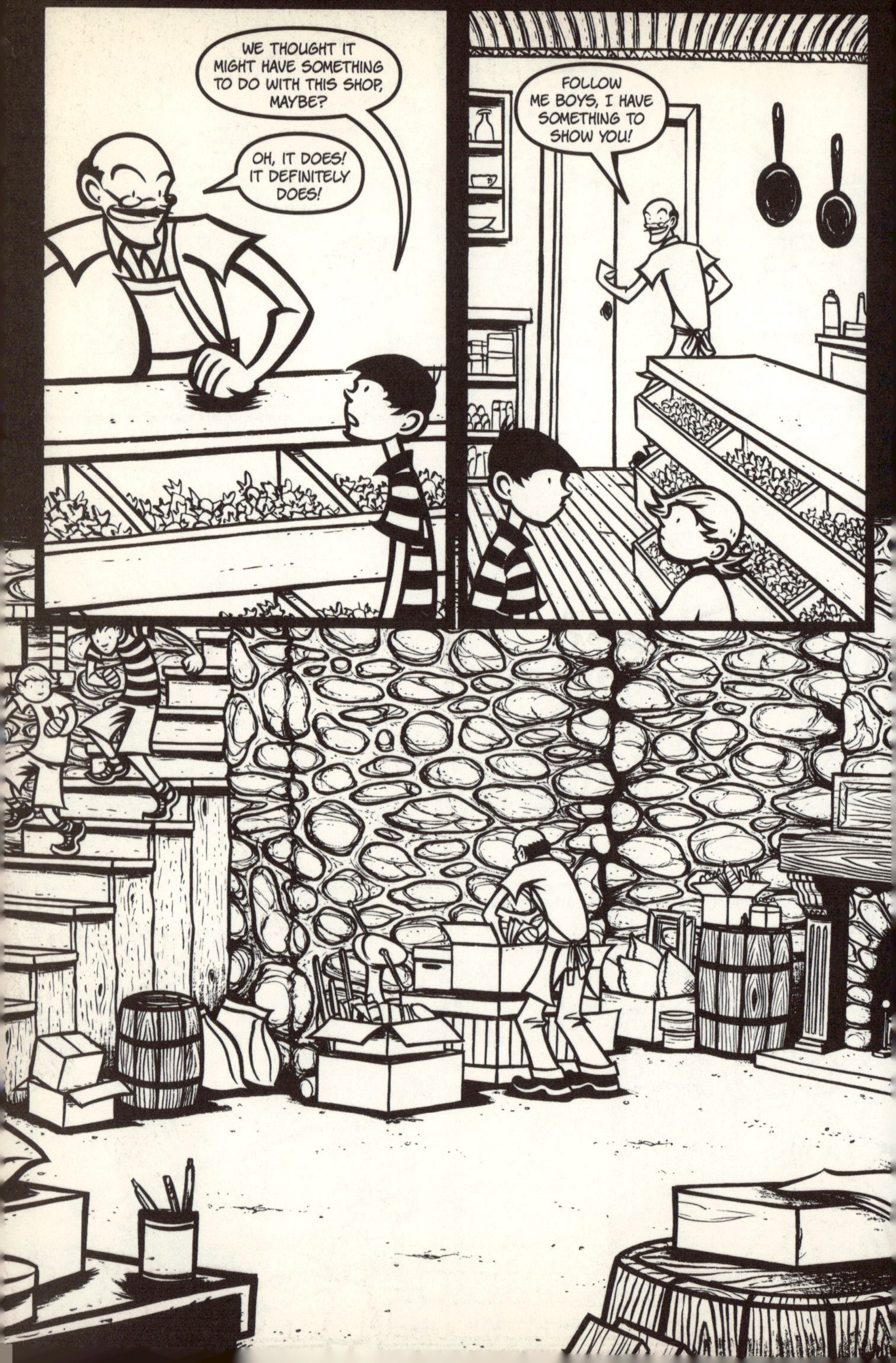
WE THOUGHT IT MIGHT HAVE SOMETHING TO DO WITH THIS SHOP, MAYBE?
OH, IT DOES! IT DEFINITELY DOES!
FOLLOW ME BOYS, I HAVE SOMETHING TO SHOW YOU!

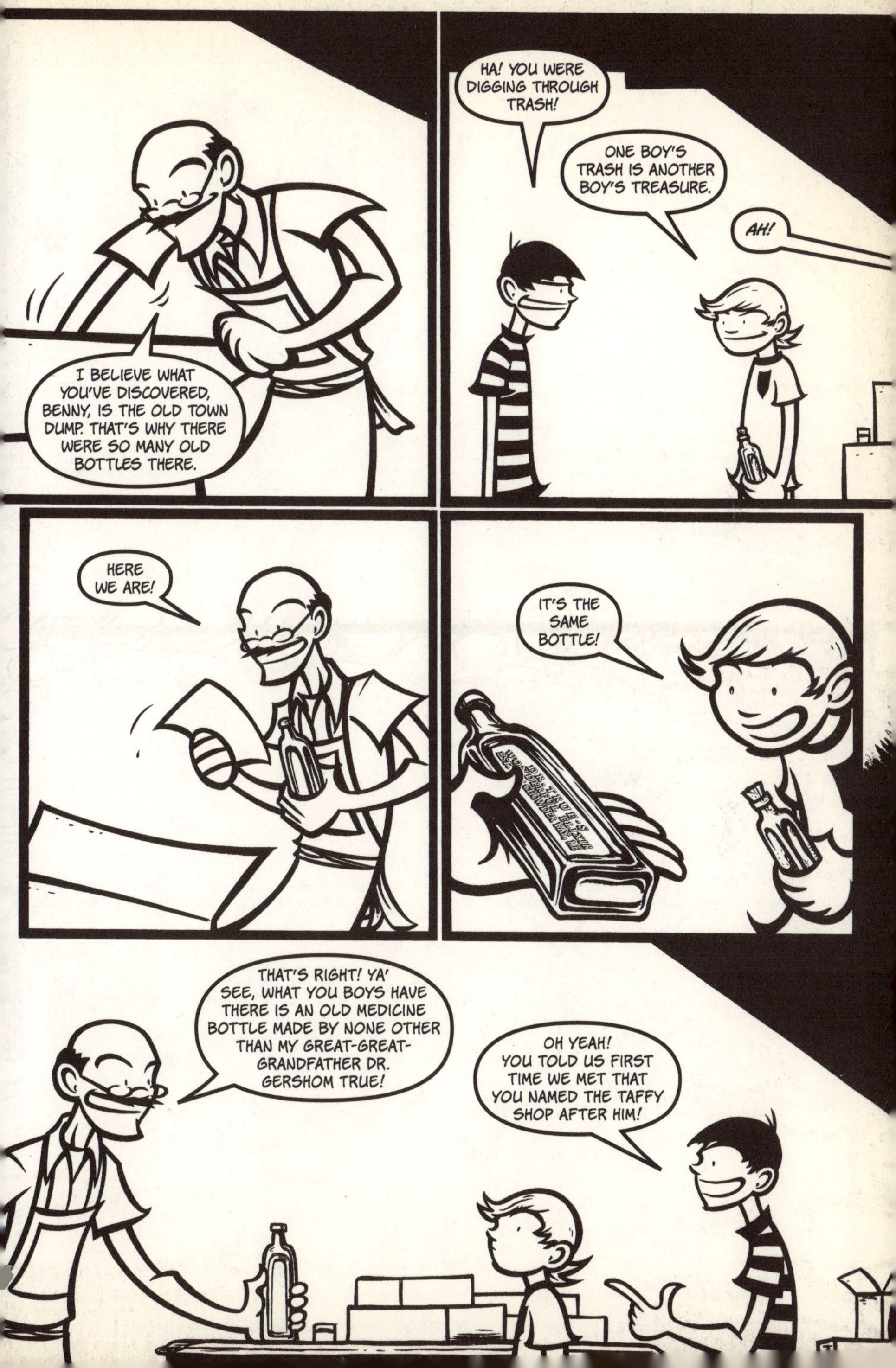
I BELIEVE WHAT YOU'VE DISCOVERED, BENNY, IS THE OLD TOWN DUMP. THAT'S WHY THERE WERE SO MANY OLD BOTTLES THERE.
HA! YOU WERE DIGGING THROUGH TRASH!
ONE BOY'S TRASH IS ANOTHER BOY'S TREASURE.
AH!
HERE WE ARE!
IT'S THE SAME BOTTLE!
THAT'S RIGHT! YA' SEE, WHAT YOU BOYS HAVE THERE IS AN OLD MEDICINE BOTTLE MADE BY NONE OTHER THAN MY GREAT-GREAT-GRANDFATHER DR. GERSHOM TRUE!
OH YEAH! YOU TOLD US FIRST TIME WE MET THAT YOU NAMED THE TAFFY SHOP AFTER HIM!

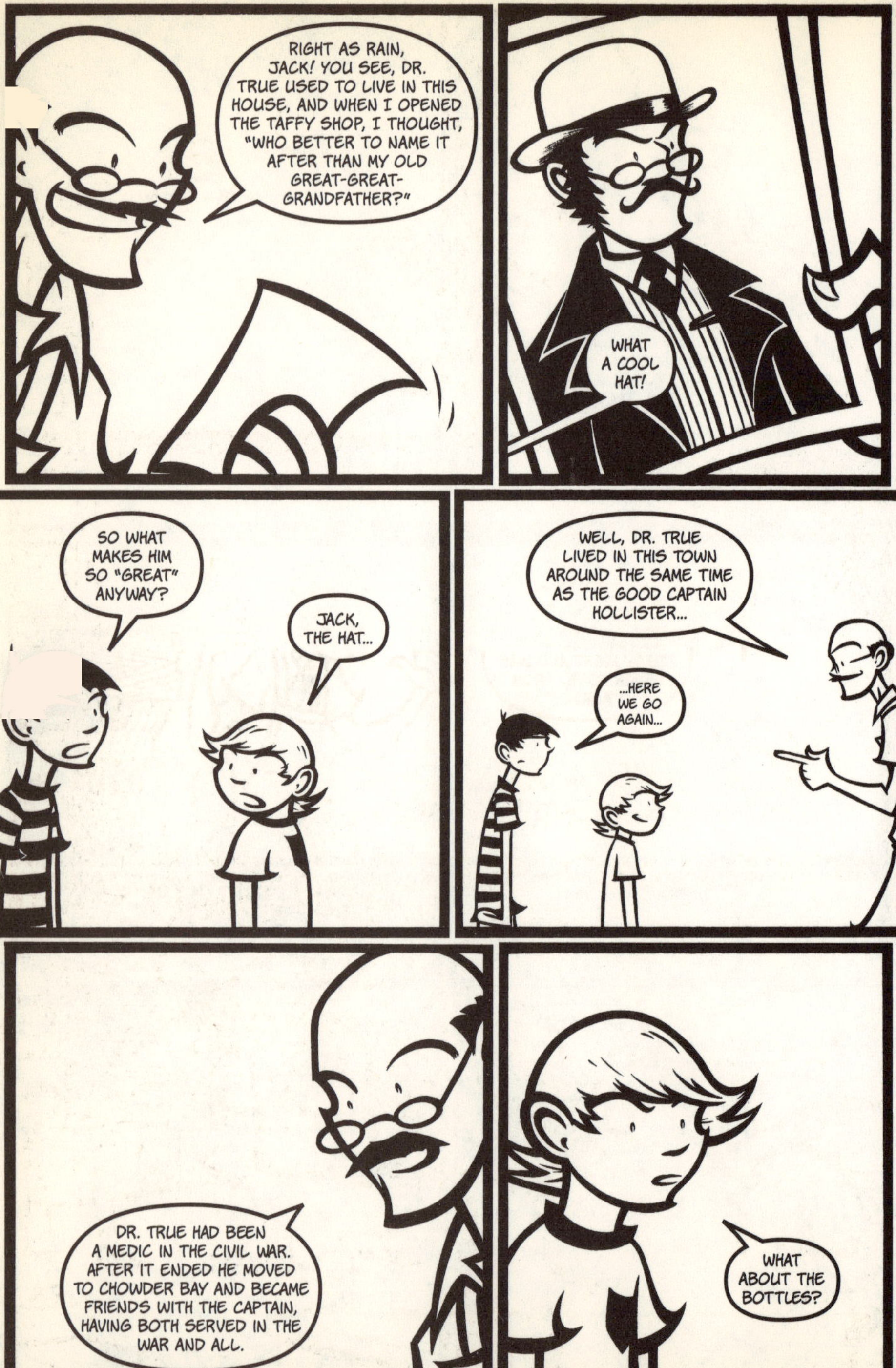
RIGHT AS RAIN, JACK! YOU SEE, DR. TRUE USED TO LIVE IN THIS HOUSE, AND WHEN I OPENED THE TAFFY SHOP, I THOUGHT, "WHO BETTER TO NAME IT AFTER THAN MY OLD GREAT-GREAT-GRANDFATHER?"
WHAT A COOL HAT!
SO WHAT MAKES HIM SO "GREAT" ANYWAY?
JACK, THE HAT...
WELL, DR. TRUE LIVED IN THIS TOWN AROUND THE SAME TIME AS THE GOOD CAPTAIN HOLLISTER...
...HERE WE GO AGAIN...
DR. TRUE HAD BEEN A MEDIC IN THE CIVIL WAR. AFTER IT ENDED HE MOVED TO CHOWDER BAY AND BECAME FRIENDS WITH THE CAPTAIN, HAVING BOTH SERVED IN THE WAR AND ALL.
WHAT ABOUT THE BOTTLES?

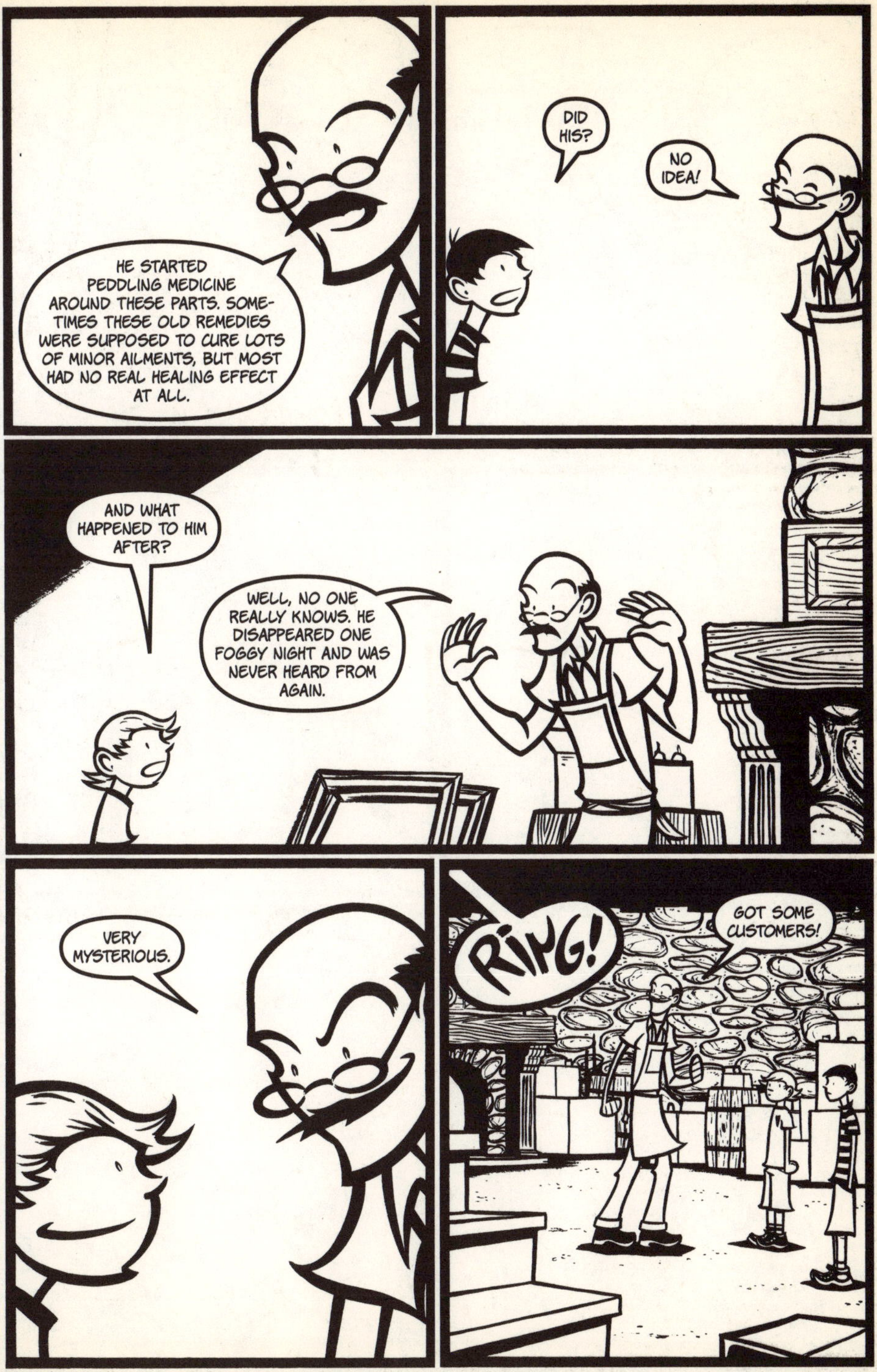

HE STARTED PEDDLING MEDICINE AROUND THESE PARTS. SOMETIMES THESE OLD REMEDIES WERE SUPPOSED TO CURE LOTS OF MINOR AILMENTS, BUT MOST HAD NO REAL HEALING EFFECT AT ALL.
DID HIS?
NO IDEA!
AND WHAT HAPPENED TO HIM AFTER?
WELL, NO ONE REALLY KNOWS. HE DISAPPEARED ONE FOGGY NIGHT AND WAS NEVER HEARD FROM AGAIN.
VERY MYSTERIOUS.
RING!
GOT SOME CUSTOMERS!

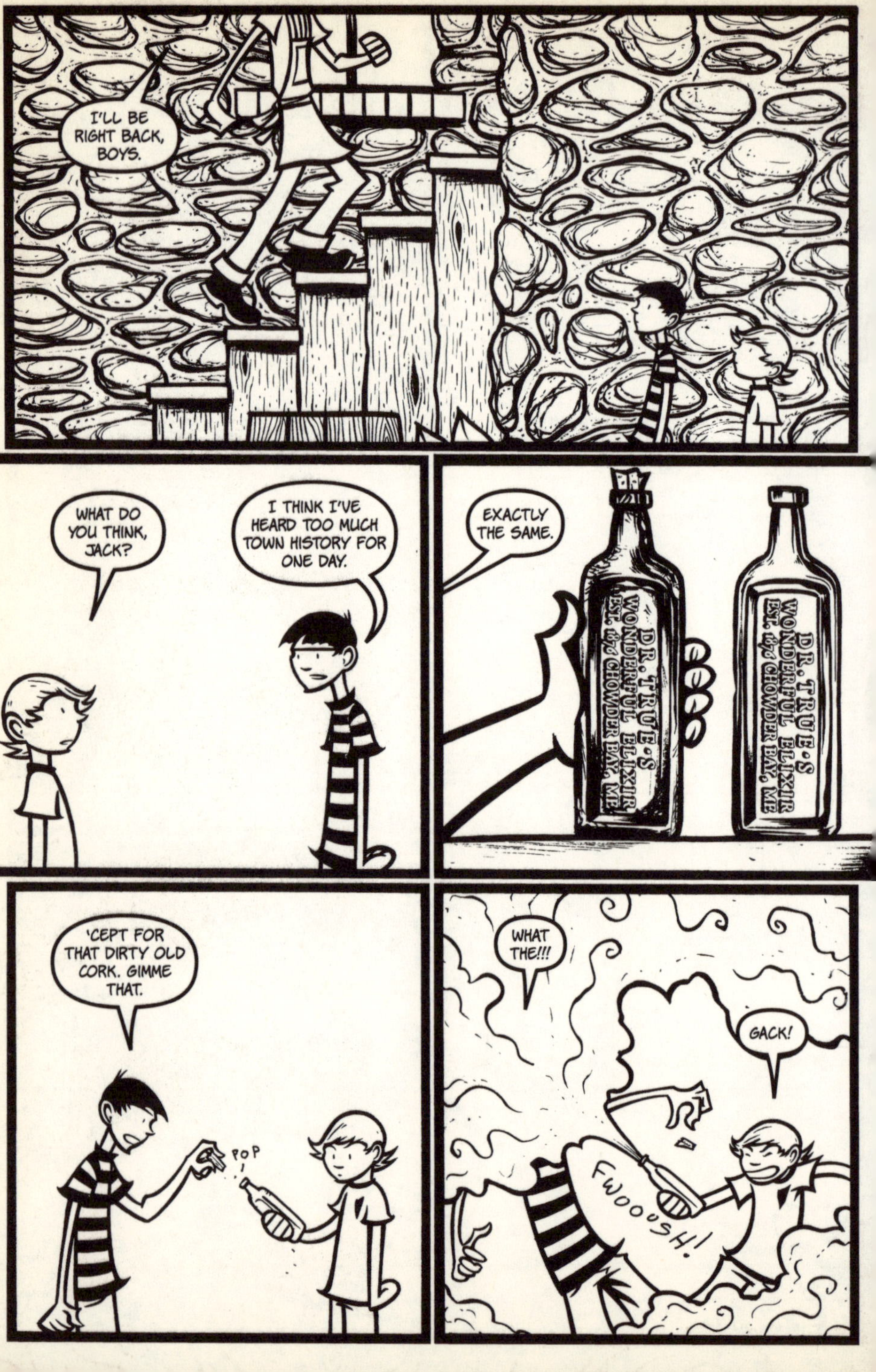
I'LL BE RIGHT BACK, BOYS.
WHAT DO YOU THINK, JACK?
I THINK I'VE HEARD TOO MUCH TOWN HISTORY FOR ONE DAY.
EXACTLY THE SAME.
DR. TRUE'S WONDERFUL ELIXIR EST. 1876 CHOWDER BAY, ME
DR. TRUE'S WONDERFUL ELIXIR EST. 1876 CHOWDER BAY, ME
'CEPT FOR THAT DIRTY OLD CORK. GIMME THAT.
POP!
WHAT THE!!!
GACK!
FWOOOSH!

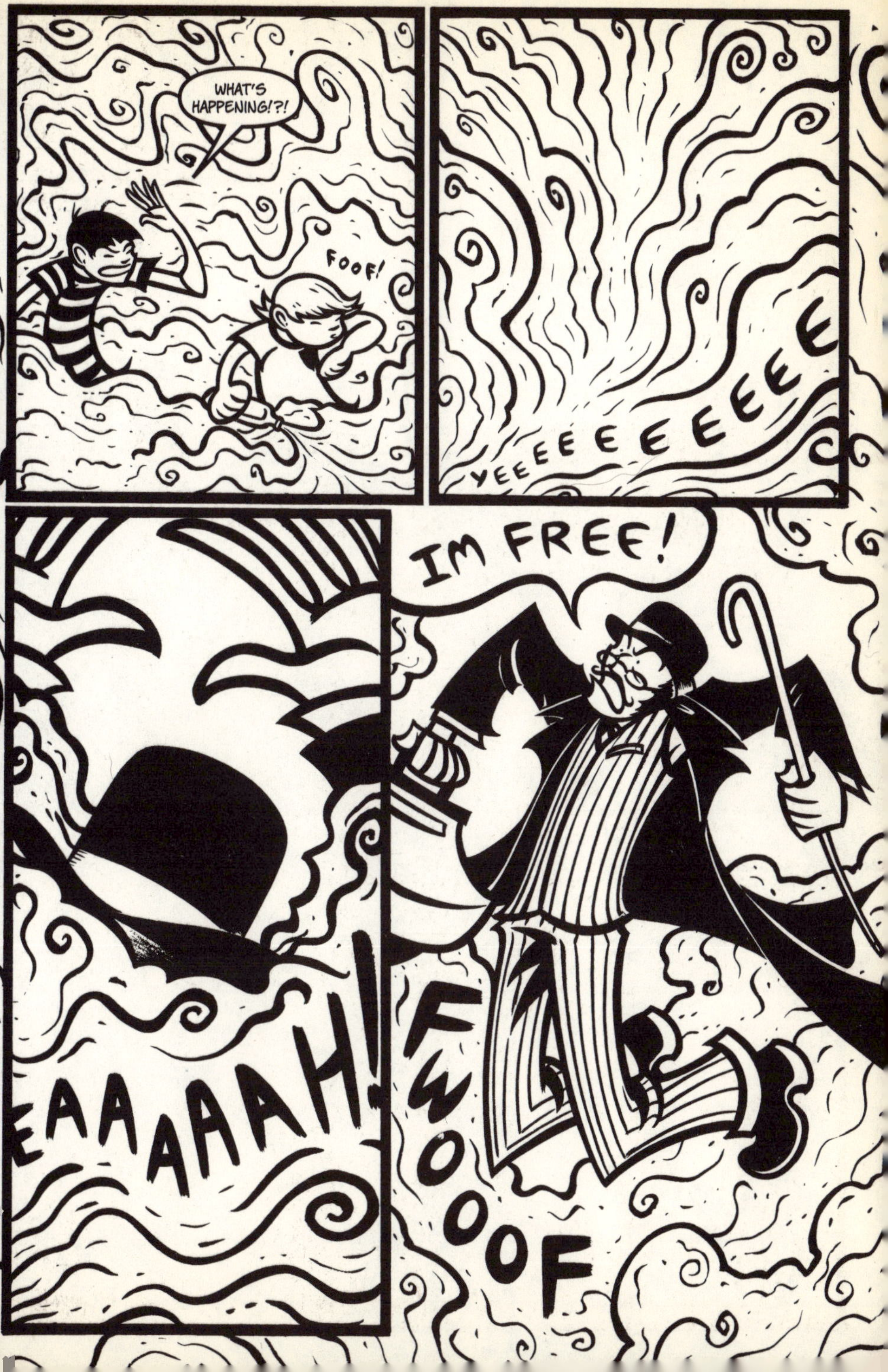
WHAT'S HAPPENING!?!
FOOF!
YEEEEEEEEEEE
IM FREE!
EAAAAAH!
FWOOOOF

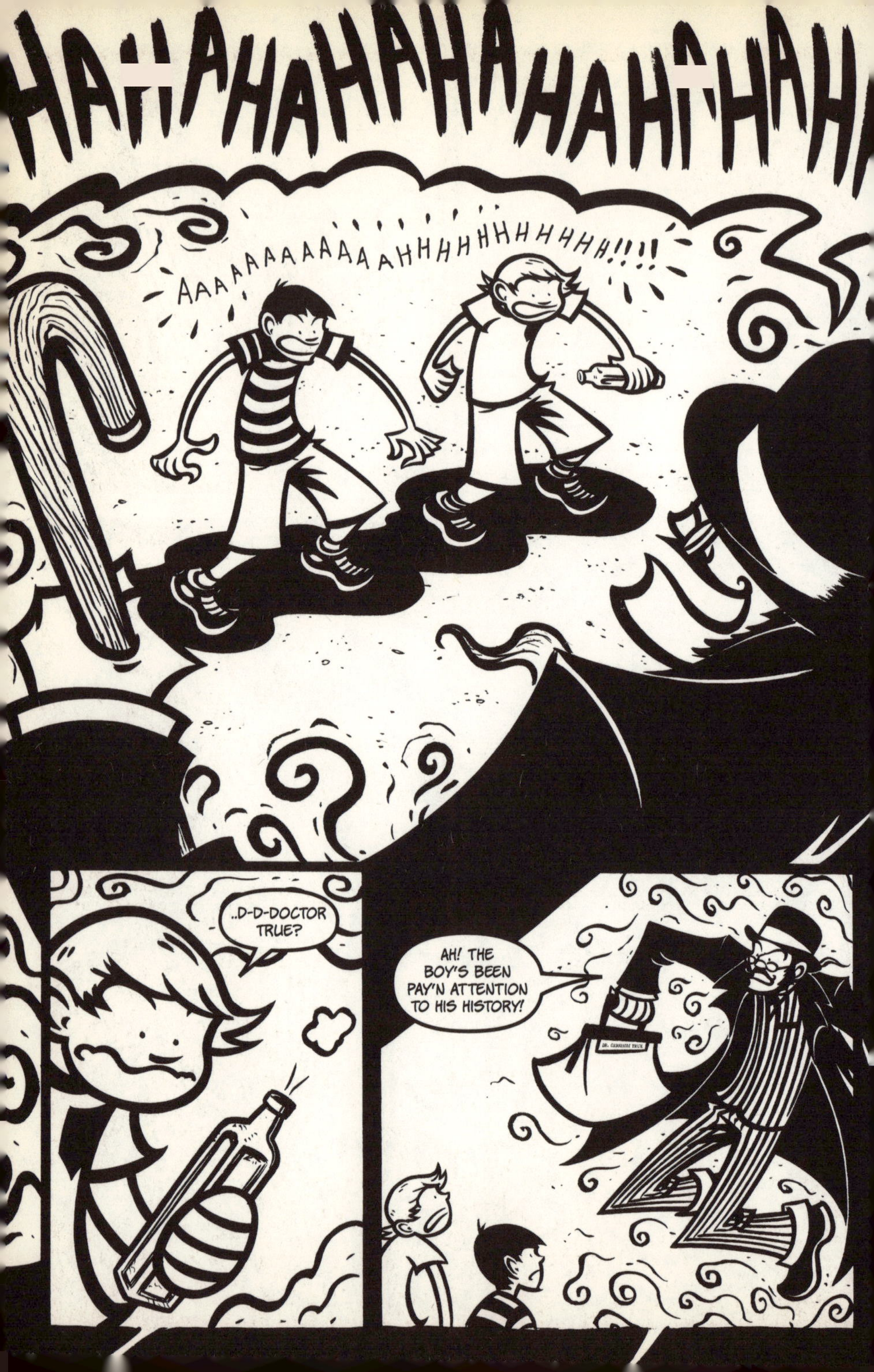
HAHAHAHAHAHAHAHAHAHAHAH
AAAAAAAAAAAAAAHHHHHHHHHHH!!!!!
..D-D-DOCTOR TRUE?
AH! THE BOY'S BEEN PAY'N ATTENTION TO HIS HISTORY!

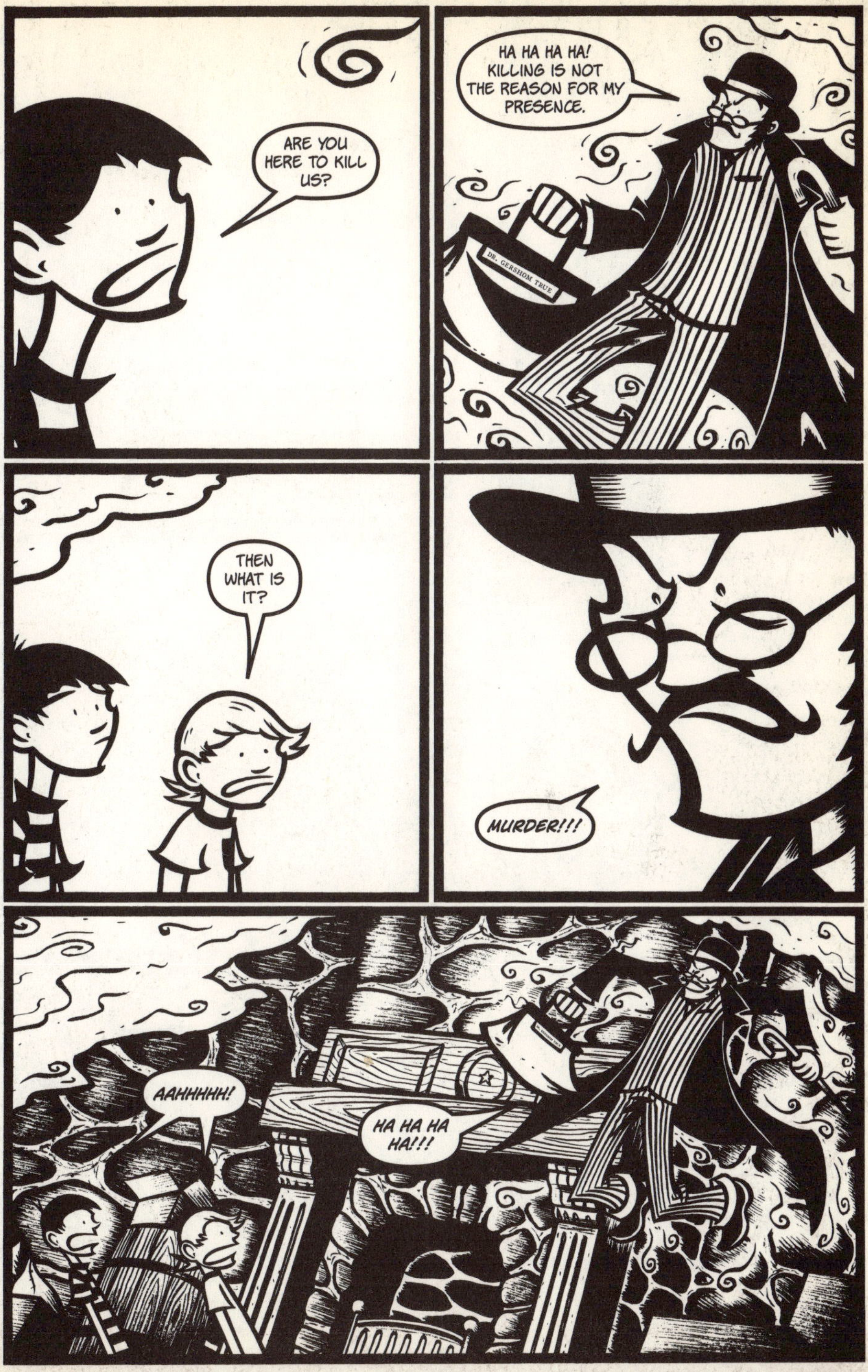
ARE YOU HERE TO KILL US?
HA HA HA HA! KILLING IS NOT THE REASON FOR MY PRESENCE.
DR. GERSHOM TRUE
THEN WHAT IS IT?
MURDER!!!
AAHHHHH!
HA HA HA HA!!!

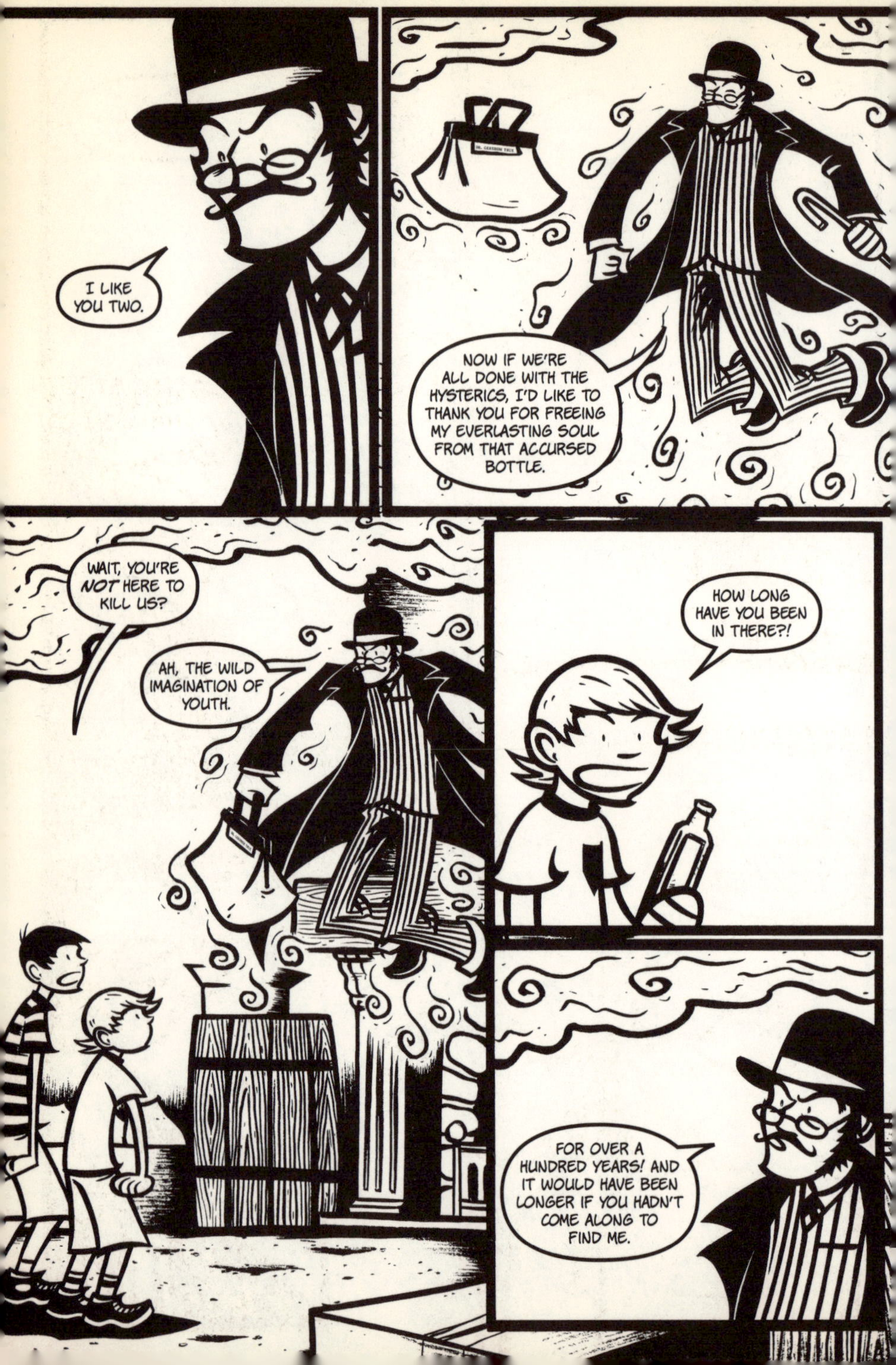
I LIKE YOU TWO.
NOW IF WE'RE ALL DONE WITH THE HYSTERICS, I'D LIKE TO THANK YOU FOR FREEING MY EVERLASTING SOUL FROM THAT ACCURSED BOTTLE.
WAIT, YOU'RE *NOT* HERE TO KILL US?
AH, THE WILD IMAGINATION OF YOUTH.
HOW LONG HAVE YOU BEEN IN THERE?!
FOR OVER A HUNDRED YEARS! AND IT WOULD HAVE BEEN LONGER IF YOU HADN'T COME ALONG TO FIND ME.

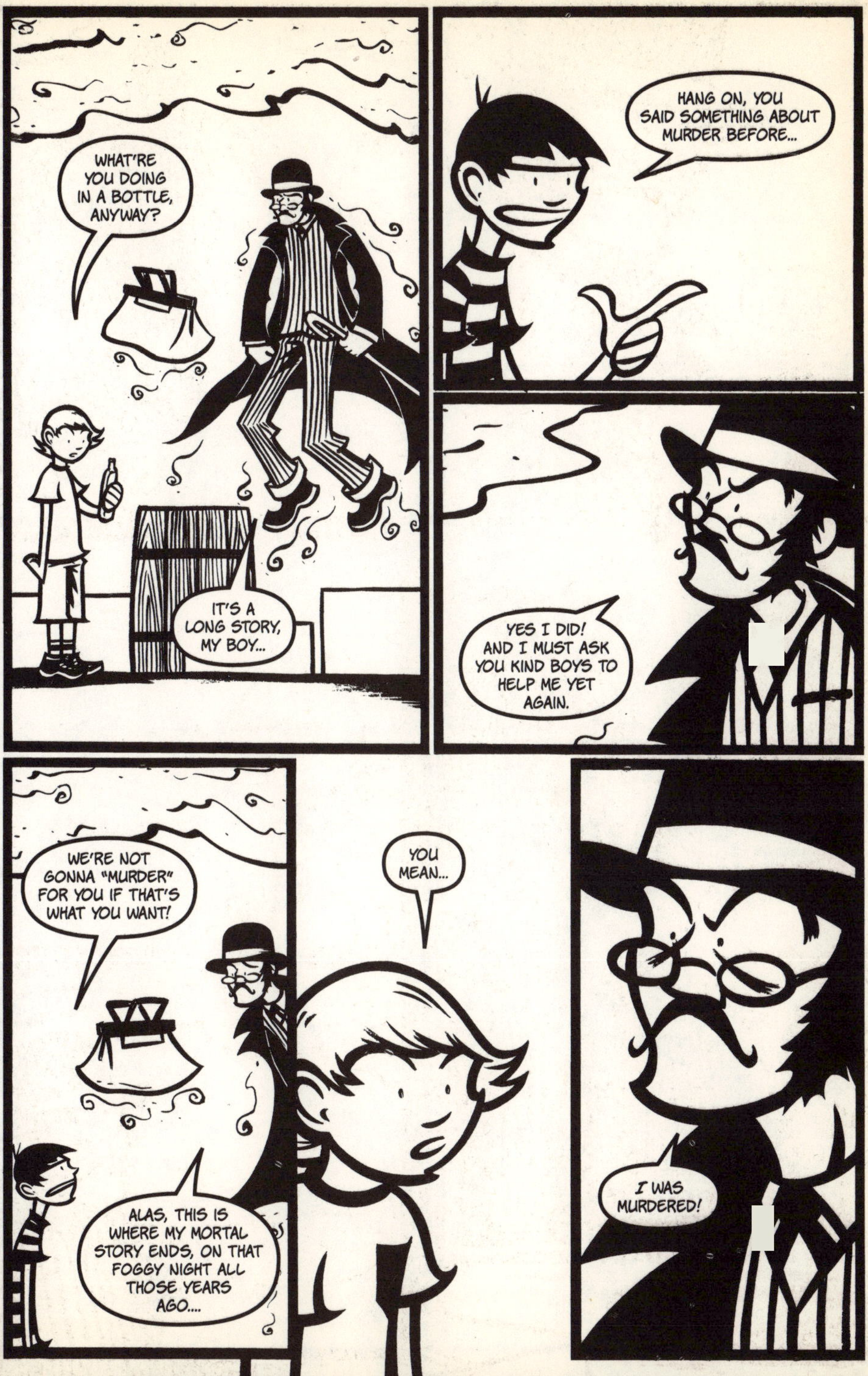
WHAT'RE YOU DOING IN A BOTTLE, ANYWAY?
IT'S A LONG STORY, MY BOY...
HANG ON, YOU SAID SOMETHING ABOUT MURDER BEFORE...
YES I DID! AND I MUST ASK YOU KIND BOYS TO HELP ME YET AGAIN.
WE'RE NOT GONNA "MURDER" FOR YOU IF THAT'S WHAT YOU WANT!
ALAS, THIS IS WHERE MY MORTAL STORY ENDS, ON THAT FOGGY NIGHT ALL THOSE YEARS AGO....
YOU MEAN...
I WAS MURDERED!

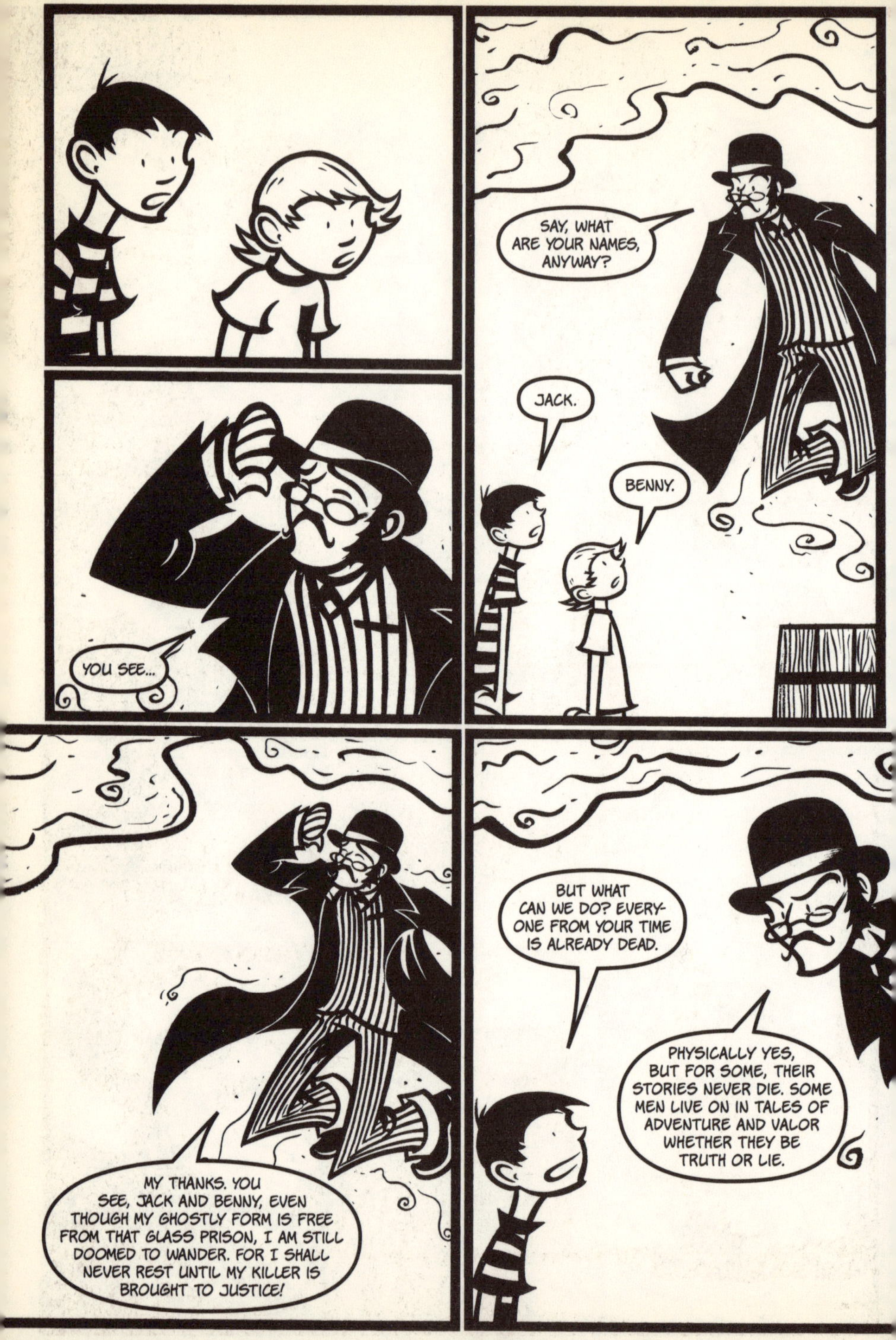
YOU SEE...
SAY, WHAT ARE YOUR NAMES, ANYWAY?
JACK.
BENNY.
MY THANKS. YOU SEE, JACK AND BENNY, EVEN THOUGH MY GHOSTLY FORM IS FREE FROM THAT GLASS PRISON, I AM STILL DOOMED TO WANDER. FOR I SHALL NEVER REST UNTIL MY KILLER IS BROUGHT TO JUSTICE!
BUT WHAT CAN WE DO? EVERY-ONE FROM YOUR TIME IS ALREADY DEAD.
PHYSICALLY YES, BUT FOR SOME, THEIR STORIES NEVER DIE. SOME MEN LIVE ON IN TALES OF ADVENTURE AND VALOR WHETHER THEY BE TRUTH OR LIE.

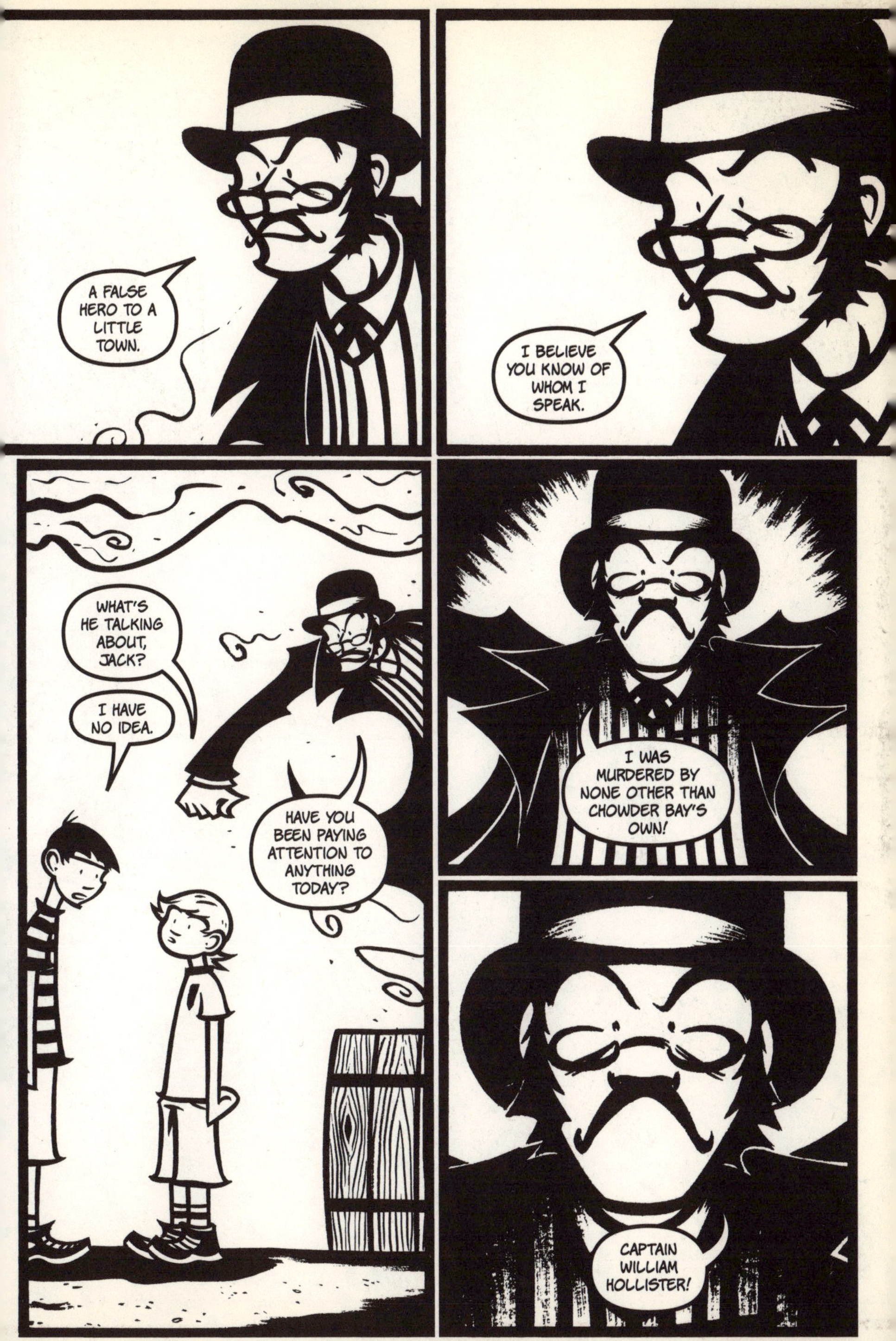
A FALSE HERO TO A LITTLE TOWN.
I BELIEVE YOU KNOW OF WHOM I SPEAK.
WHAT'S HE TALKING ABOUT, JACK?
I HAVE NO IDEA.
HAVE YOU BEEN PAYING ATTENTION TO ANYTHING TODAY?
I WAS MURDERED BY NONE OTHER THAN CHOWDER BAY'S OWN!
CAPTAIN WILLIAM HOLLISTER!

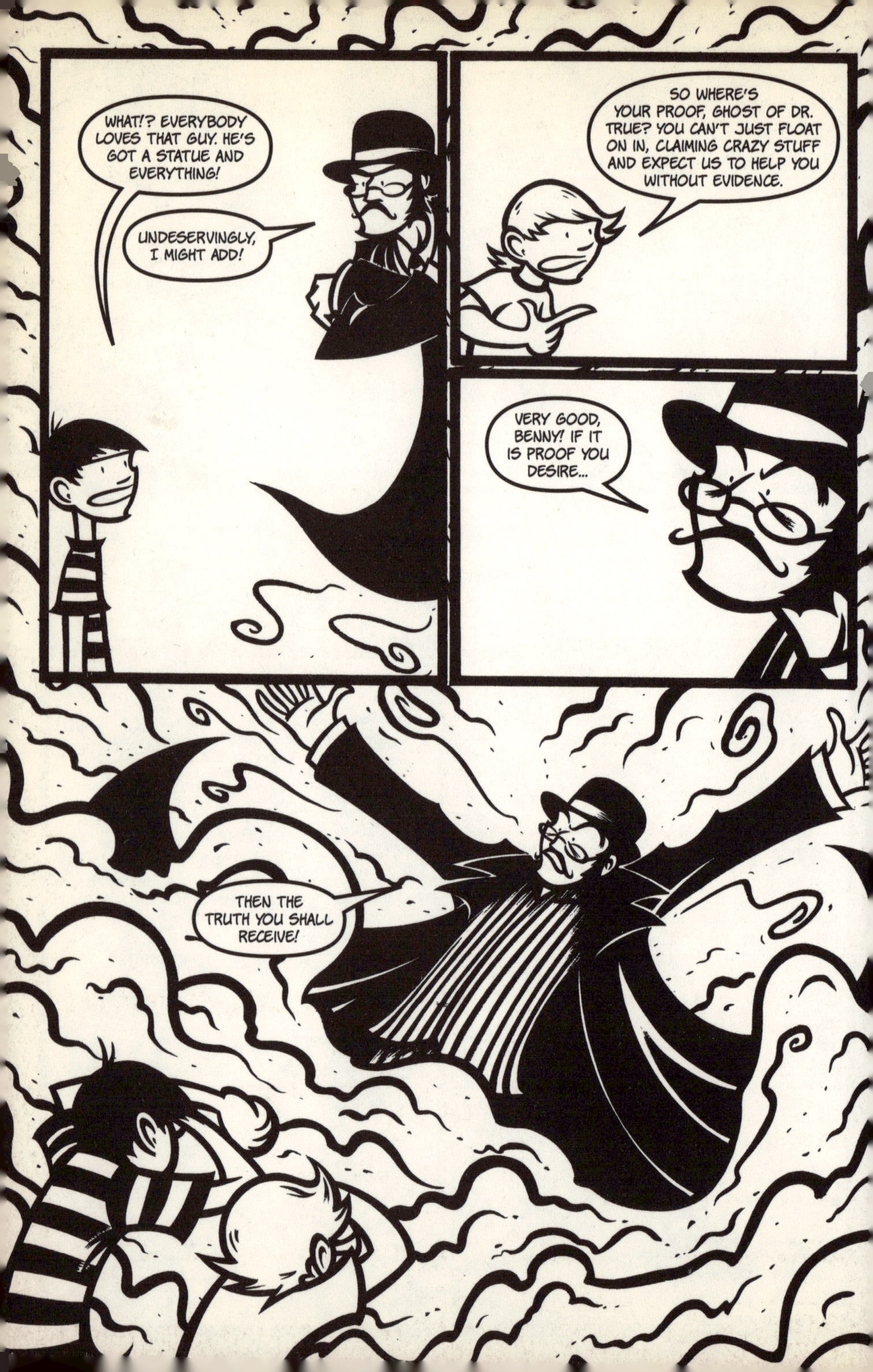
WHAT!? EVERYBODY LOVES THAT GUY. HE'S GOT A STATUE AND EVERYTHING!
UNDESERVINGLY, I MIGHT ADD!
SO WHERE'S YOUR PROOF, GHOST OF DR. TRUE? YOU CAN'T JUST FLOAT ON IN, CLAIMING CRAZY STUFF AND EXPECT US TO HELP YOU WITHOUT EVIDENCE.
VERY GOOD, BENNY! IF IT IS PROOF YOU DESIRE...
THEN THE TRUTH YOU SHALL RECEIVE!

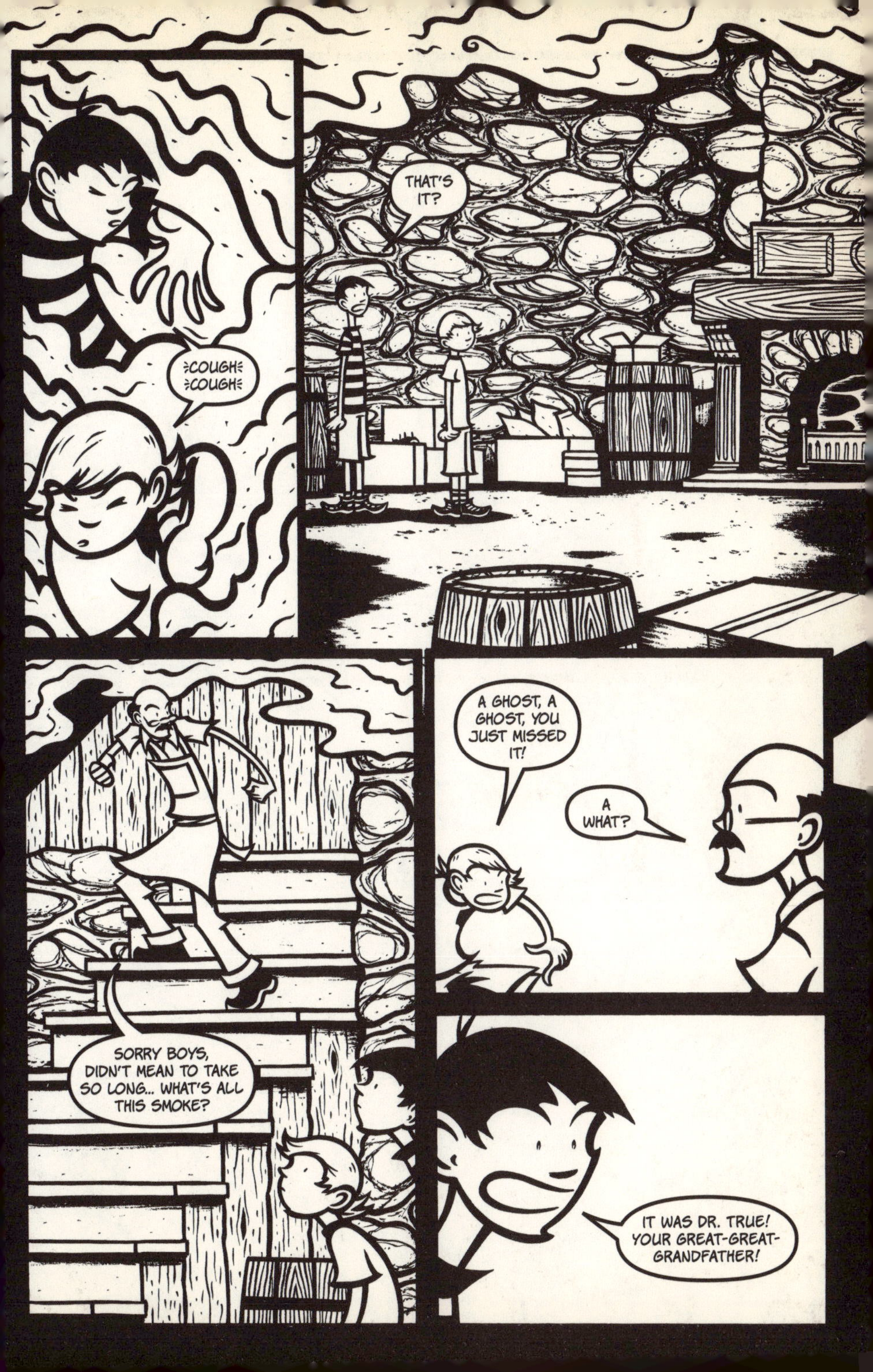

COUGH COUGH
THAT'S IT?
SORRY BOYS, DIDN'T MEAN TO TAKE SO LONG... WHAT'S ALL THIS SMOKE?
A GHOST, A GHOST, YOU JUST MISSED IT!
A WHAT?
IT WAS DR. TRUE! YOUR GREAT-GREAT-GRANDFATHER!

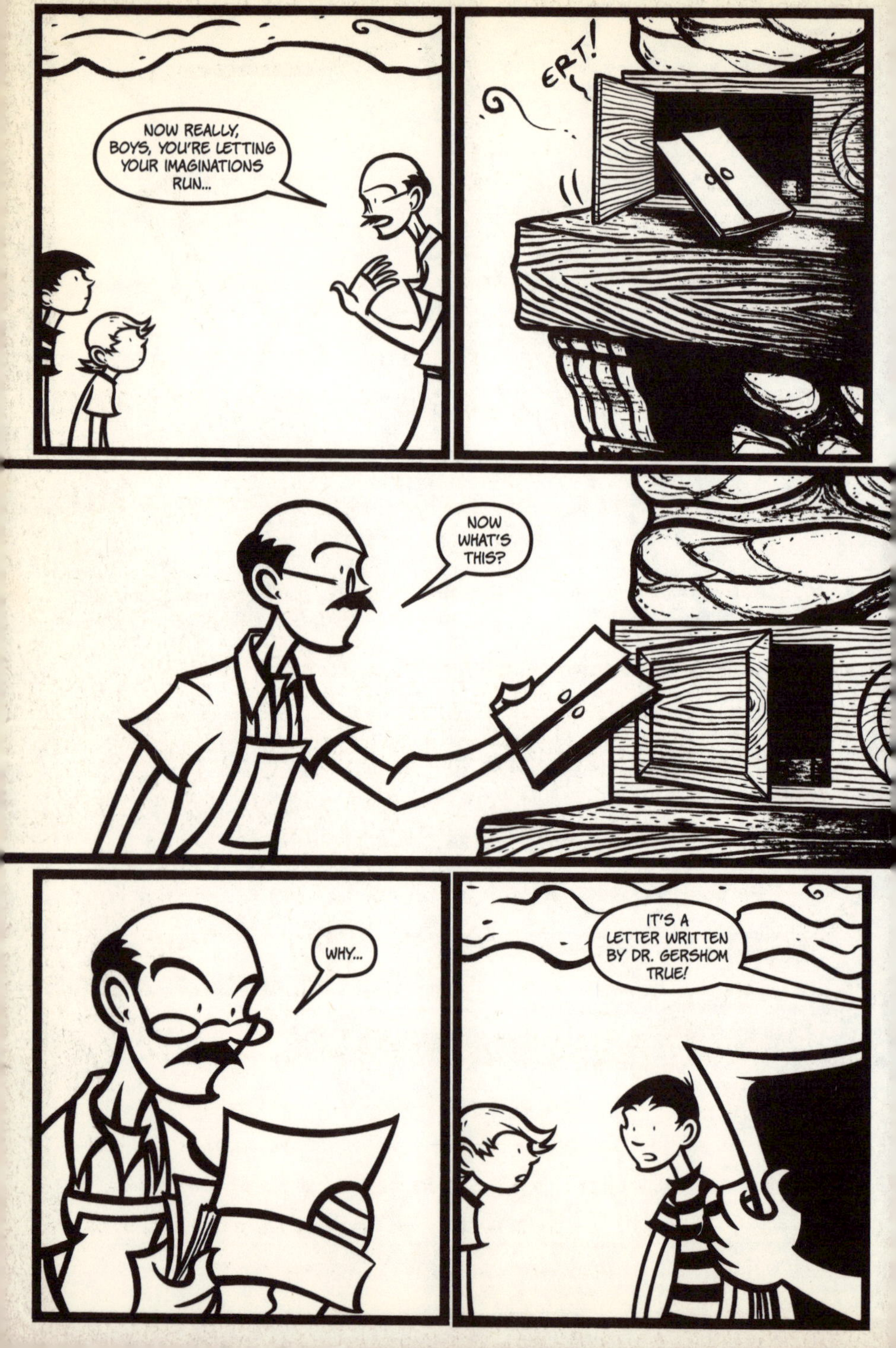
NOW REALLY, BOYS, YOU'RE LETTING YOUR IMAGINATIONS RUN...
ERT!
NOW WHAT'S THIS?
WHY...
IT'S A LETTER WRITTEN BY DR. GERSHOM TRUE!

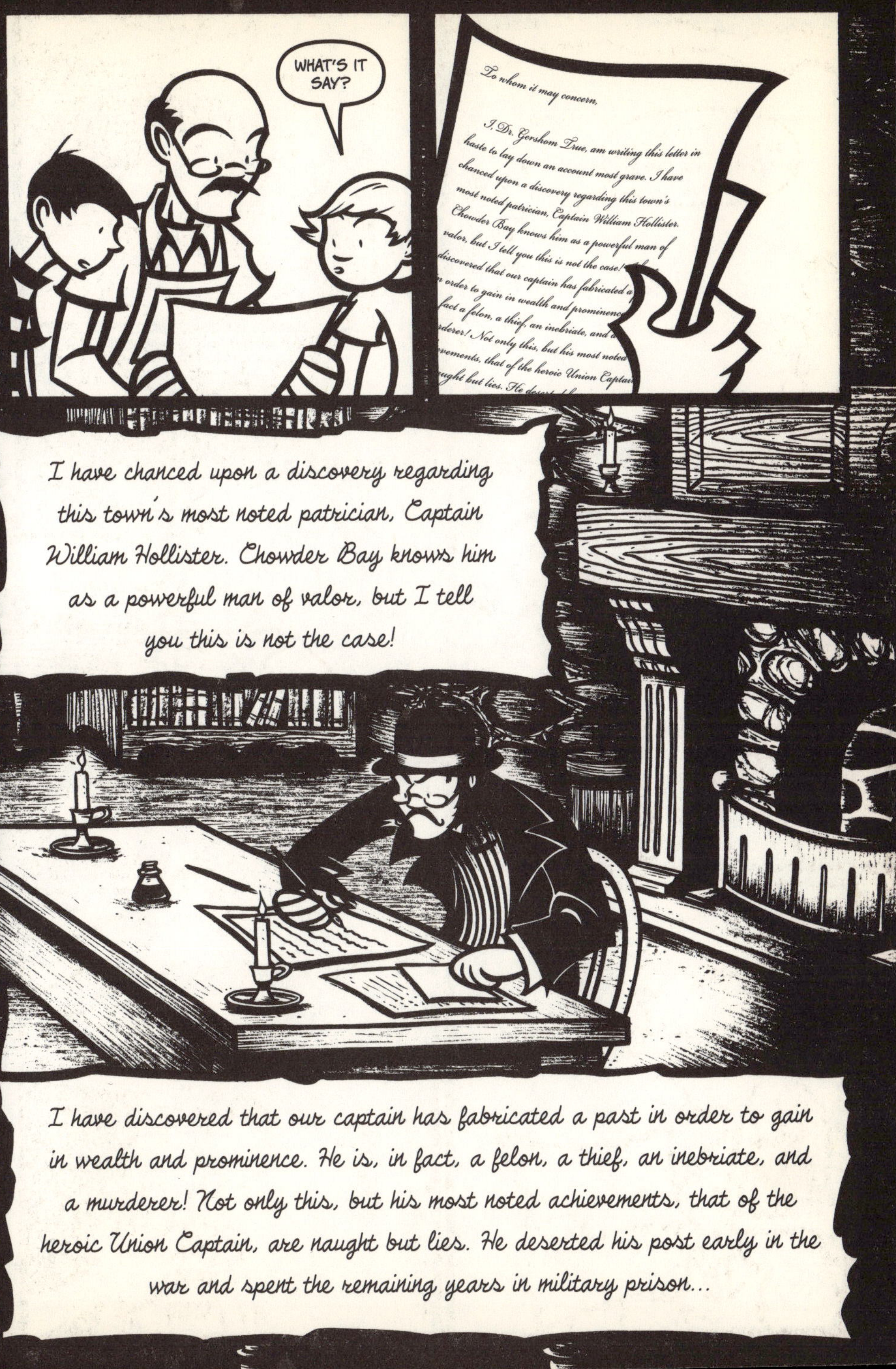
WHAT'S IT SAY?
To whom it may concern,
I, Dr. Gershom True, am writing this letter in
haste to lay down an account most grave. I have
chanced upon a discovery regarding this town's
most noted patrician, Captain William Hollister.
Chowder Bay knows him as a powerful man of
valor, but I tell you this is not the case!
discovered that our captain has fabricated a
order to gain in wealth and
fact a felon, a thief, an inebriate, and
Not only this, but his most
that of the heroic Union
but lies.
I have chanced upon a discovery regarding this town's most noted patrician, Captain William Hollister. Chowder Bay knows him as a powerful man of valor, but I tell you this is not the case!
I have discovered that our captain has fabricated a past in order to gain in wealth and prominence. He is, in fact, a felon, a thief, an inebriate, and a murderer! Not only this, but his most noted achievements, that of the heroic Union Captain, are naught but lies. He deserted his post early in the war and spent the remaining years in military prison...

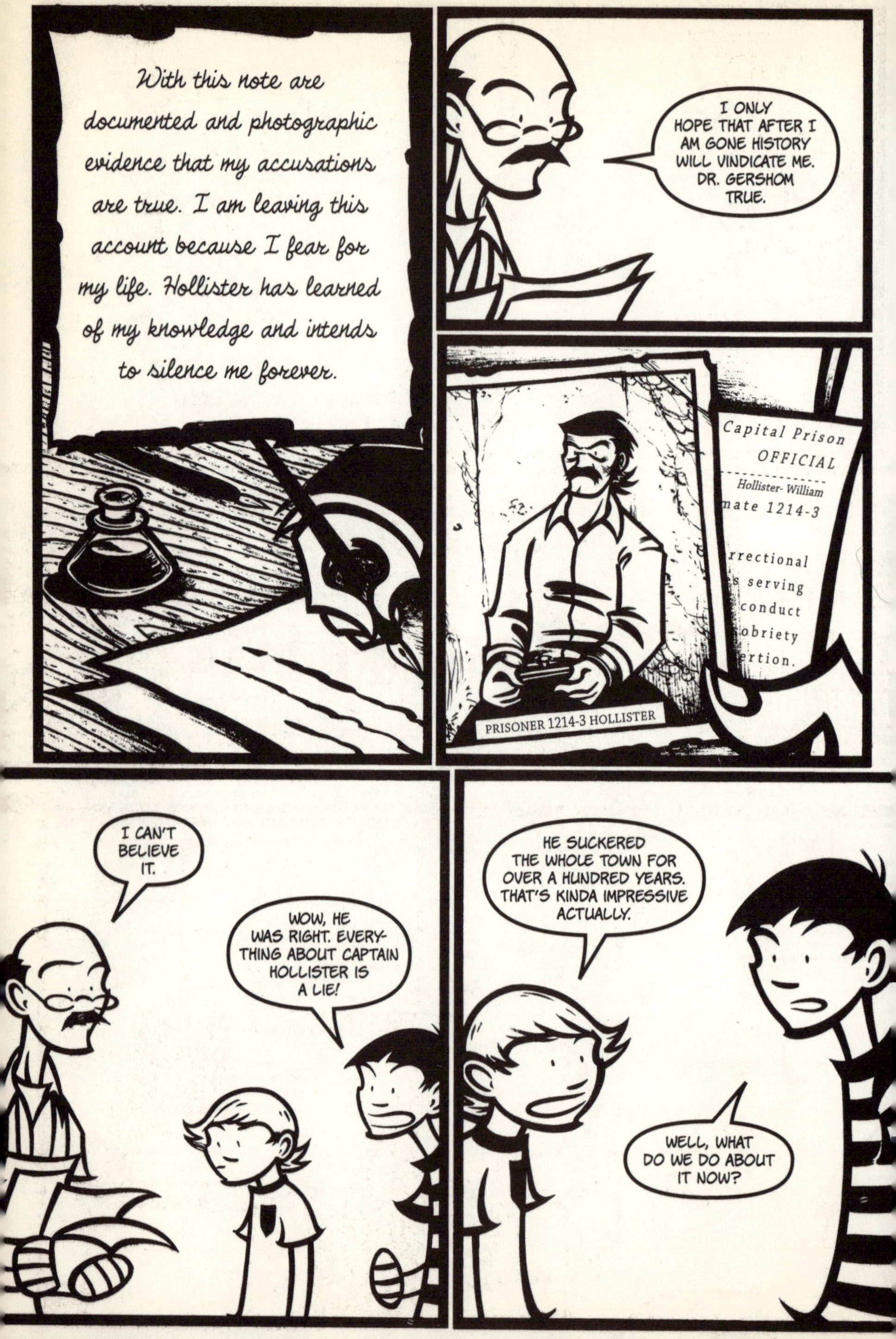
With this note are documented and photographic evidence that my accusations are true. I am leaving this account because I fear for my life. Hollister has learned of my knowledge and intends to silence me forever.
I ONLY HOPE THAT AFTER I AM GONE HISTORY WILL VINDICATE ME. DR. GERSHOM TRUE.
Capital Prison
OFFICIAL
Hollister- William
mate 1214-3
rrectional
s serving
conduct
obriety
ertion.
PRISONER 1214-3 HOLLISTER
I CAN'T BELIEVE IT.
WOW, HE WAS RIGHT. EVERYTHING ABOUT CAPTAIN HOLLISTER IS A LIE!
HE SUCKERED THE WHOLE TOWN FOR OVER A HUNDRED YEARS. THAT'S KINDA IMPRESSIVE ACTUALLY.
WELL, WHAT DO WE DO ABOUT IT NOW?

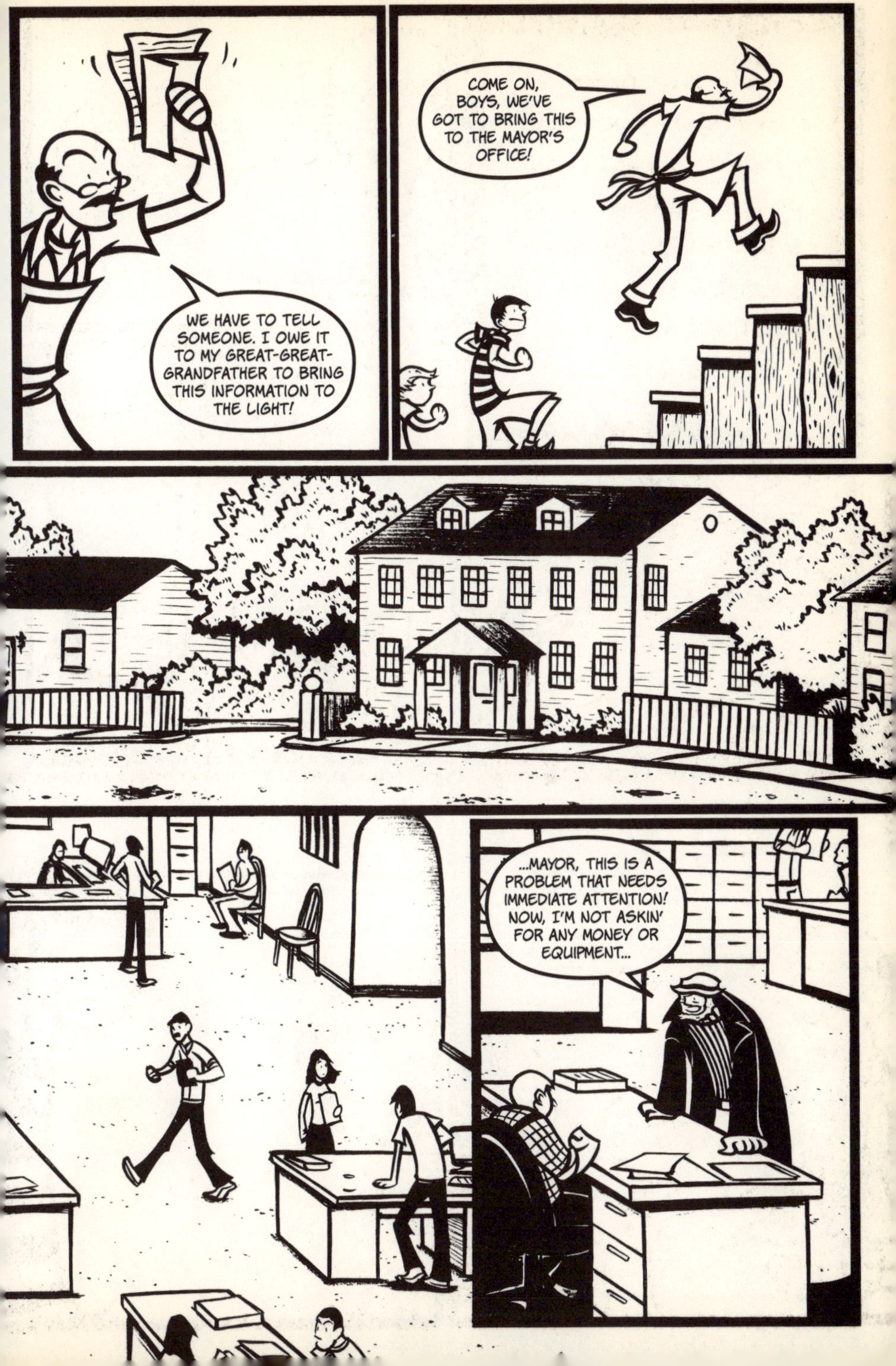
WE HAVE TO TELL SOMEONE. I OWE IT TO MY GREAT-GREAT-GRANDFATHER TO BRING THIS INFORMATION TO THE LIGHT!
COME ON, BOYS, WE'VE GOT TO BRING THIS TO THE MAYOR'S OFFICE!
...MAYOR, THIS IS A PROBLEM THAT NEEDS IMMEDIATE ATTENTION! NOW, I'M NOT ASKIN' FOR ANY MONEY OR EQUIPMENT...

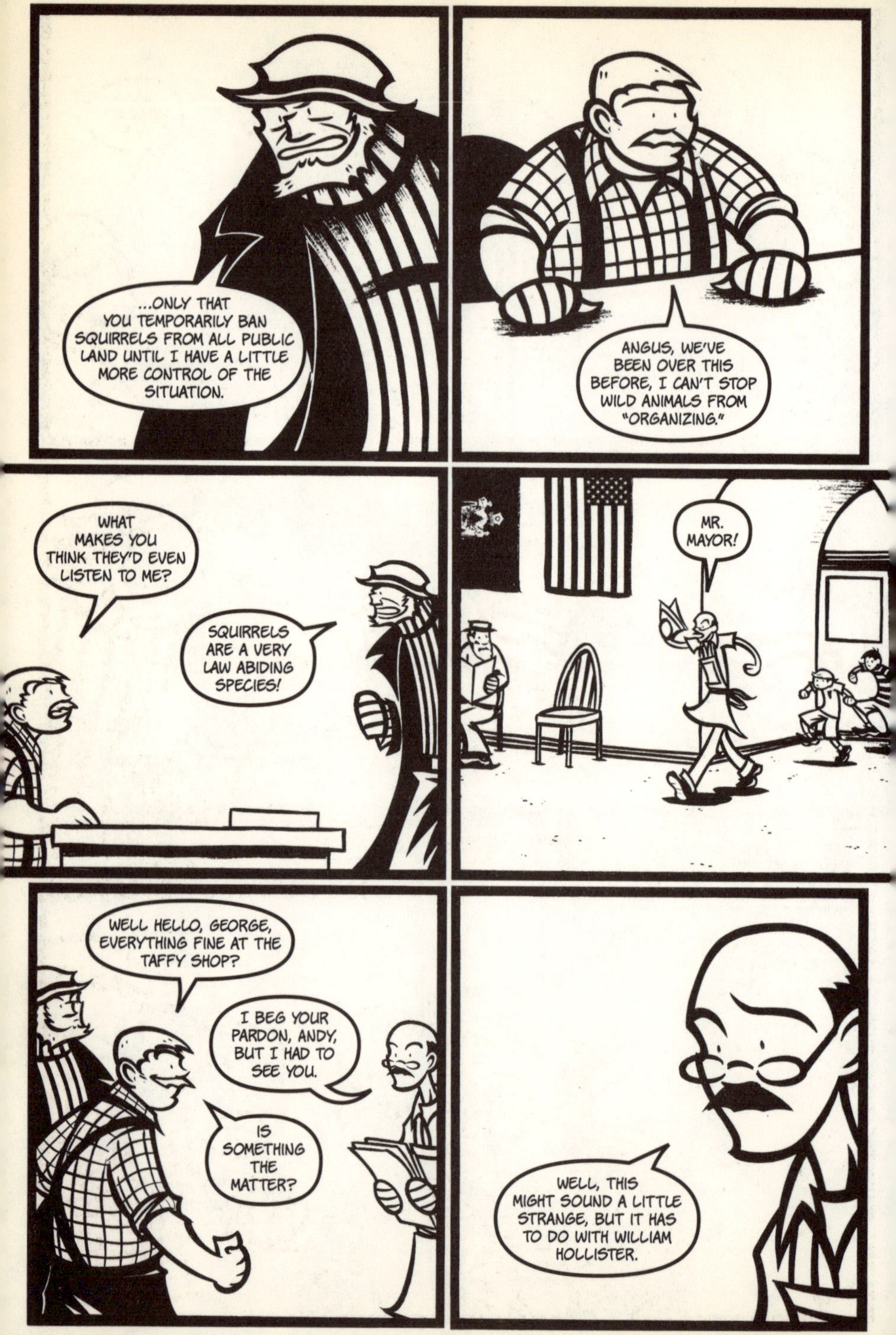
...ONLY THAT YOU TEMPORARILY BAN SQUIRRELS FROM ALL PUBLIC LAND UNTIL I HAVE A LITTLE MORE CONTROL OF THE SITUATION.
ANGUS, WE'VE BEEN OVER THIS BEFORE, I CAN'T STOP WILD ANIMALS FROM "ORGANIZING."
WHAT MAKES YOU THINK THEY'D EVEN LISTEN TO ME?
SQUIRRELS ARE A VERY LAW ABIDING SPECIES!
MR. MAYOR!
WELL HELLO, GEORGE, EVERYTHING FINE AT THE TAFFY SHOP?
I BEG YOUR PARDON, ANDY, BUT I HAD TO SEE YOU.
IS SOMETHING THE MATTER?
WELL, THIS MIGHT SOUND A LITTLE STRANGE, BUT IT HAS TO DO WITH WILLIAM HOLLISTER.

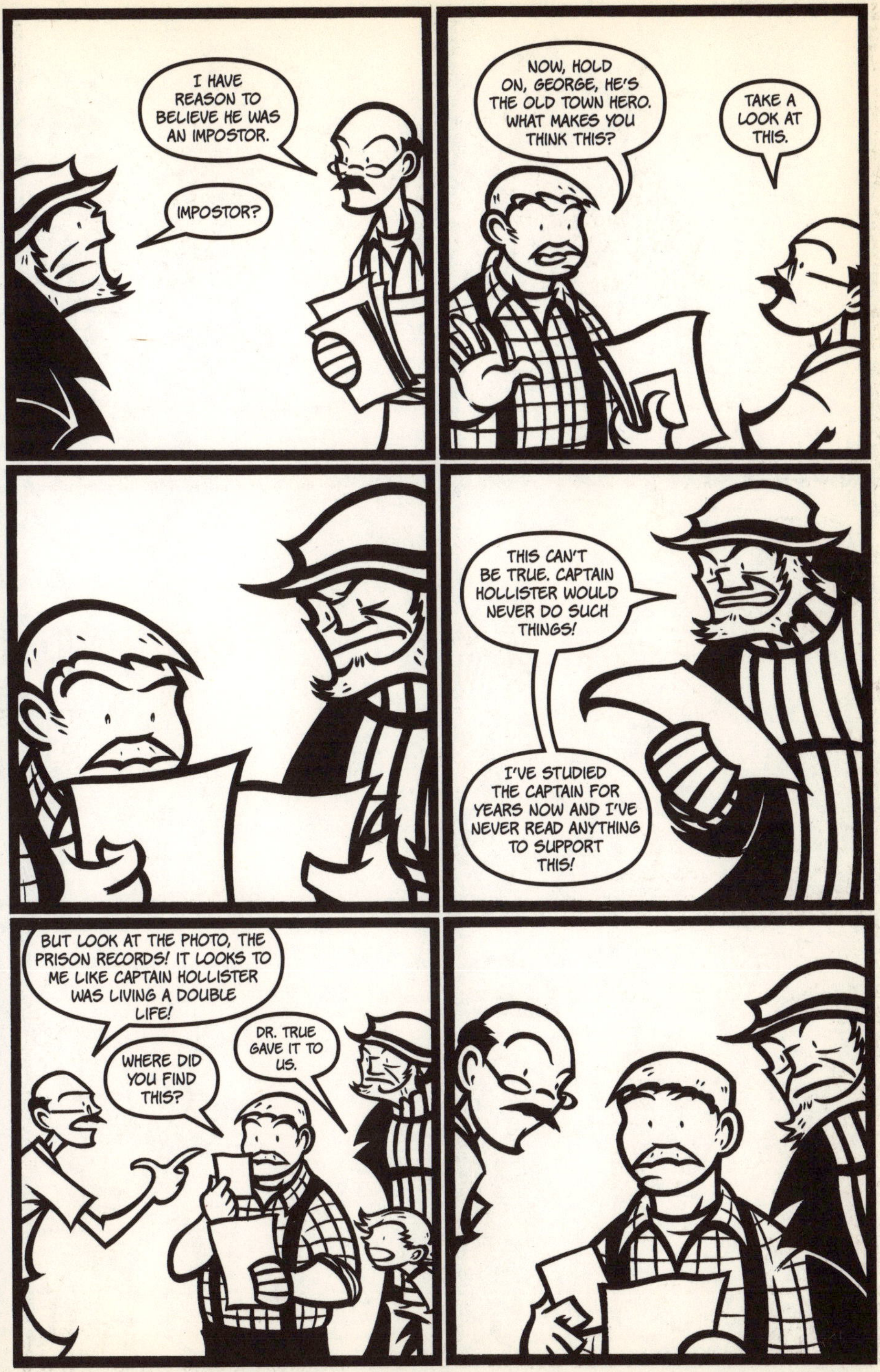
I HAVE REASON TO BELIEVE HE WAS AN IMPOSTOR.
IMPOSTOR?
NOW, HOLD ON, GEORGE, HE'S THE OLD TOWN HERO. WHAT MAKES YOU THINK THIS?
TAKE A LOOK AT THIS.
THIS CAN'T BE TRUE. CAPTAIN HOLLISTER WOULD NEVER DO SUCH THINGS!
I'VE STUDIED THE CAPTAIN FOR YEARS NOW AND I'VE NEVER READ ANYTHING TO SUPPORT THIS!
BUT LOOK AT THE PHOTO, THE PRISON RECORDS! IT LOOKS TO ME LIKE CAPTAIN HOLLISTER WAS LIVING A DOUBLE LIFE!
WHERE DID YOU FIND THIS?
DR. TRUE GAVE IT TO US.

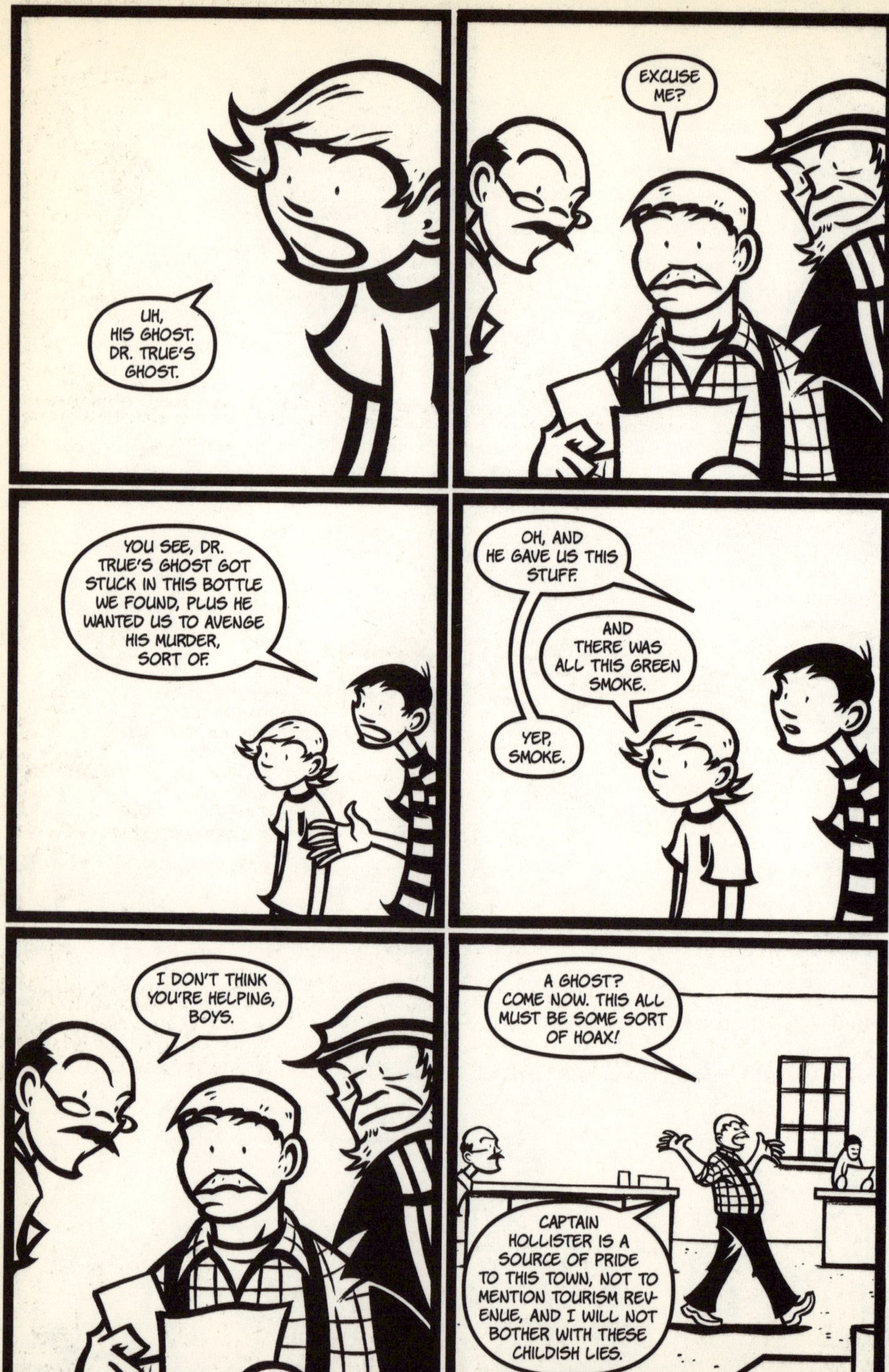
UH, HIS GHOST. DR. TRUE'S GHOST.
EXCUSE ME?
YOU SEE, DR. TRUE'S GHOST GOT STUCK IN THIS BOTTLE WE FOUND, PLUS HE WANTED US TO AVENGE HIS MURDER, SORT OF.
OH, AND HE GAVE US THIS STUFF.
AND THERE WAS ALL THIS GREEN SMOKE.
YEP, SMOKE.
I DON'T THINK YOU'RE HELPING, BOYS.
A GHOST? COME NOW. THIS ALL MUST BE SOME SORT OF HOAX!
CAPTAIN HOLLISTER IS A SOURCE OF PRIDE TO THIS TOWN, NOT TO MENTION TOURISM REV-ENUE, AND I WILL NOT BOTHER WITH THESE CHILDISH LIES.

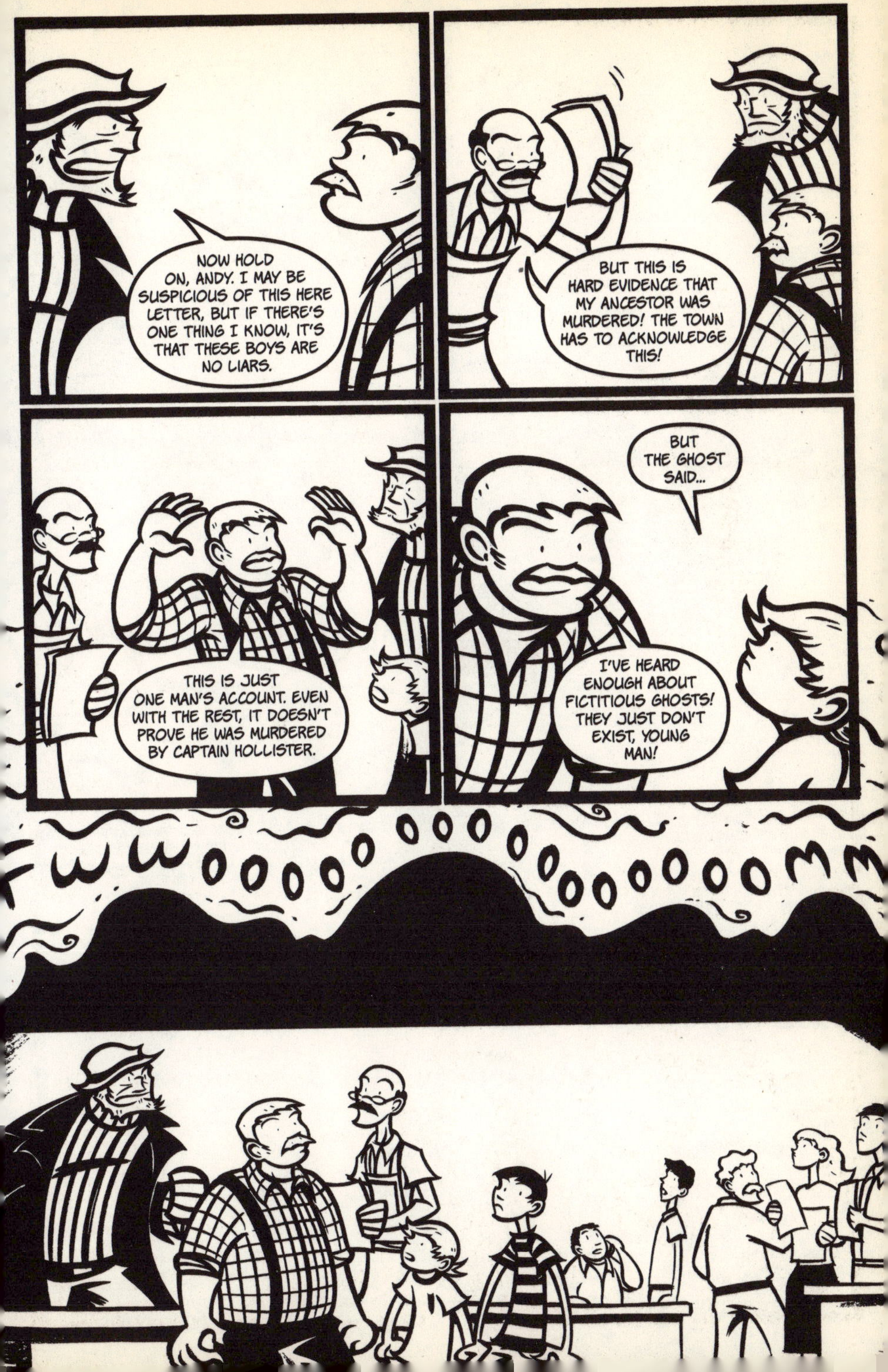
NOW HOLD ON, ANDY. I MAY BE SUSPICIOUS OF THIS HERE LETTER, BUT IF THERE'S ONE THING I KNOW, IT'S THAT THESE BOYS ARE NO LIARS.
BUT THIS IS HARD EVIDENCE THAT MY ANCESTOR WAS MURDERED! THE TOWN HAS TO ACKNOWLEDGE THIS!
THIS IS JUST ONE MAN'S ACCOUNT. EVEN WITH THE REST, IT DOESN'T PROVE HE WAS MURDERED BY CAPTAIN HOLLISTER.
BUT THE GHOST SAID...
I'VE HEARD ENOUGH ABOUT FICTITIOUS GHOSTS! THEY JUST DON'T EXIST, YOUNG MAN!
FWWOOOOOOOOOOOOOOOOOMM

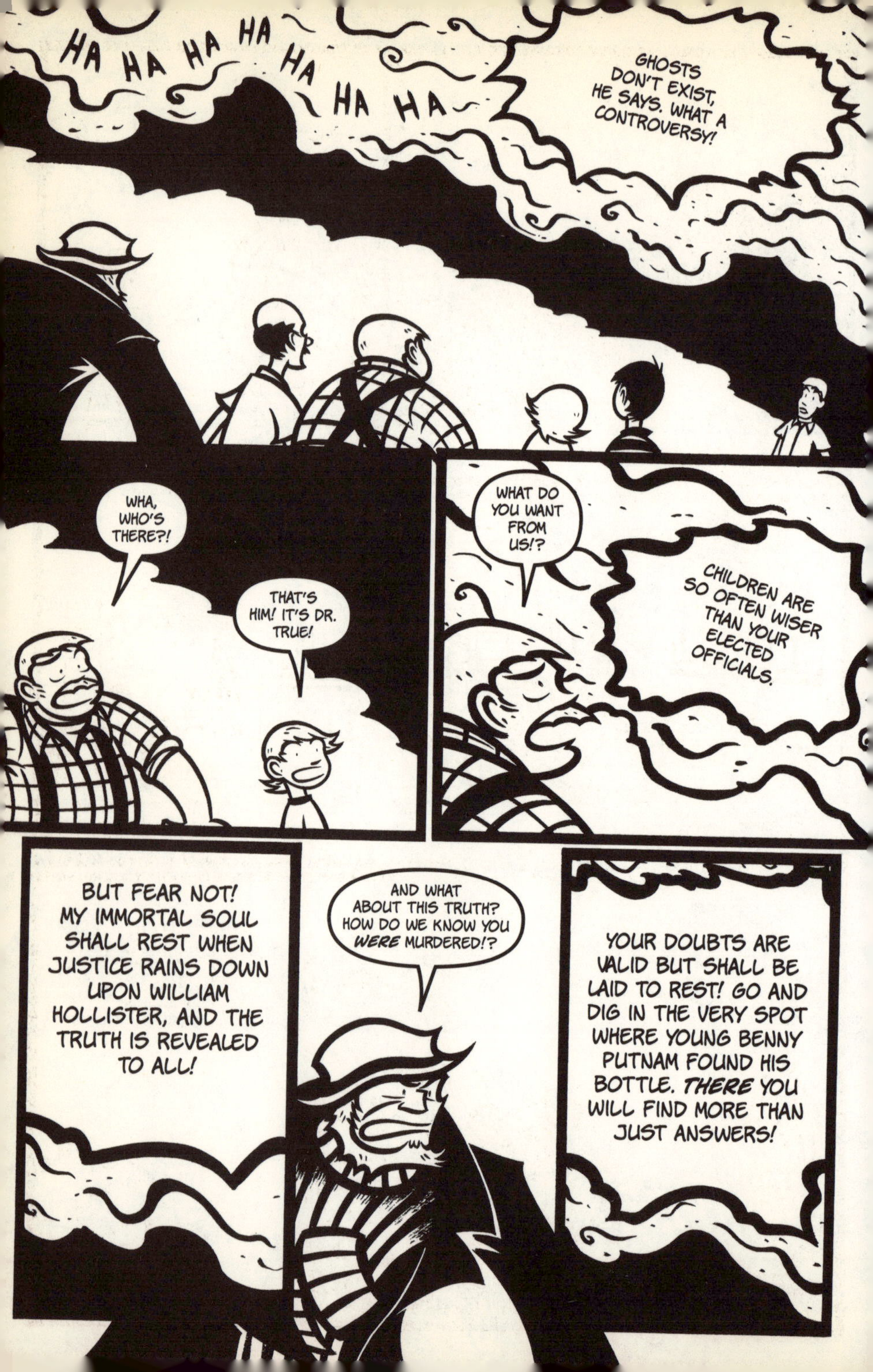
HA HA HA HA HA HA HA
GHOSTS DON'T EXIST, HE SAYS. WHAT A CONTROVERSY!
WHA, WHO'S THERE?!
THAT'S HIM! IT'S DR. TRUE!
WHAT DO YOU WANT FROM US!?
CHILDREN ARE SO OFTEN WISER THAN YOUR ELECTED OFFICIALS.
BUT FEAR NOT! MY IMMORTAL SOUL SHALL REST WHEN JUSTICE RAINS DOWN UPON WILLIAM HOLLISTER, AND THE TRUTH IS REVEALED TO ALL!
AND WHAT ABOUT THIS TRUTH? HOW DO WE KNOW YOU *WERE* MURDERED!?
YOUR DOUBTS ARE VALID BUT SHALL BE LAID TO REST! GO AND DIG IN THE VERY SPOT WHERE YOUNG BENNY PUTNAM FOUND HIS BOTTLE. *THERE* YOU WILL FIND MORE THAN JUST ANSWERS!

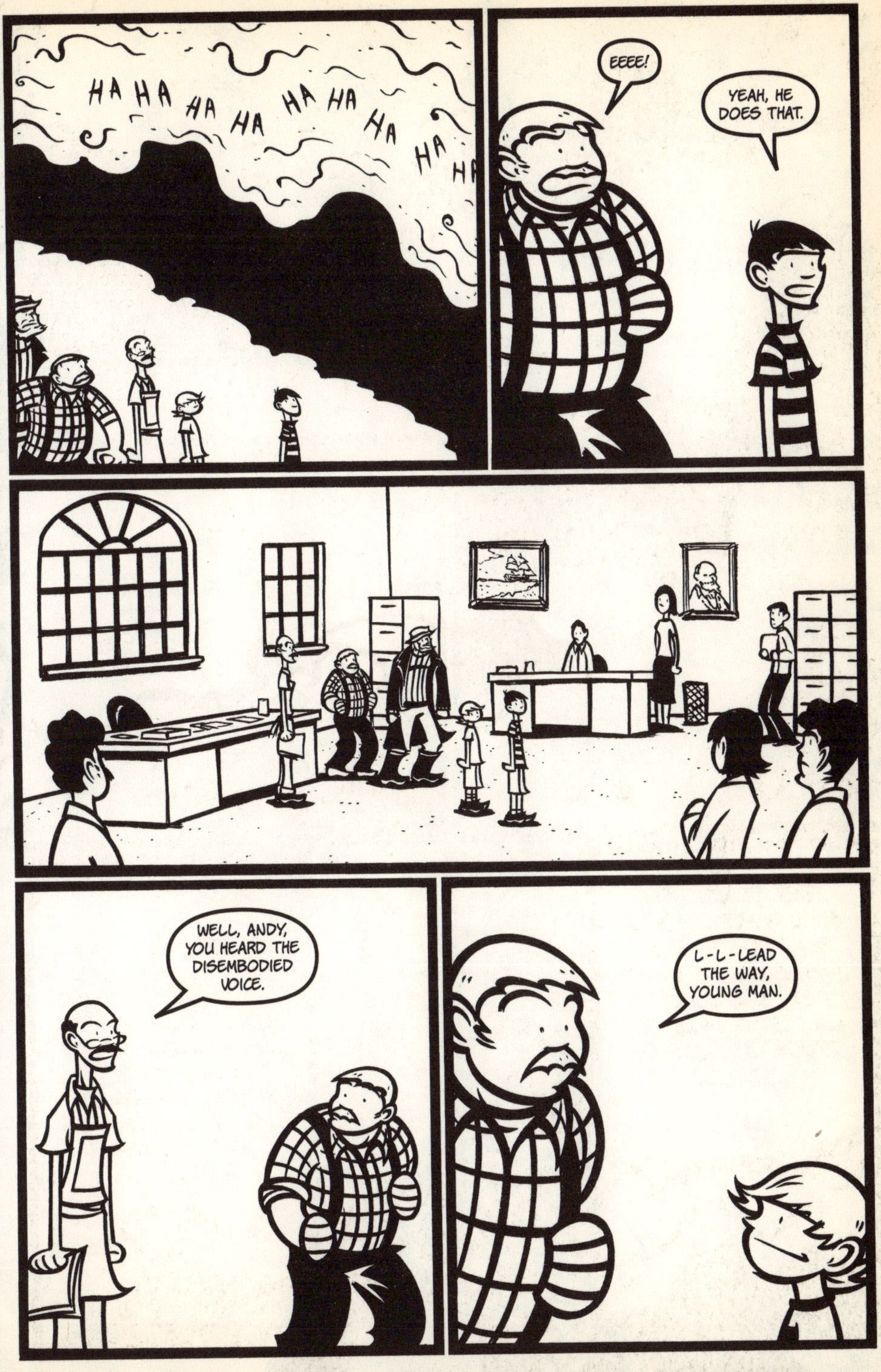
HA HA HA HA HA HA HA HA HA HA
EEEE!
YEAH, HE DOES THAT.
WELL, ANDY, YOU HEARD THE DISEMBODIED VOICE.
L-L-LEAD THE WAY, YOUNG MAN.

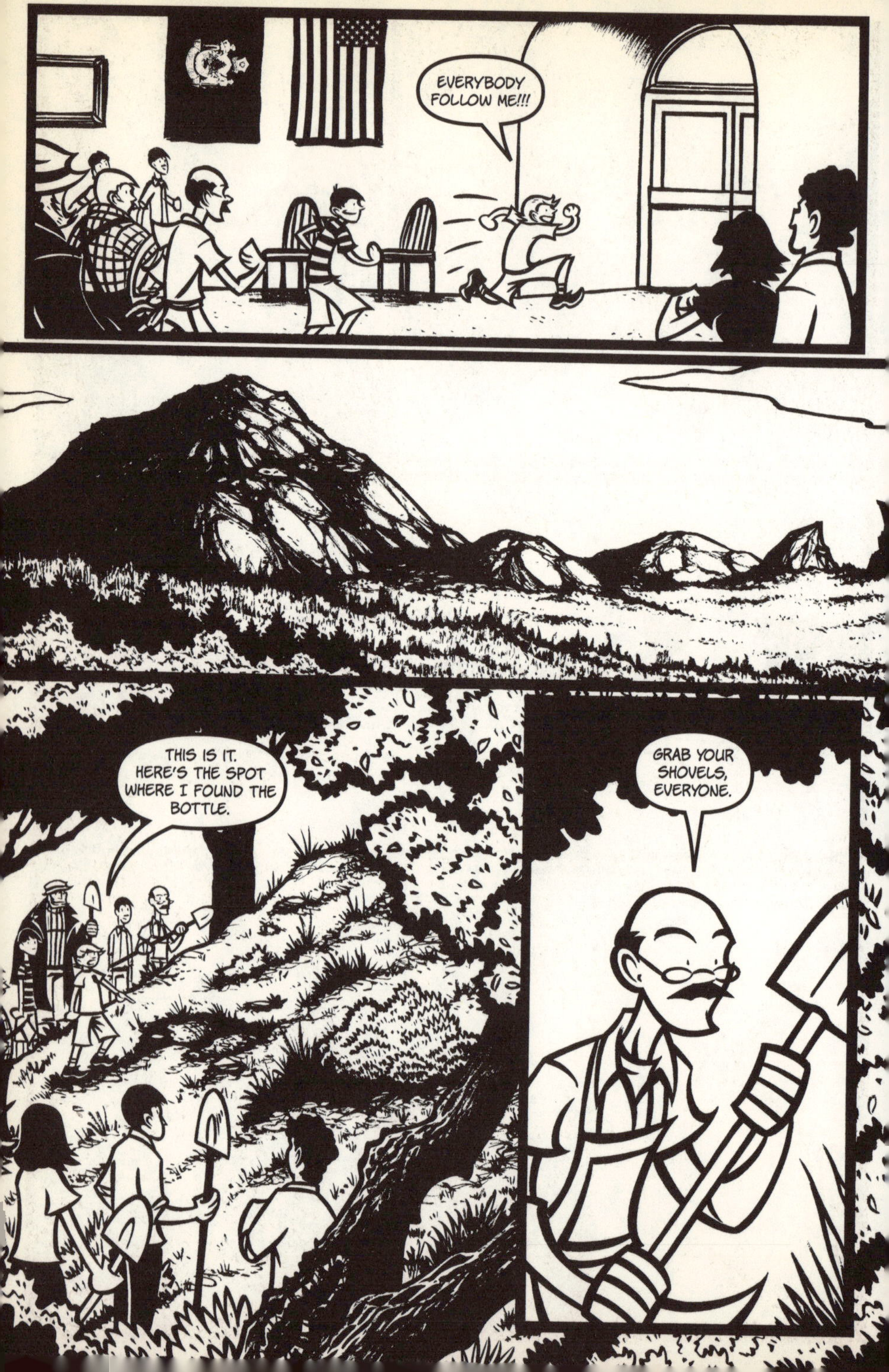
EVERYBODY FOLLOW ME!!!
THIS IS IT. HERE'S THE SPOT WHERE I FOUND THE BOTTLE.
GRAB YOUR SHOVELS, EVERYONE.

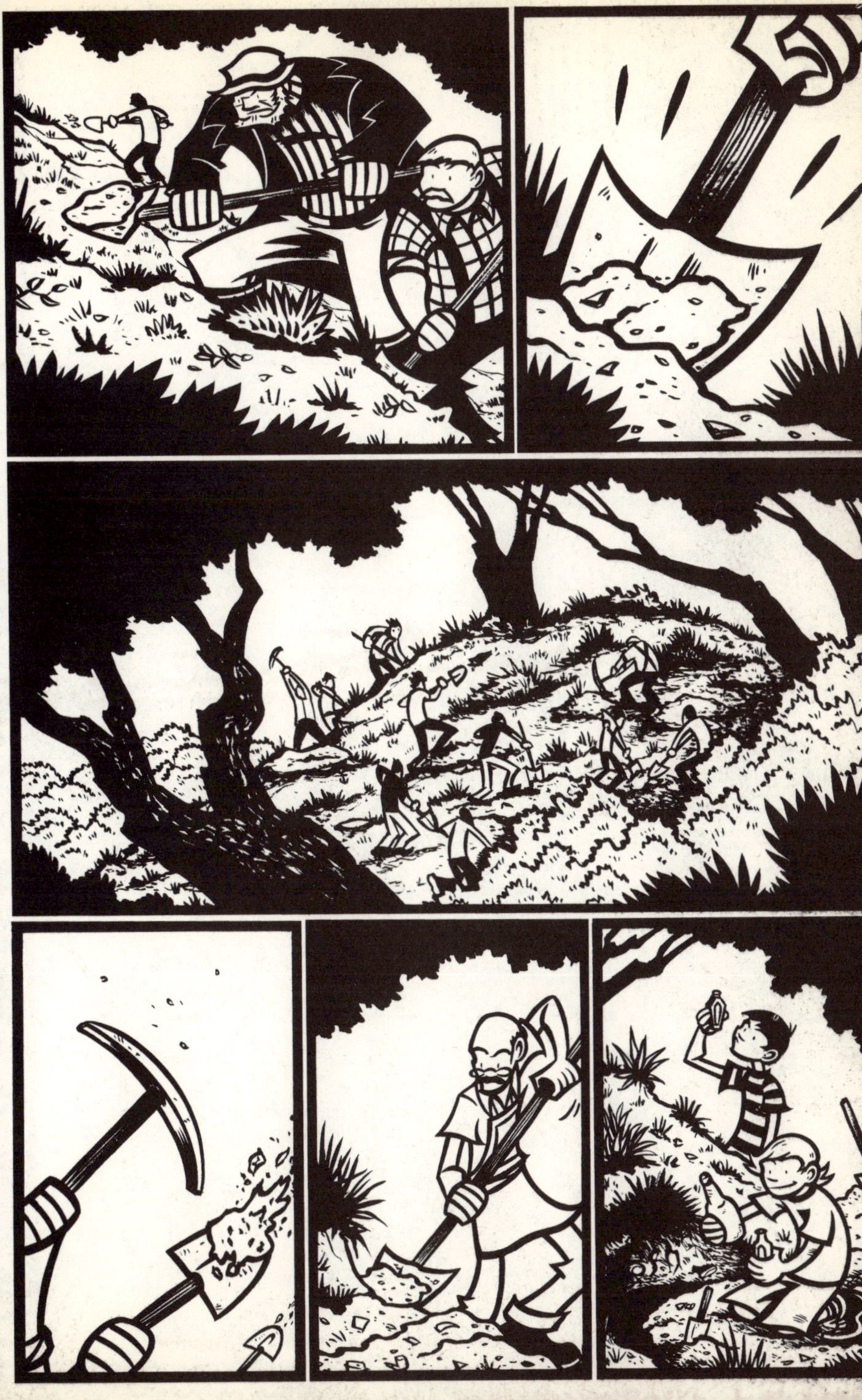

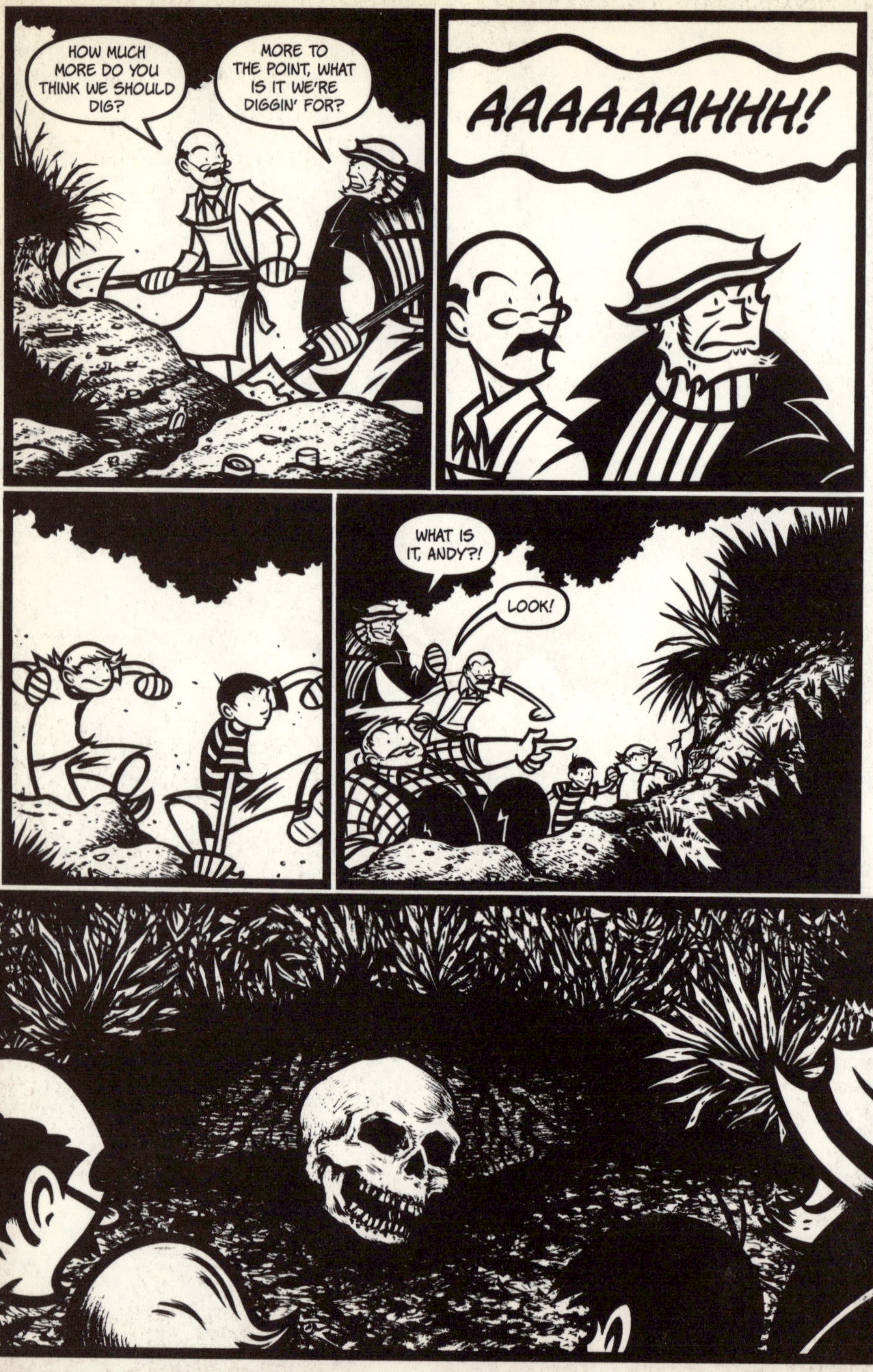
HOW MUCH MORE DO YOU THINK WE SHOULD DIG?
MORE TO THE POINT, WHAT IS IT WE'RE DIGGIN' FOR?
AAAAAAHHH!
WHAT IS IT, ANDY?!
LOOK!

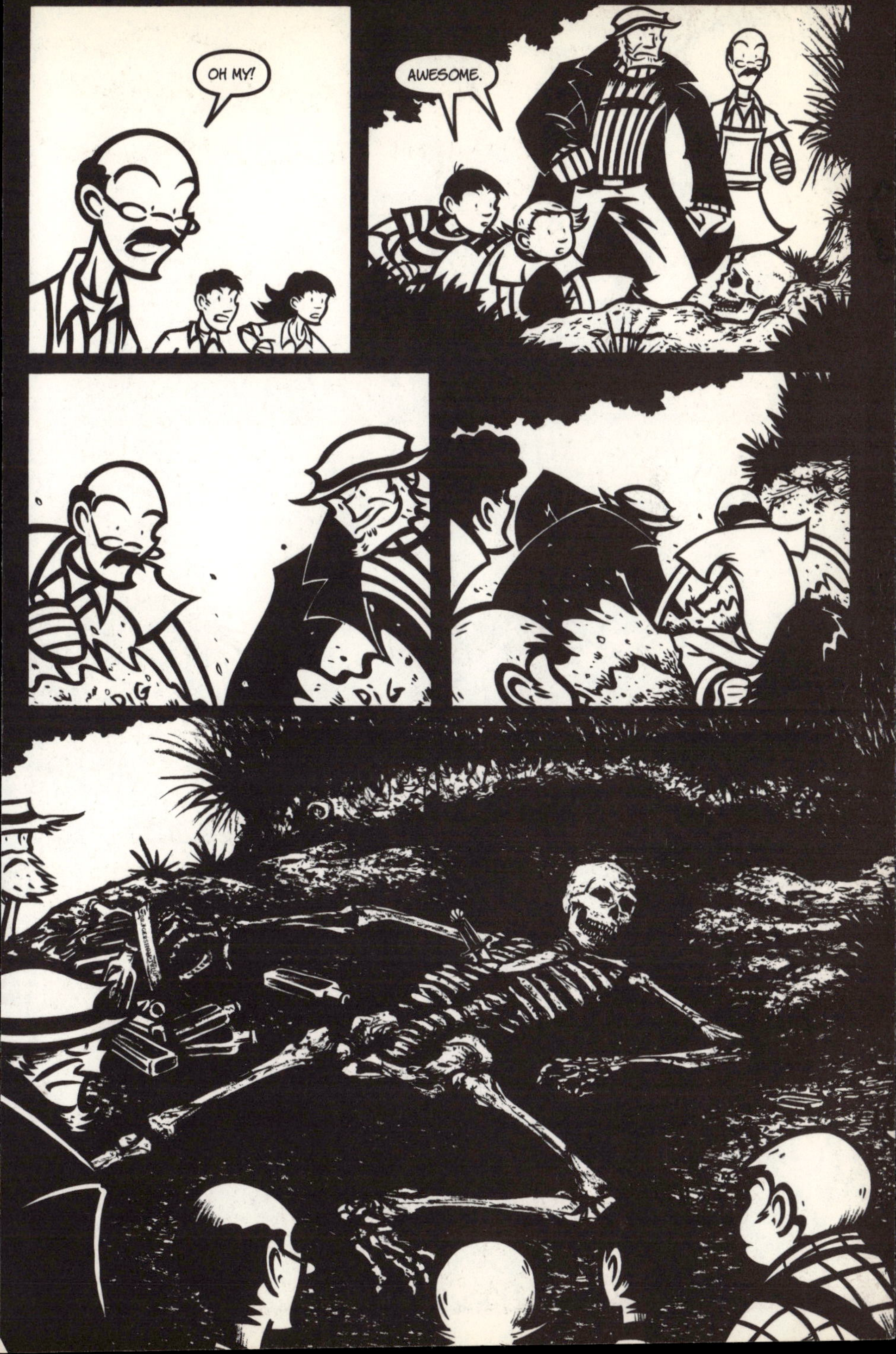
OH MY!
AWESOME.
DIG
DIG

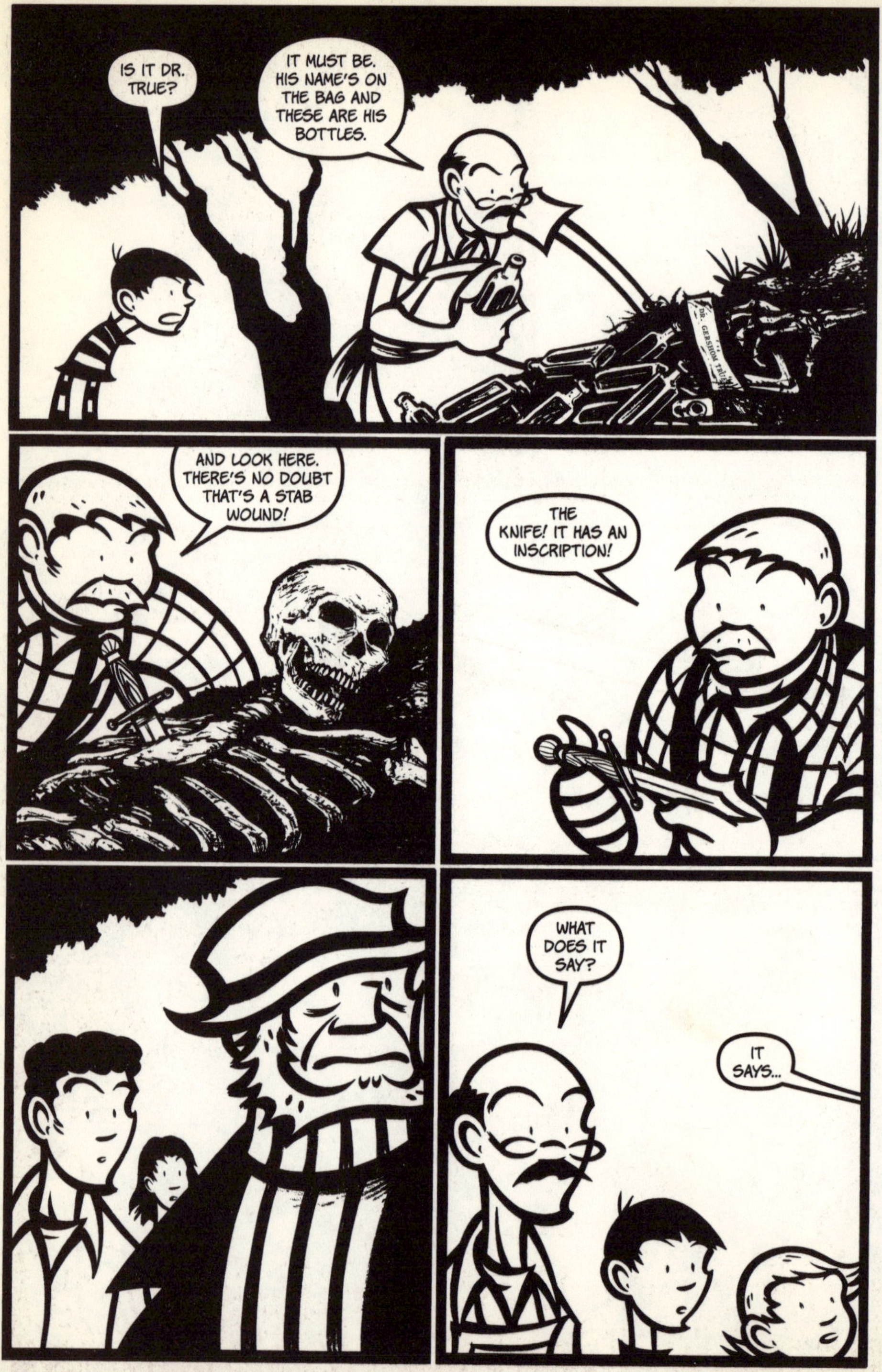
IS IT DR. TRUE?
IT MUST BE. HIS NAME'S ON THE BAG AND THESE ARE HIS BOTTLES.
DR. GERSHOM TRUE
AND LOOK HERE. THERE'S NO DOUBT THAT'S A STAB WOUND!
THE KNIFE! IT HAS AN INSCRIPTION!
WHAT DOES IT SAY?
IT SAYS...

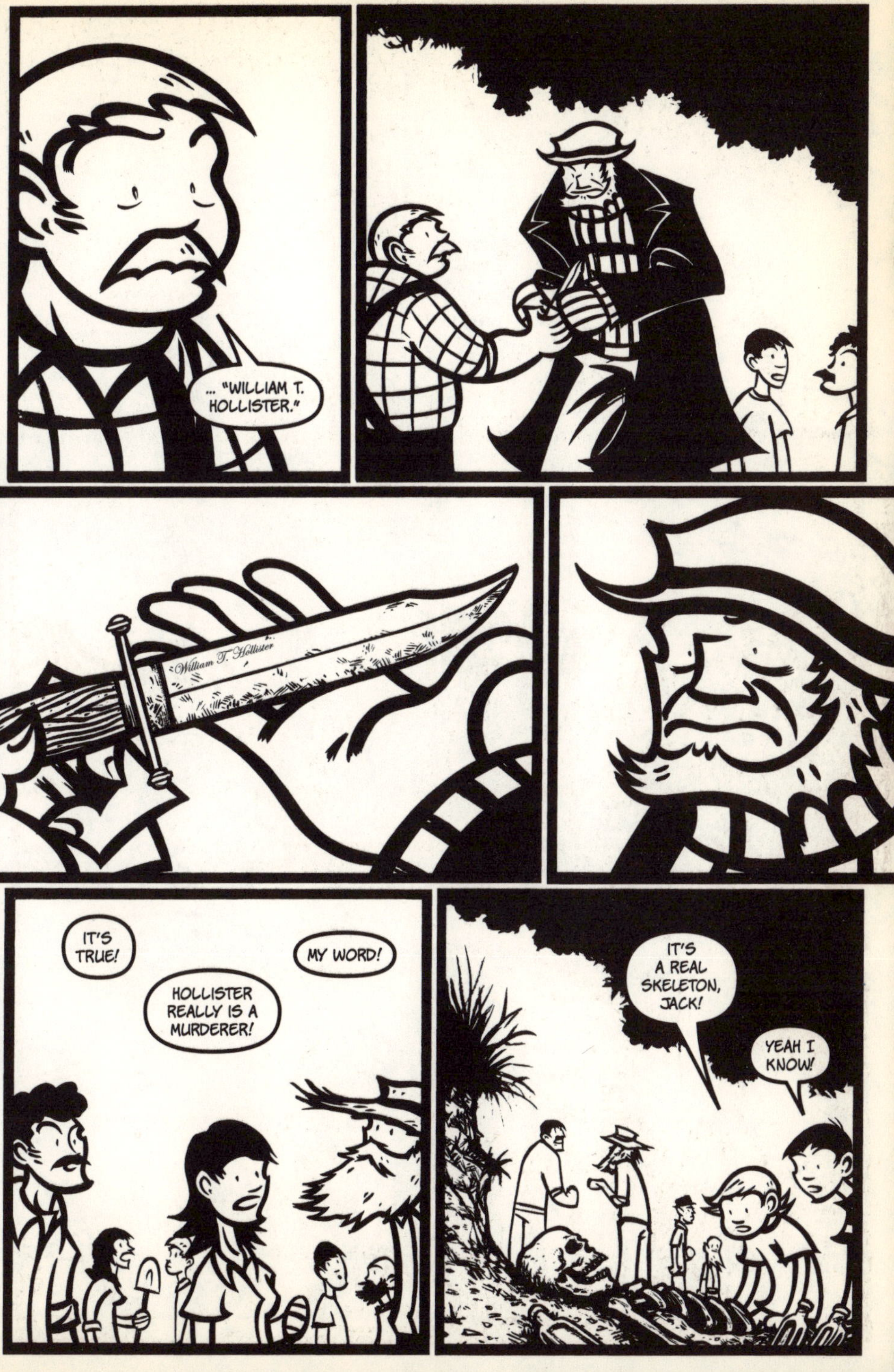
... "WILLIAM T. HOLLISTER."
William T. Hollister
IT'S TRUE!
MY WORD!
HOLLISTER REALLY IS A MURDERER!
IT'S A REAL SKELETON, JACK!
YEAH I KNOW!

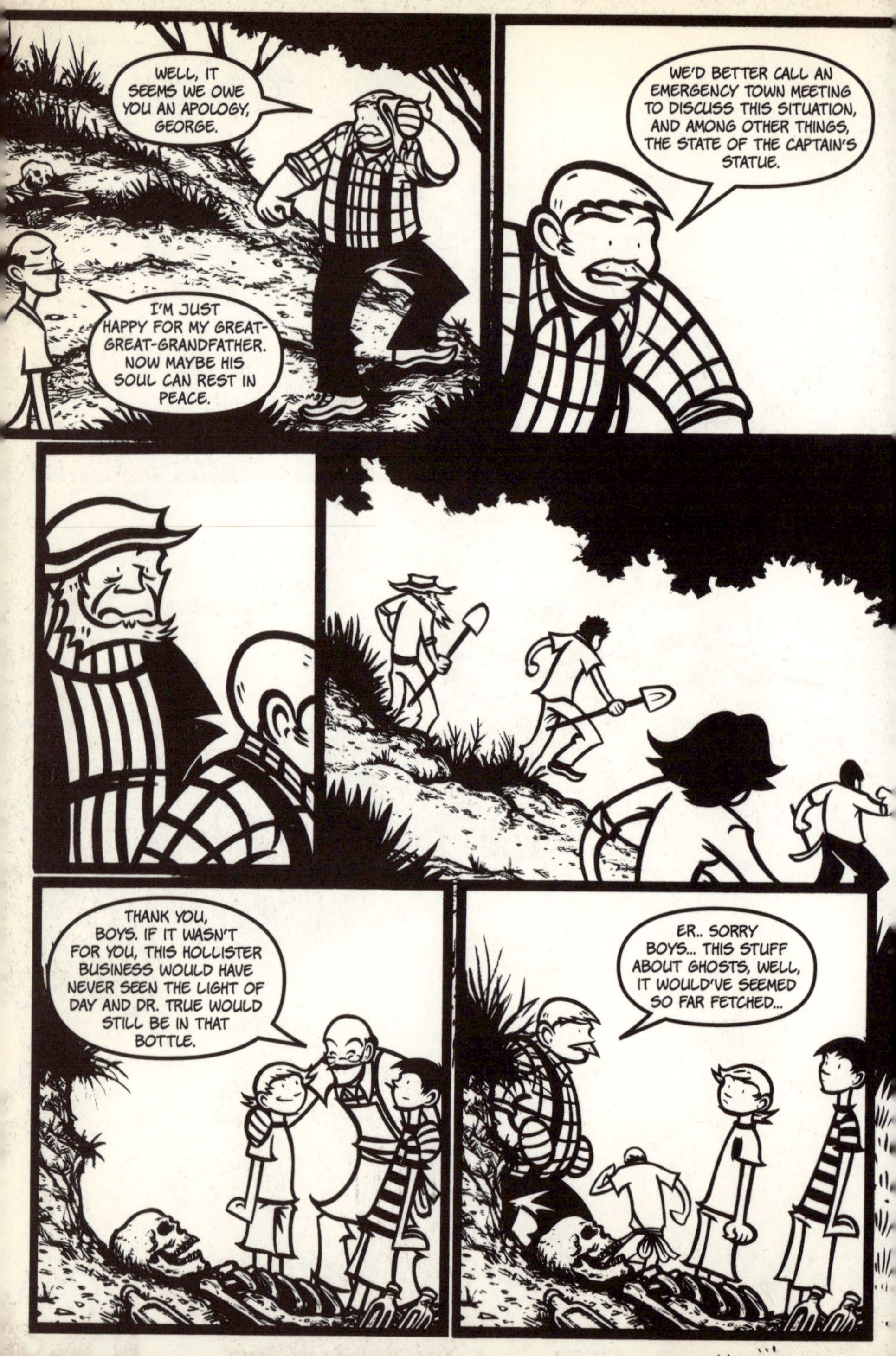
WELL, IT SEEMS WE OWE YOU AN APOLOGY, GEORGE.
I'M JUST HAPPY FOR MY GREAT-GREAT-GRANDFATHER. NOW MAYBE HIS SOUL CAN REST IN PEACE.
WE'D BETTER CALL AN EMERGENCY TOWN MEETING TO DISCUSS THIS SITUATION, AND AMONG OTHER THINGS, THE STATE OF THE CAPTAIN'S STATUE.
THANK YOU, BOYS. IF IT WASN'T FOR YOU, THIS HOLLISTER BUSINESS WOULD HAVE NEVER SEEN THE LIGHT OF DAY AND DR. TRUE WOULD STILL BE IN THAT BOTTLE.
ER.. SORRY BOYS... THIS STUFF ABOUT GHOSTS, WELL, IT WOULD'VE SEEMED SO FAR FETCHED...

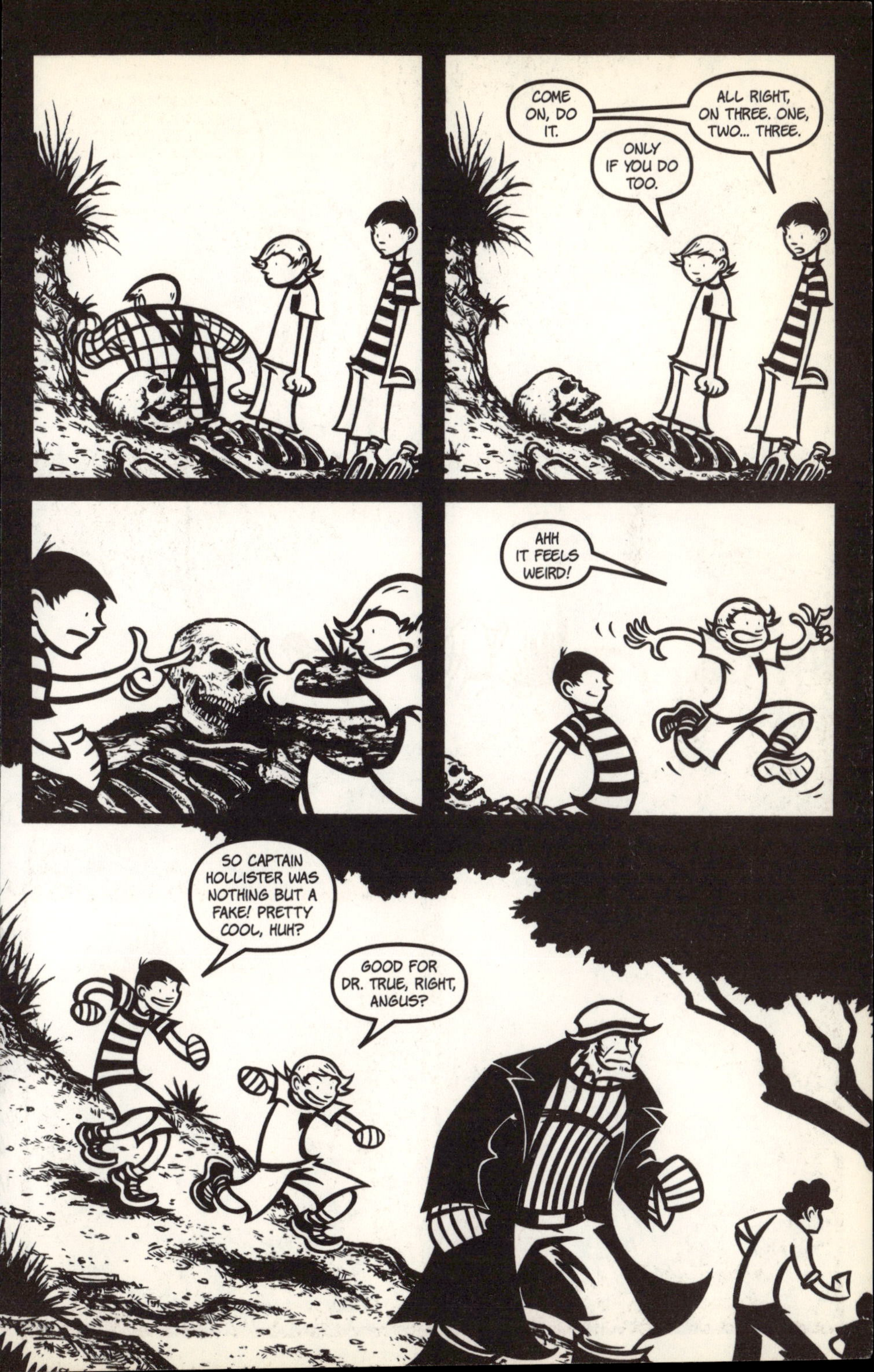
COME ON, DO IT.
ONLY IF YOU DO TOO.
ALL RIGHT, ON THREE. ONE, TWO... THREE.
AHH IT FEELS WEIRD!
SO CAPTAIN HOLLISTER WAS NOTHING BUT A FAKE! PRETTY COOL, HUH?
GOOD FOR DR. TRUE, RIGHT, ANGUS?

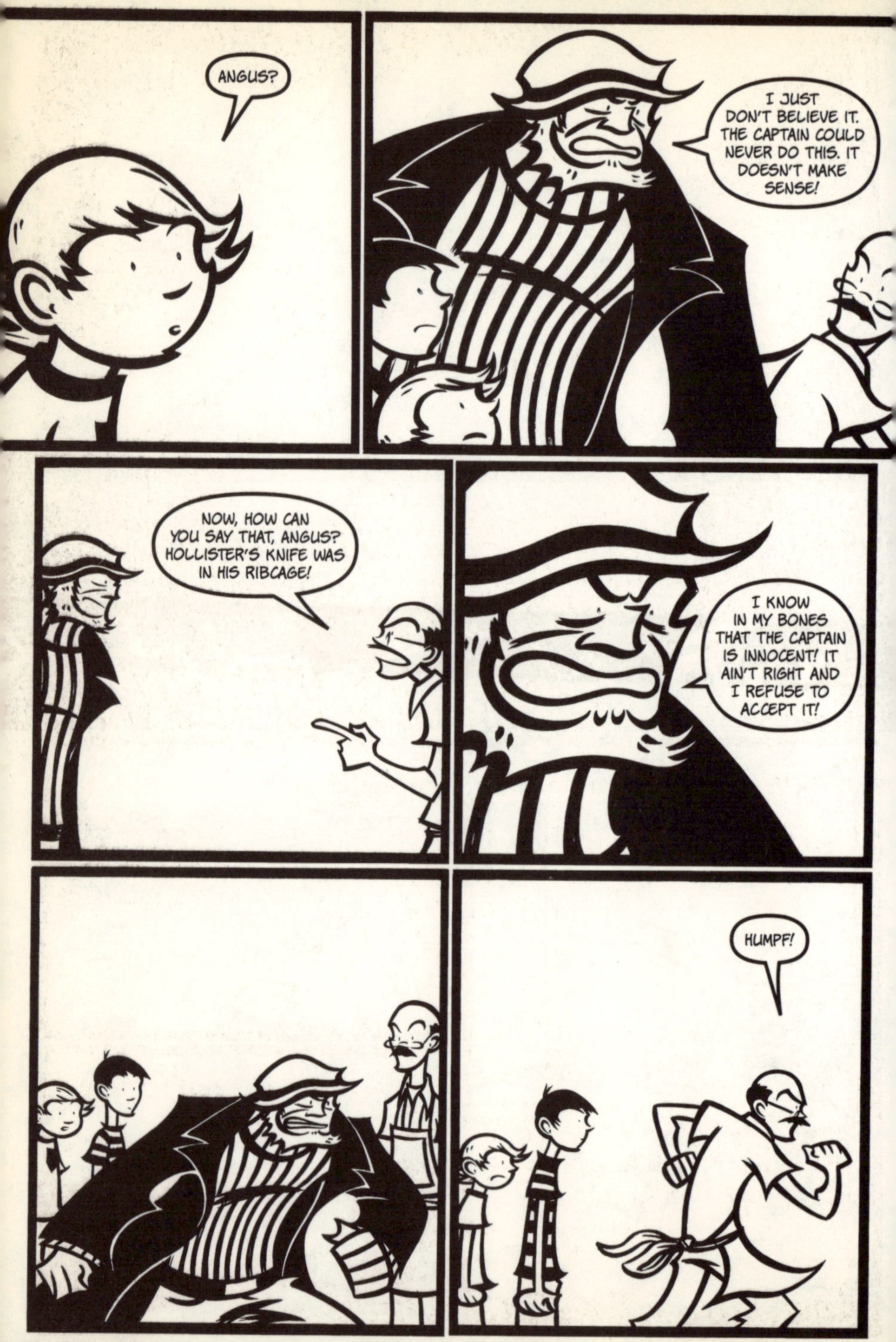
ANGUS?
I JUST DON'T BELIEVE IT. THE CAPTAIN COULD NEVER DO THIS. IT DOESN'T MAKE SENSE!
NOW, HOW CAN YOU SAY THAT, ANGUS? HOLLISTER'S KNIFE WAS IN HIS RIBCAGE!
I KNOW IN MY BONES THAT THE CAPTAIN IS INNOCENT! IT AIN'T RIGHT AND I REFUSE TO ACCEPT IT!
HUMPF!

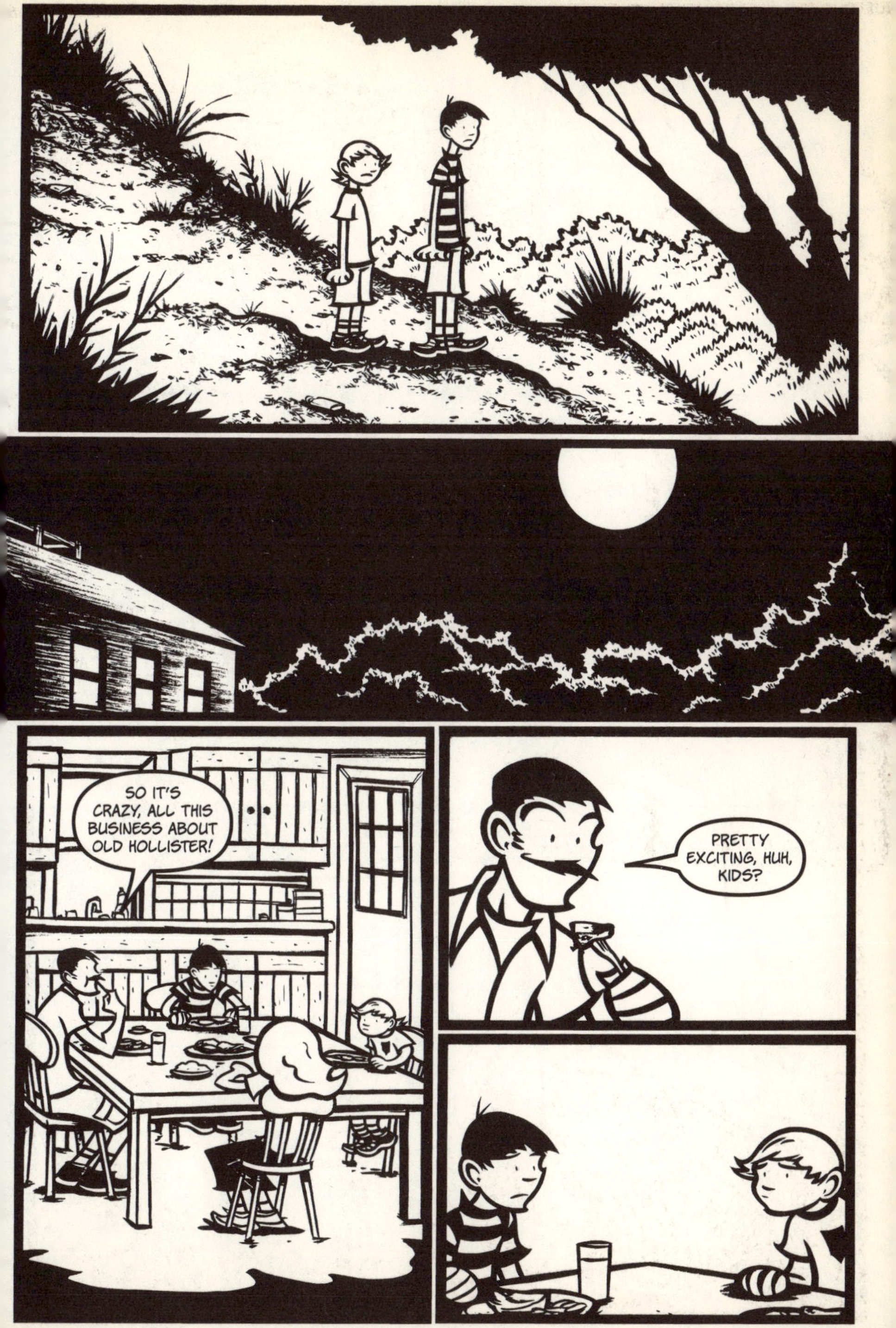
SO IT'S CRAZY, ALL THIS BUSINESS ABOUT OLD HOLLISTER!
PRETTY EXCITING, HUH, KIDS?

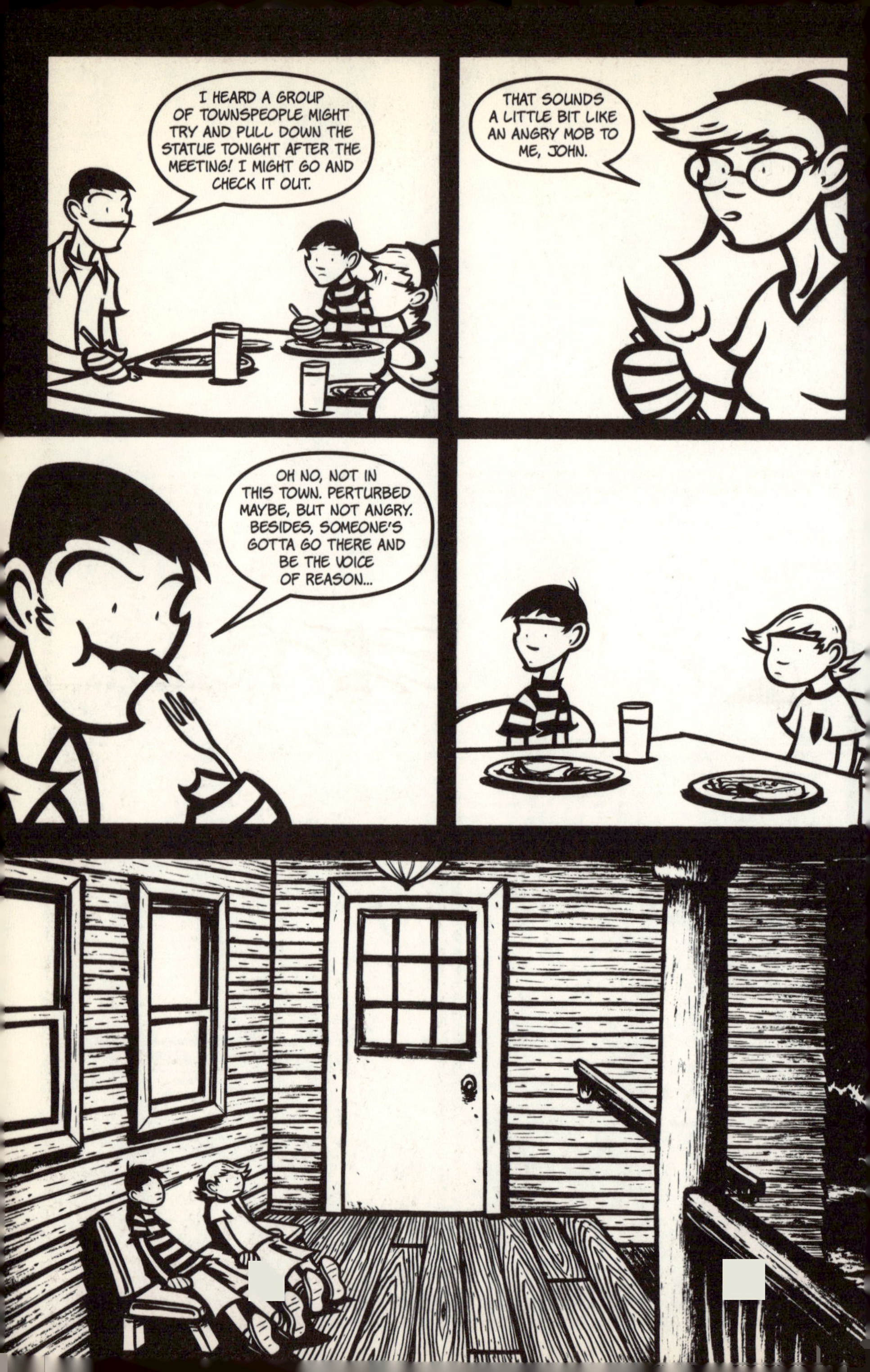
I HEARD A GROUP OF TOWNSPEOPLE MIGHT TRY AND PULL DOWN THE STATUE TONIGHT AFTER THE MEETING! I MIGHT GO AND CHECK IT OUT.
THAT SOUNDS A LITTLE BIT LIKE AN ANGRY MOB TO ME, JOHN.
OH NO, NOT IN THIS TOWN. PERTURBED MAYBE, BUT NOT ANGRY. BESIDES, SOMEONE'S GOTTA GO THERE AND BE THE VOICE OF REASON...

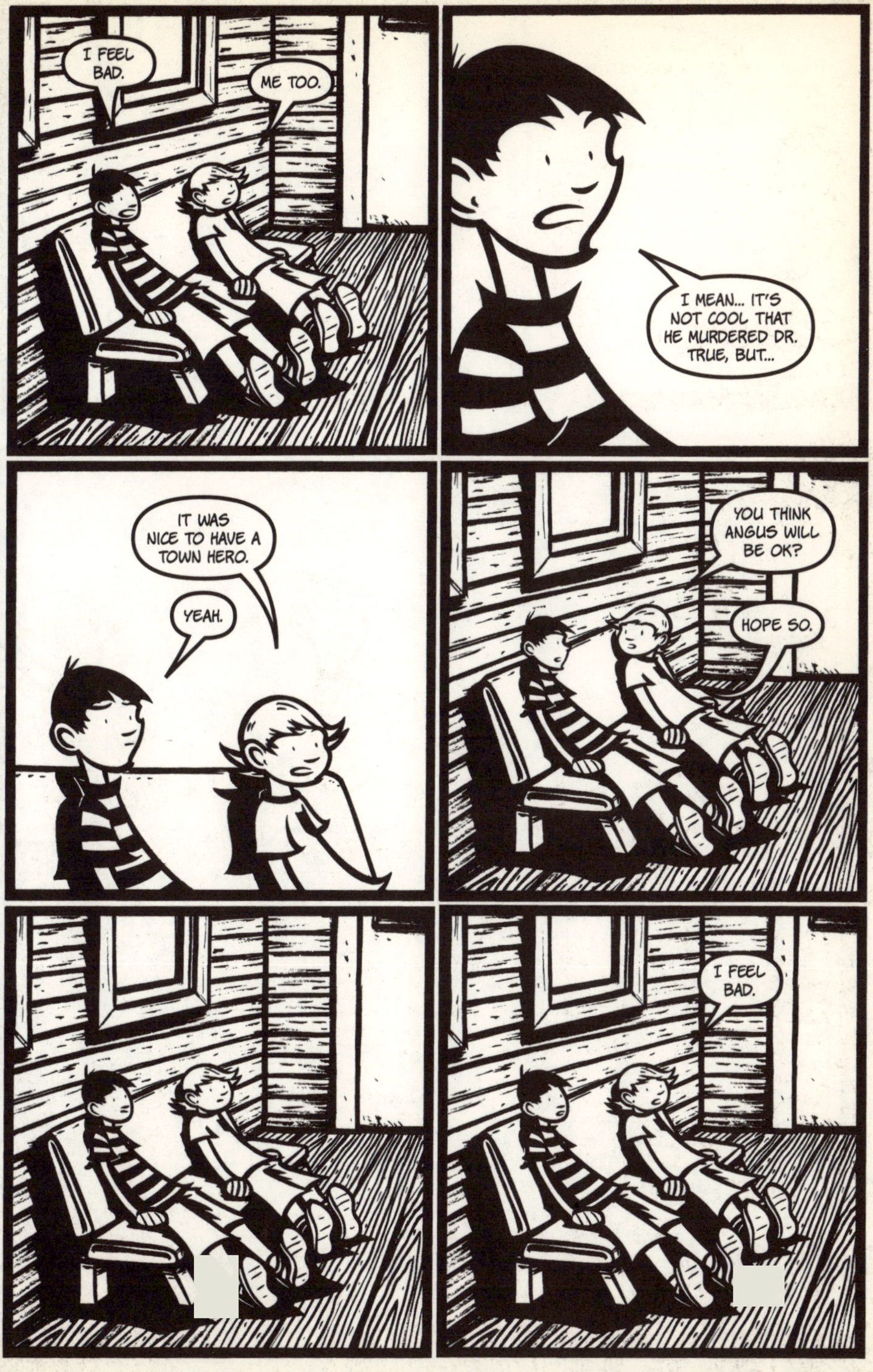
I FEEL BAD.
ME TOO.
I MEAN... IT'S NOT COOL THAT HE MURDERED DR. TRUE, BUT...
IT WAS NICE TO HAVE A TOWN HERO.
YEAH.
YOU THINK ANGUS WILL BE OK?
HOPE SO.
I FEEL BAD.

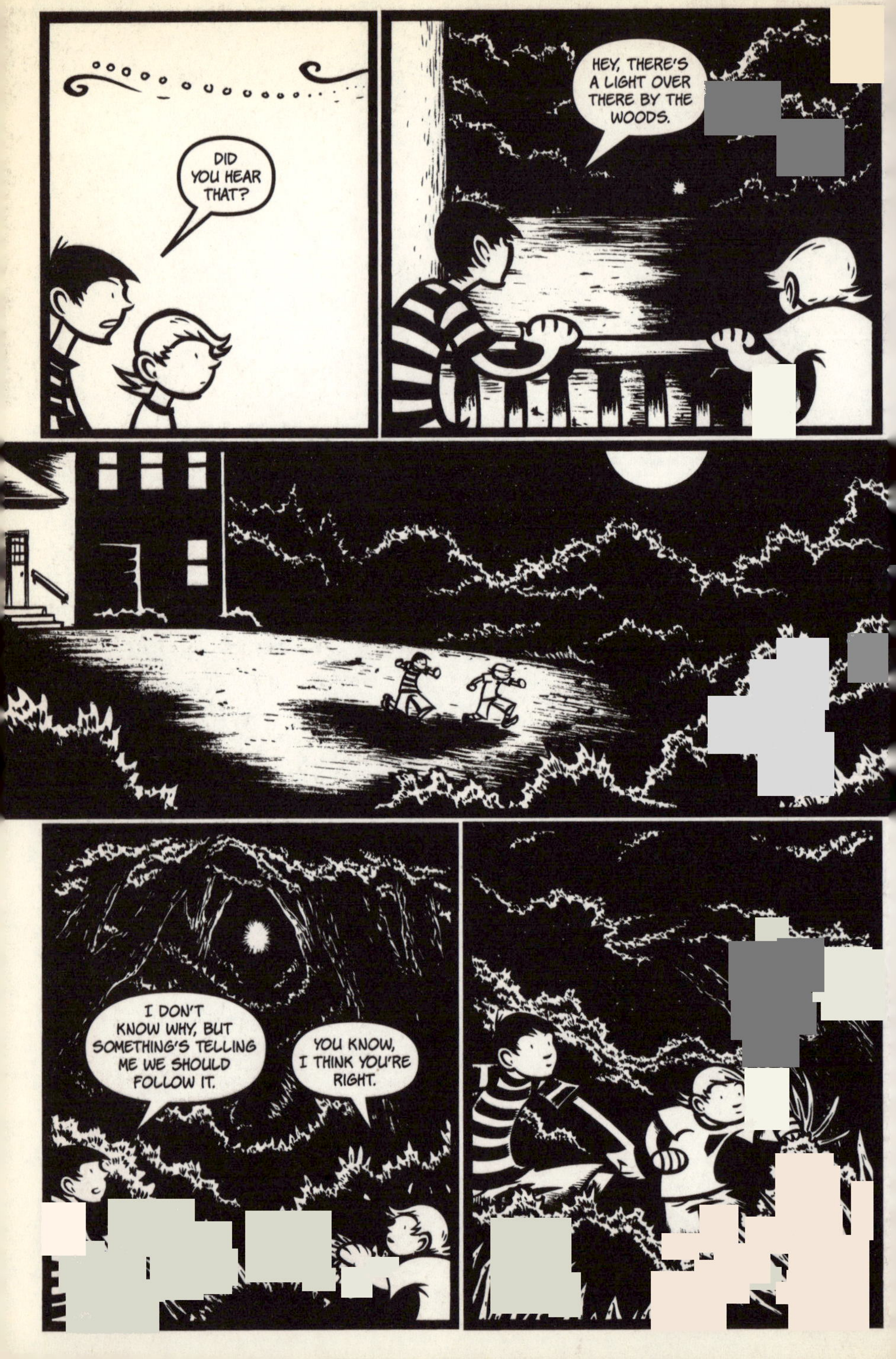
DID YOU HEAR THAT?
HEY, THERE'S A LIGHT OVER THERE BY THE WOODS.
I DON'T KNOW WHY, BUT SOMETHING'S TELLING ME WE SHOULD FOLLOW IT.
YOU KNOW, I THINK YOU'RE RIGHT.

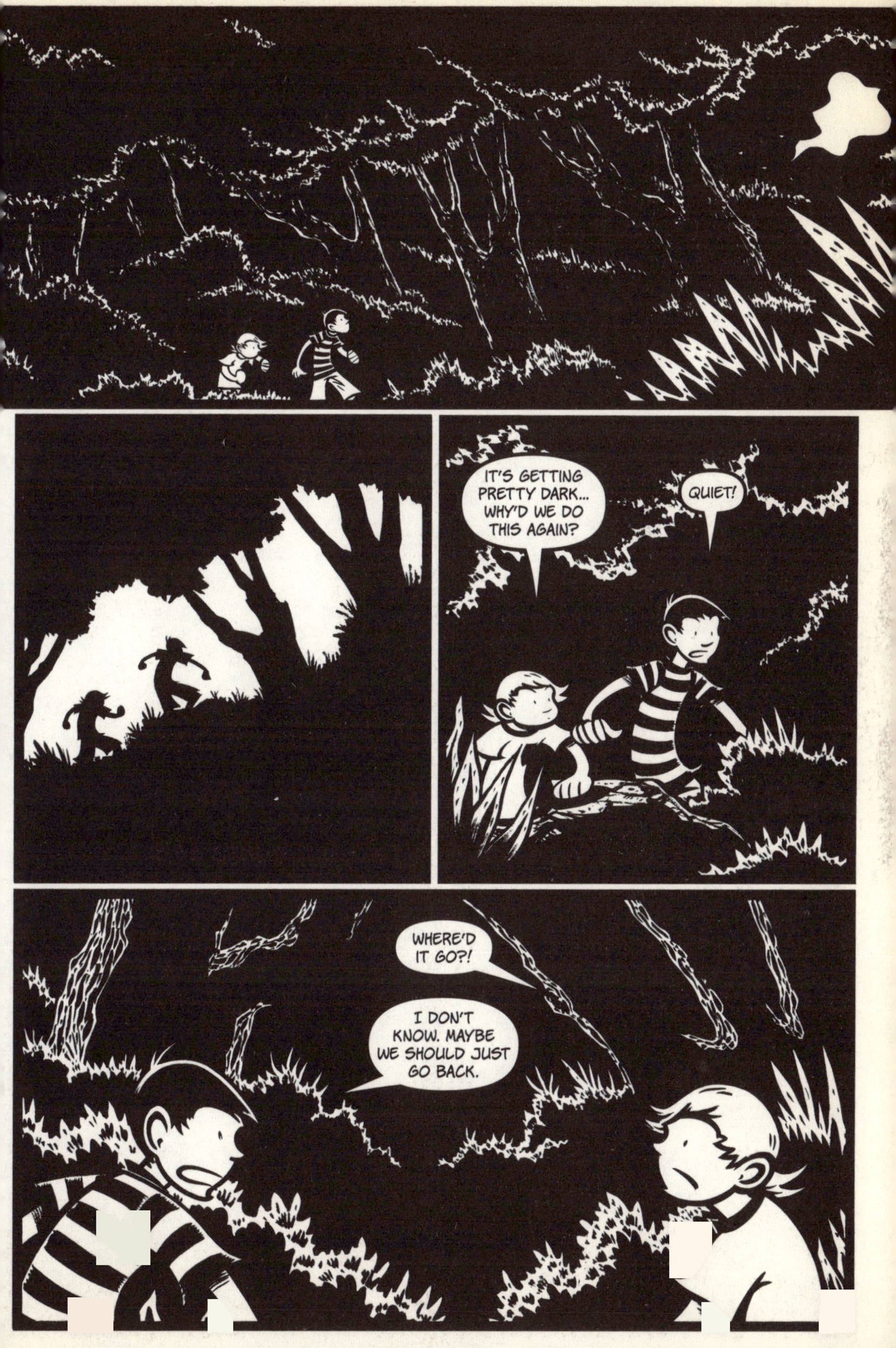
IT'S GETTING PRETTY DARK... WHY'D WE DO THIS AGAIN?
QUIET!
WHERE'D IT GO?!
I DON'T KNOW. MAYBE WE SHOULD JUST GO BACK.

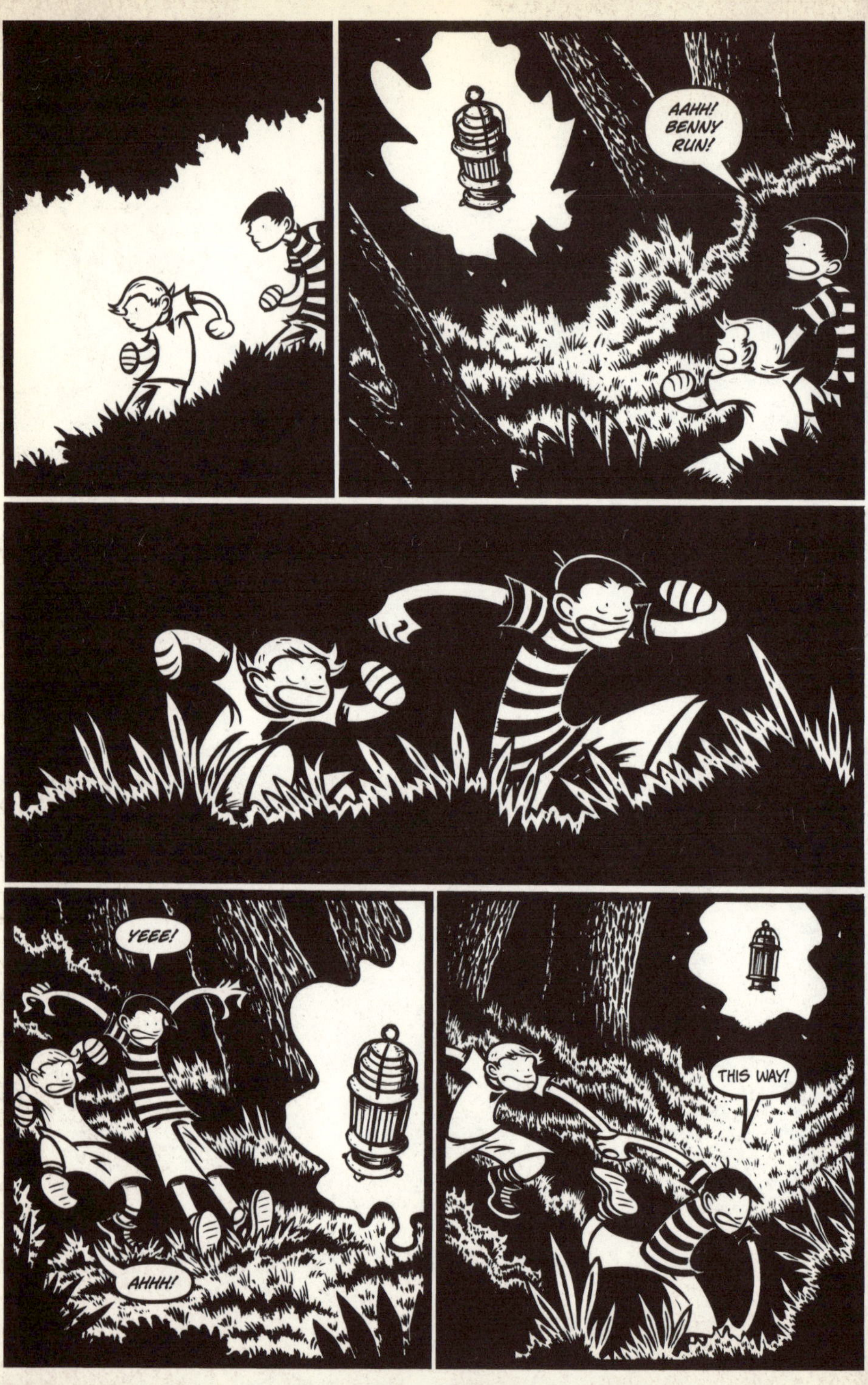
AAHH! BENNY RUN!
YEEE!
AHHH!
THIS WAY!

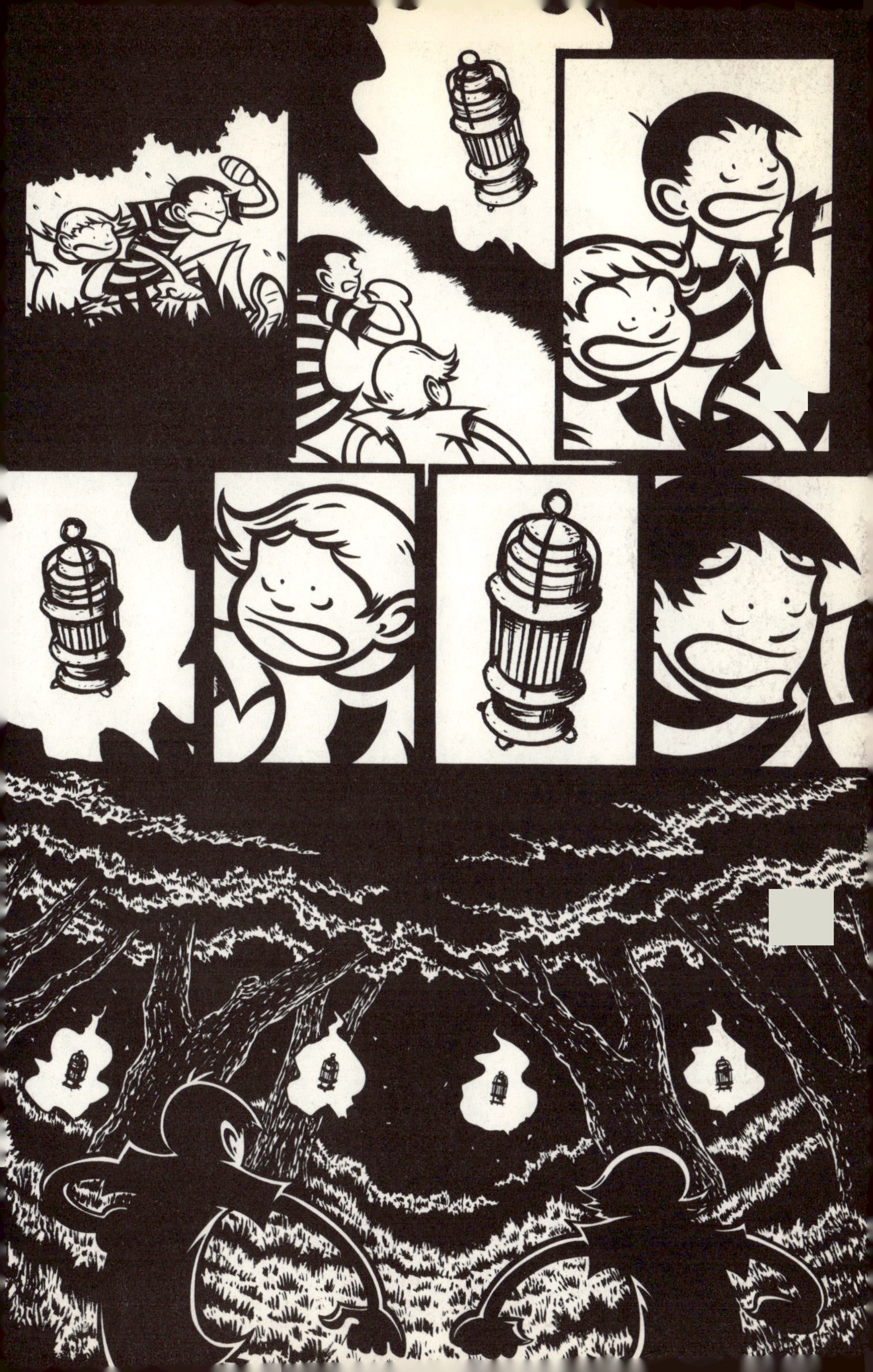

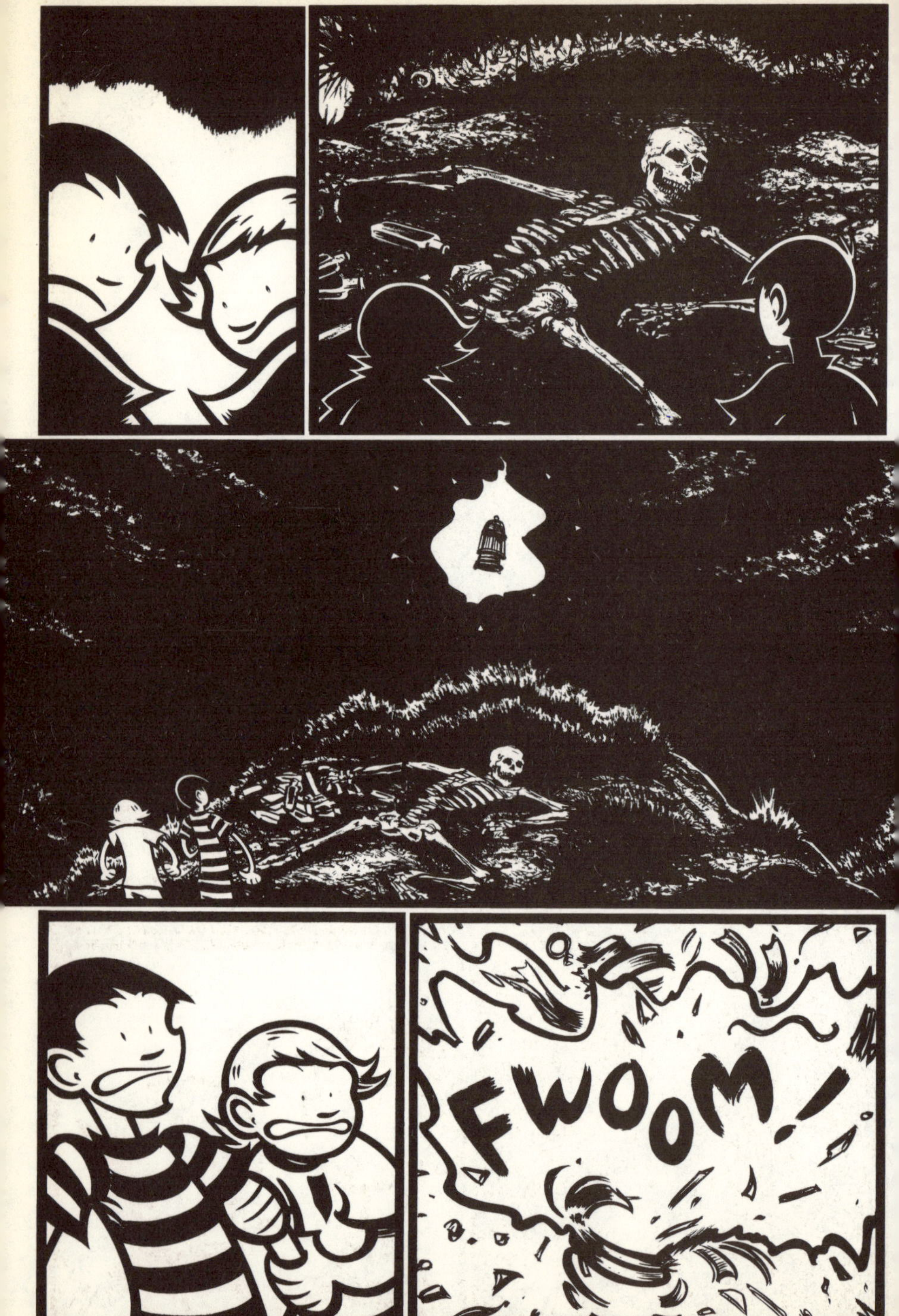
FWOOM!

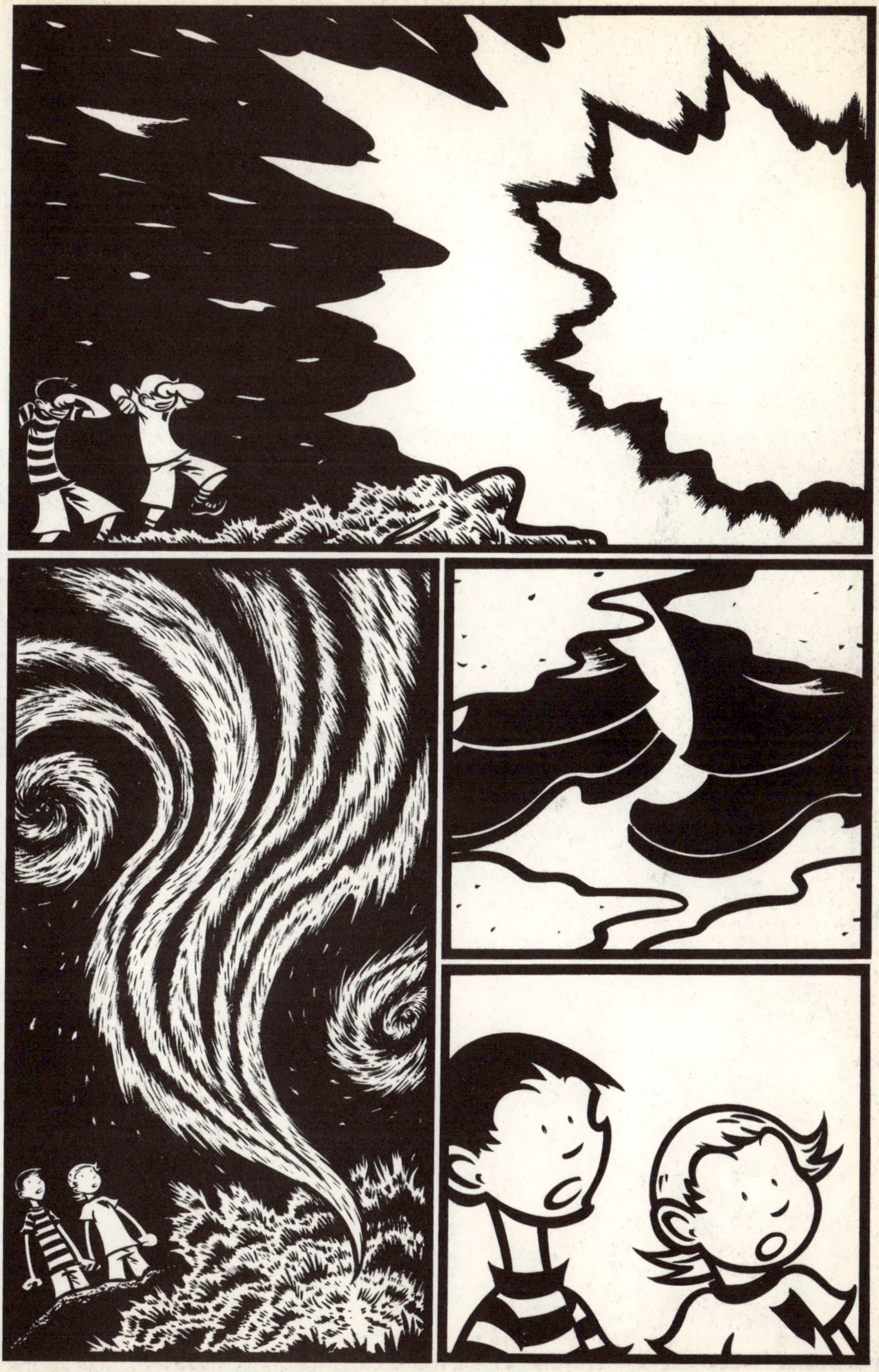

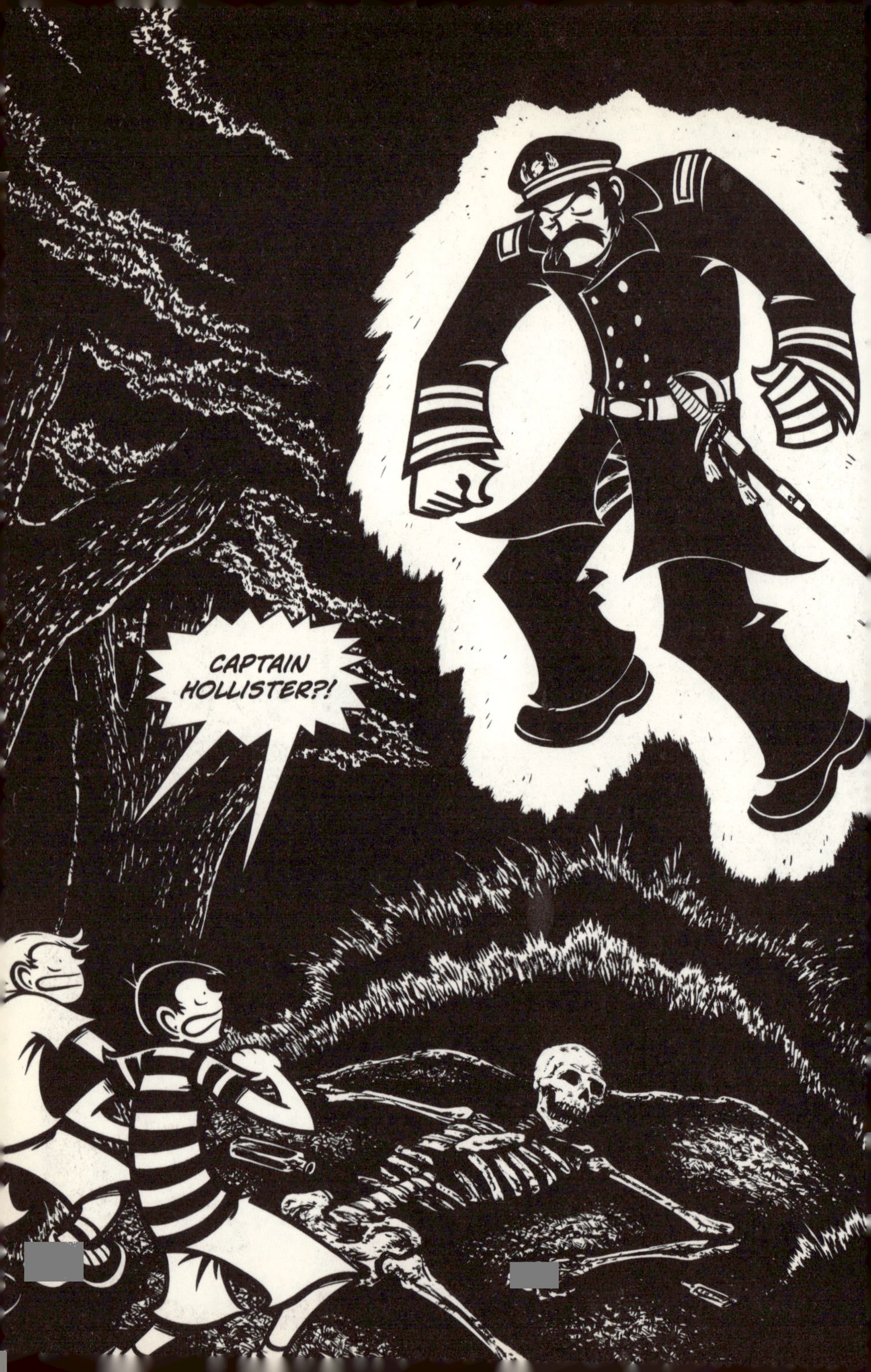
CAPTAIN HOLLISTER?!

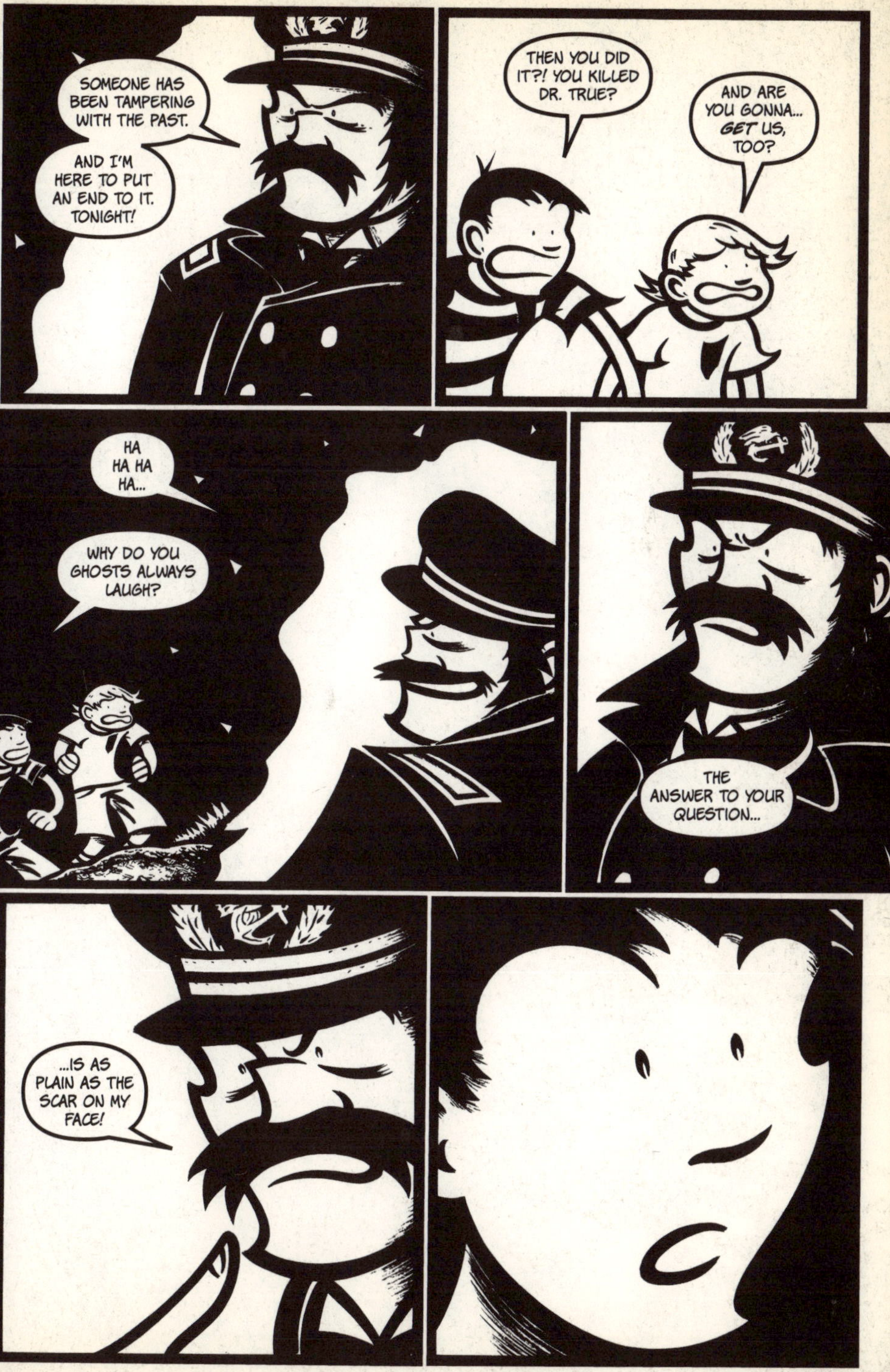
SOMEONE HAS BEEN TAMPERING WITH THE PAST.
AND I'M HERE TO PUT AN END TO IT. TONIGHT!
THEN YOU DID IT?! YOU KILLED DR. TRUE?
AND ARE YOU GONNA... GET US, TOO?
HA HA HA HA...
WHY DO YOU GHOSTS ALWAYS LAUGH?
THE ANSWER TO YOUR QUESTION...
...IS AS PLAIN AS THE SCAR ON MY FACE!

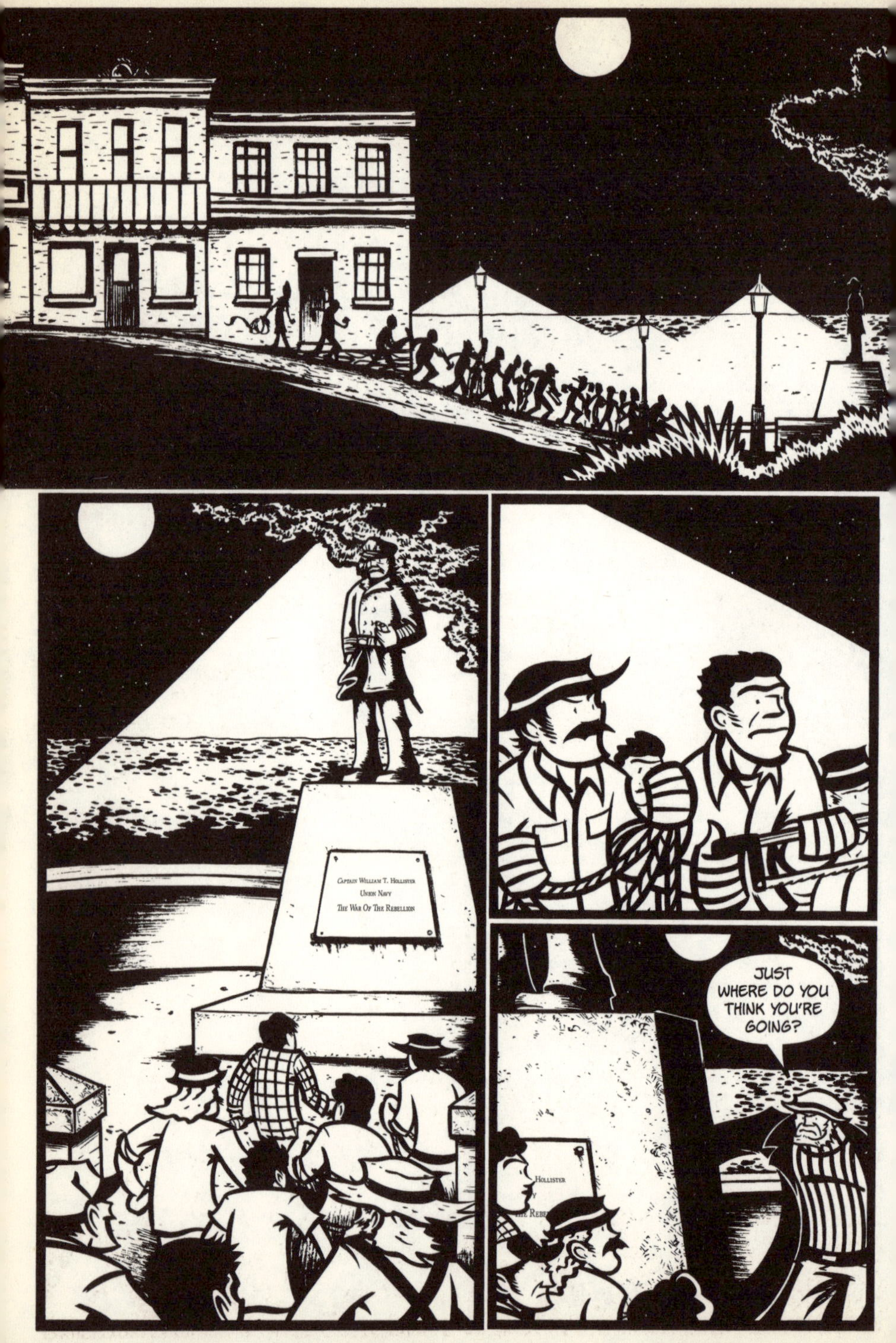
Captain William T. Hollister
Union Navy
The War Of The Rebellion
JUST WHERE DO YOU THINK YOU'RE GOING?

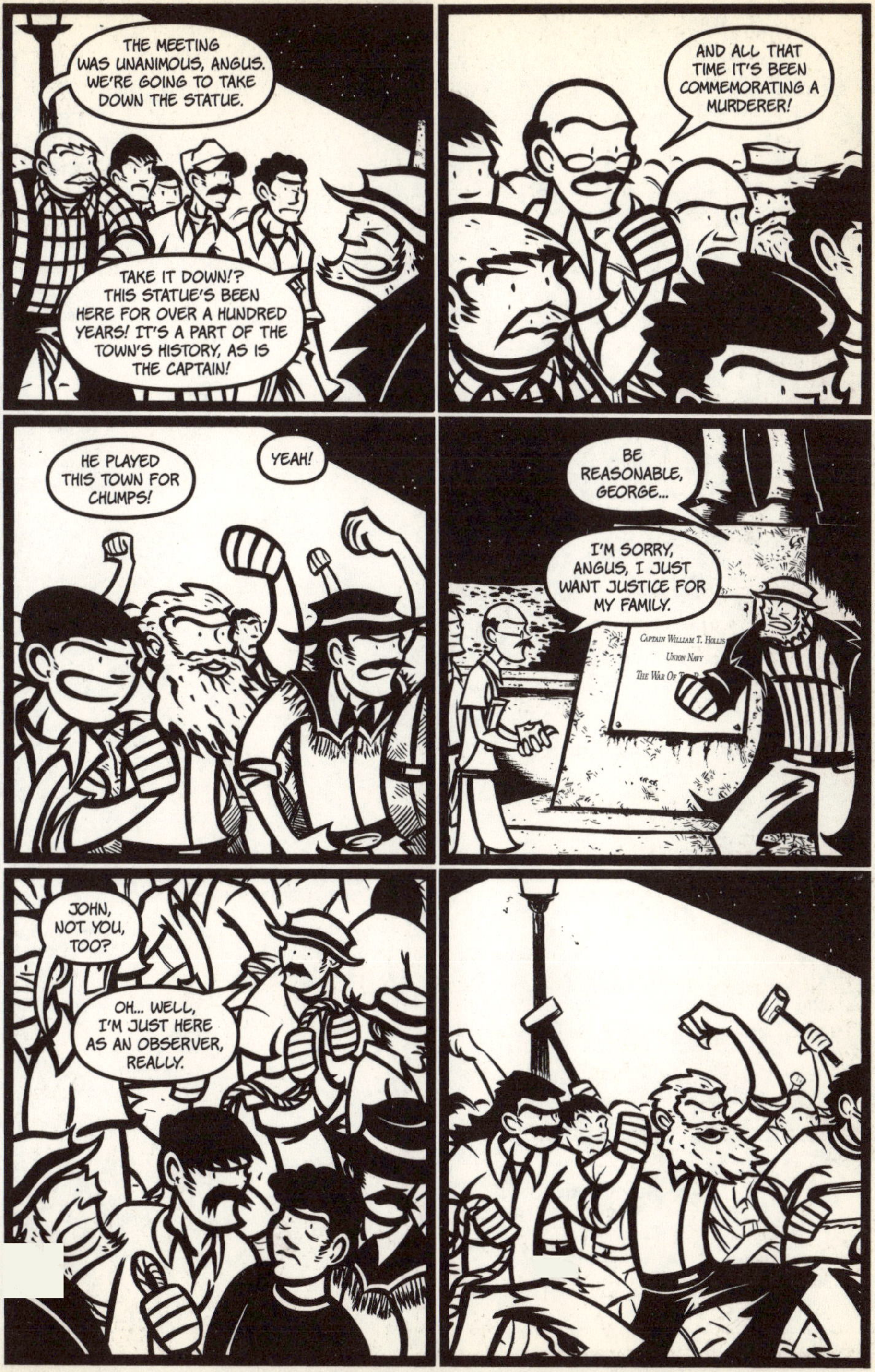
THE MEETING WAS UNANIMOUS, ANGUS. WE'RE GOING TO TAKE DOWN THE STATUE.
TAKE IT DOWN!? THIS STATUE'S BEEN HERE FOR OVER A HUNDRED YEARS! IT'S A PART OF THE TOWN'S HISTORY, AS IS THE CAPTAIN!
AND ALL THAT TIME IT'S BEEN COMMEMORATING A MURDERER!
HE PLAYED THIS TOWN FOR CHUMPS!
YEAH!
BE REASONABLE, GEORGE...
I'M SORRY, ANGUS, I JUST WANT JUSTICE FOR MY FAMILY.
CAPTAIN WILLIAM T. HOLLIS
UNION NAVY
JOHN, NOT YOU, TOO?
OH... WELL, I'M JUST HERE AS AN OBSERVER, REALLY.

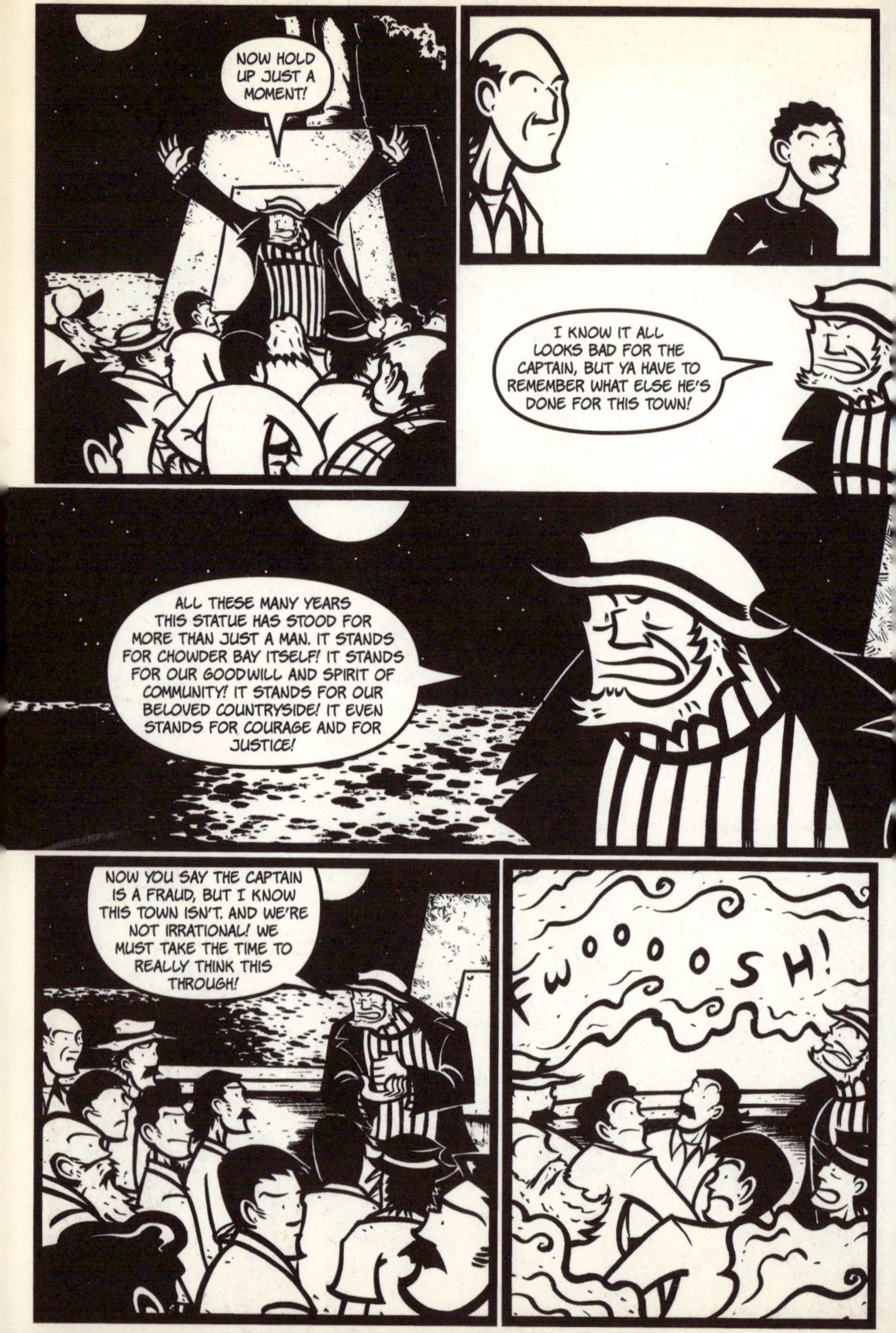
NOW HOLD UP JUST A MOMENT!
I KNOW IT ALL LOOKS BAD FOR THE CAPTAIN, BUT YA HAVE TO REMEMBER WHAT ELSE HE'S DONE FOR THIS TOWN!
ALL THESE MANY YEARS THIS STATUE HAS STOOD FOR MORE THAN JUST A MAN. IT STANDS FOR CHOWDER BAY ITSELF! IT STANDS FOR OUR GOODWILL AND SPIRIT OF COMMUNITY! IT STANDS FOR OUR BELOVED COUNTRYSIDE! IT EVEN STANDS FOR COURAGE AND FOR JUSTICE!
NOW YOU SAY THE CAPTAIN IS A FRAUD, BUT I KNOW THIS TOWN ISN'T. AND WE'RE NOT IRRATIONAL! WE MUST TAKE THE TIME TO REALLY THINK THIS THROUGH!
WOOOOSH!

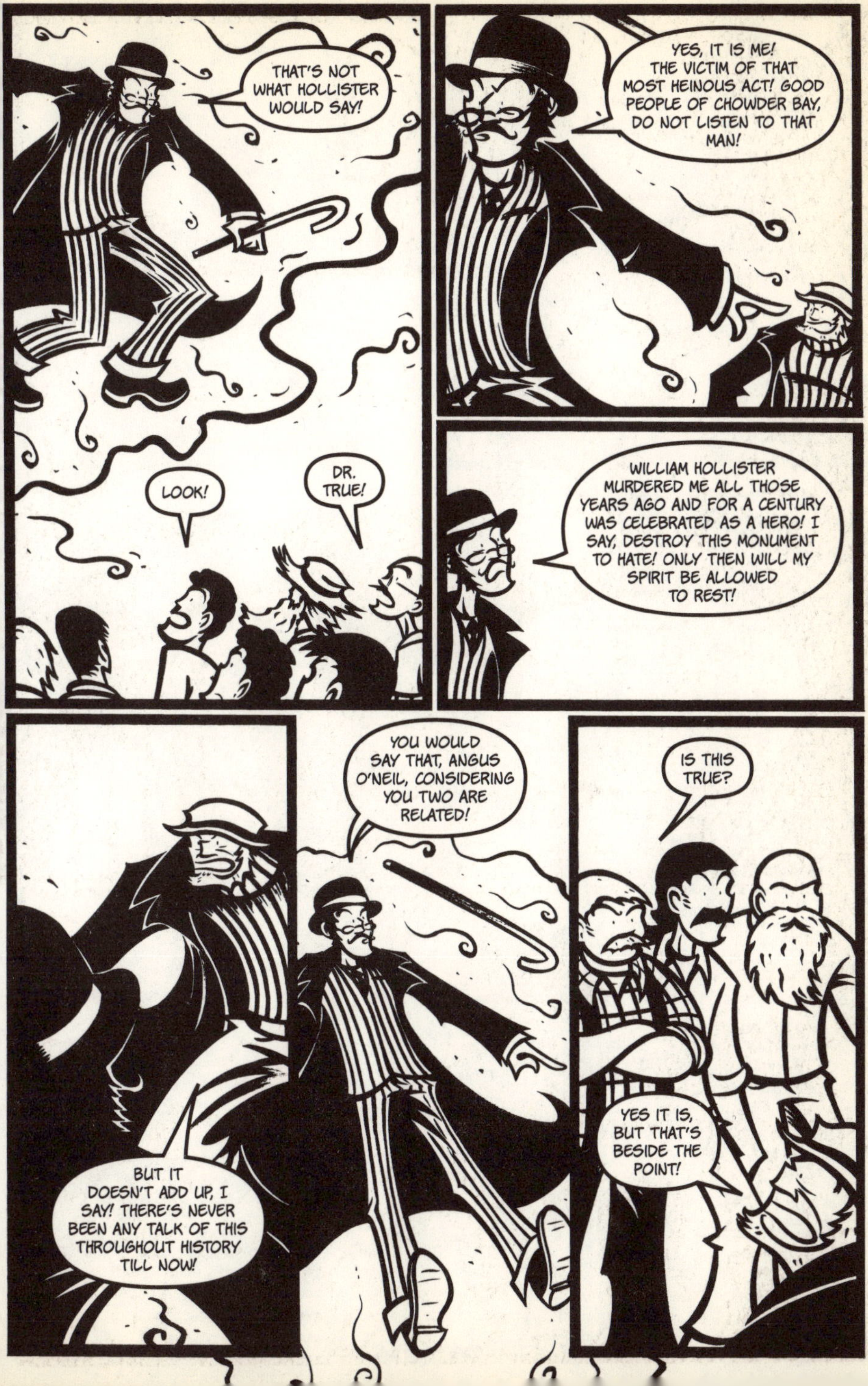

THAT'S NOT WHAT HOLLISTER WOULD SAY!
YES, IT IS ME! THE VICTIM OF THAT MOST HEINOUS ACT! GOOD PEOPLE OF CHOWDER BAY, DO NOT LISTEN TO THAT MAN!
LOOK!
DR. TRUE!
WILLIAM HOLLISTER MURDERED ME ALL THOSE YEARS AGO AND FOR A CENTURY WAS CELEBRATED AS A HERO! I SAY, DESTROY THIS MONUMENT TO HATE! ONLY THEN WILL MY SPIRIT BE ALLOWED TO REST!
BUT IT DOESN'T ADD UP, I SAY! THERE'S NEVER BEEN ANY TALK OF THIS THROUGHOUT HISTORY TILL NOW!
YOU WOULD SAY THAT, ANGUS O'NEIL, CONSIDERING YOU TWO ARE RELATED!
IS THIS TRUE?
YES IT IS, BUT THAT'S BESIDE THE POINT!

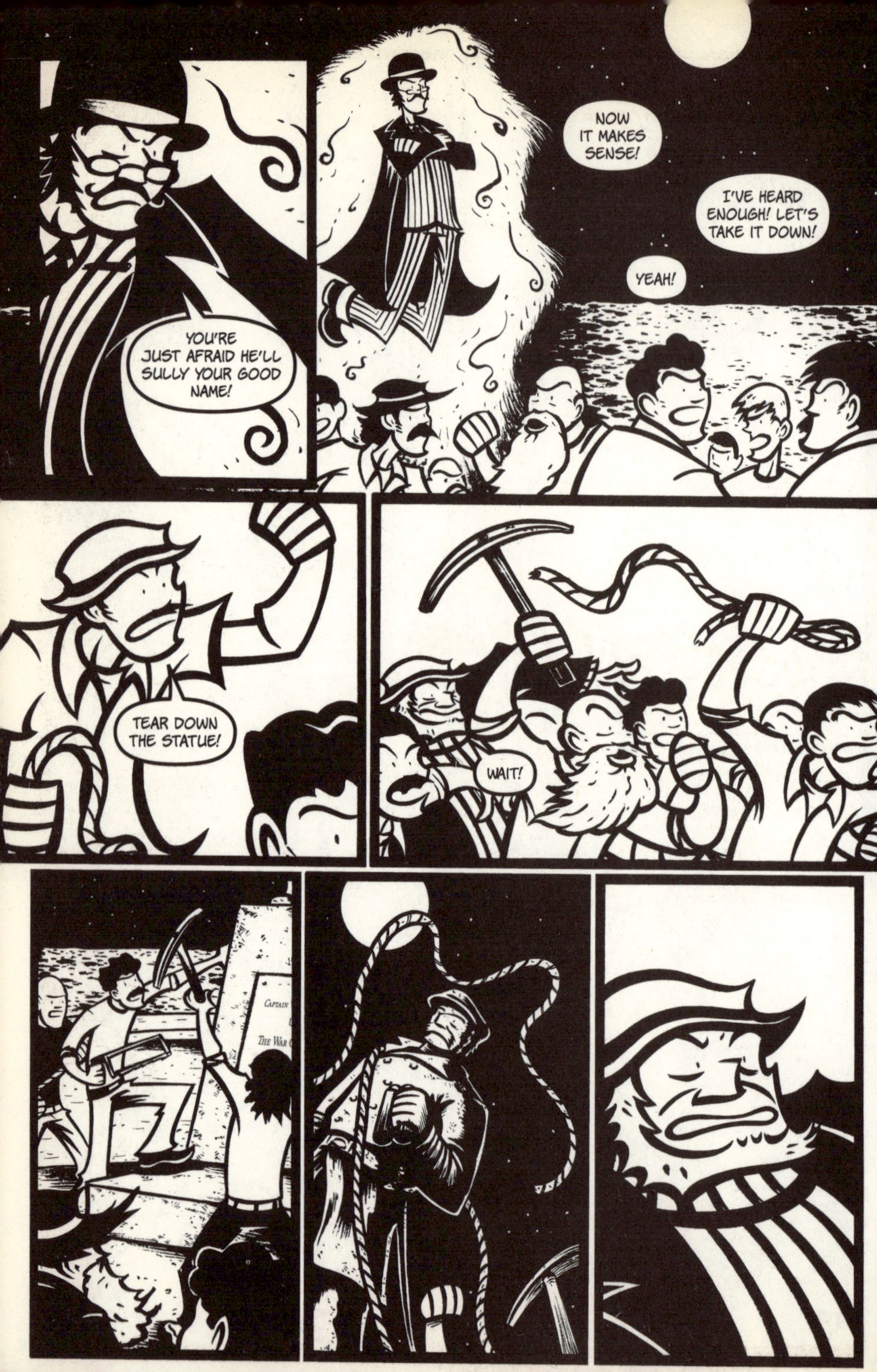
YOU'RE JUST AFRAID HE'LL SULLY YOUR GOOD NAME!
NOW IT MAKES SENSE!
I'VE HEARD ENOUGH! LET'S TAKE IT DOWN!
YEAH!
TEAR DOWN THE STATUE!
WAIT!

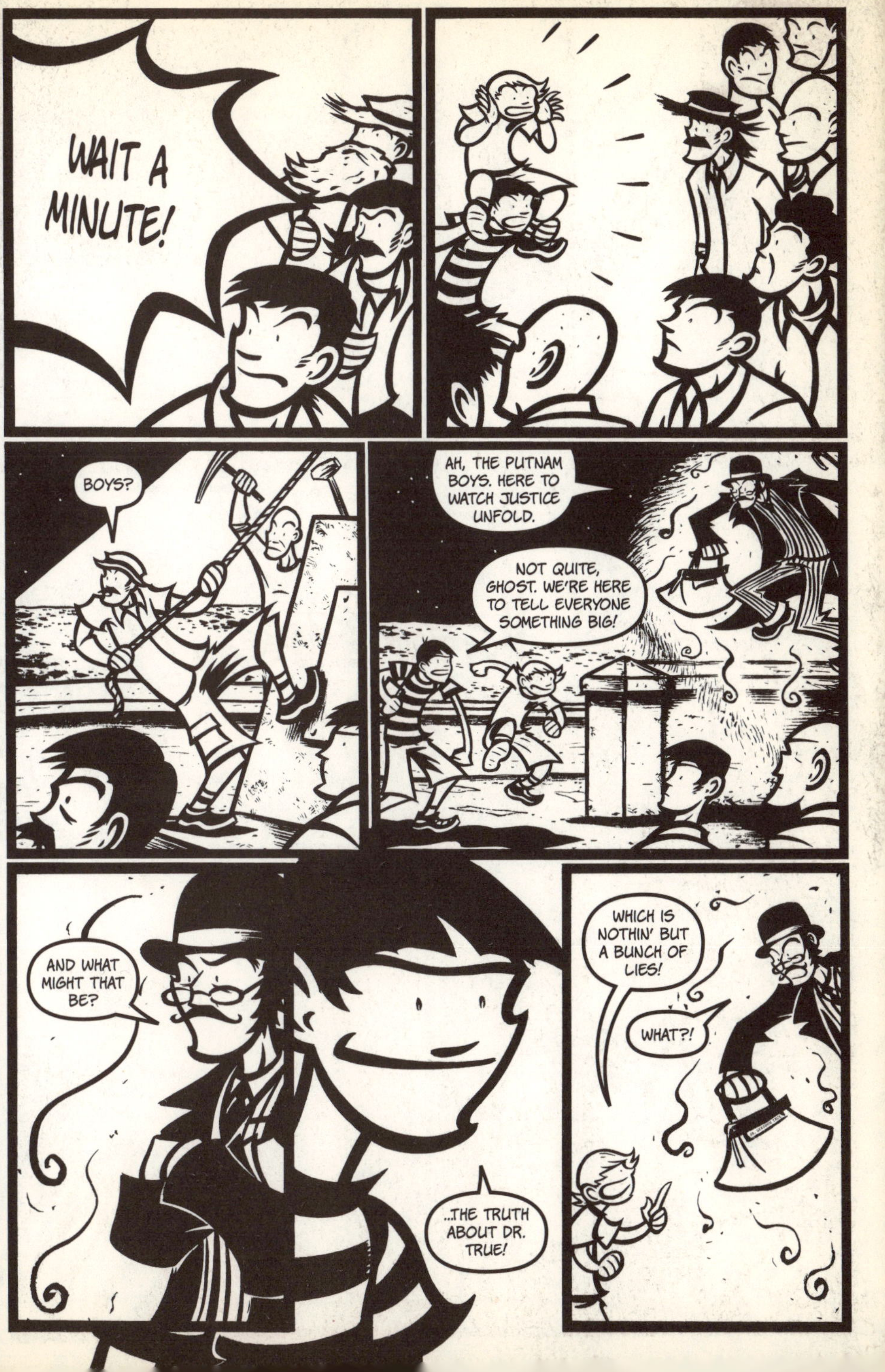
WAIT A MINUTE!
BOYS?
AH, THE PUTNAM BOYS. HERE TO WATCH JUSTICE UNFOLD.
NOT QUITE, GHOST. WE'RE HERE TO TELL EVERYONE SOMETHING BIG!
AND WHAT MIGHT THAT BE?
...THE TRUTH ABOUT DR. TRUE!
WHICH IS NOTHIN' BUT A BUNCH OF LIES!
WHAT?!

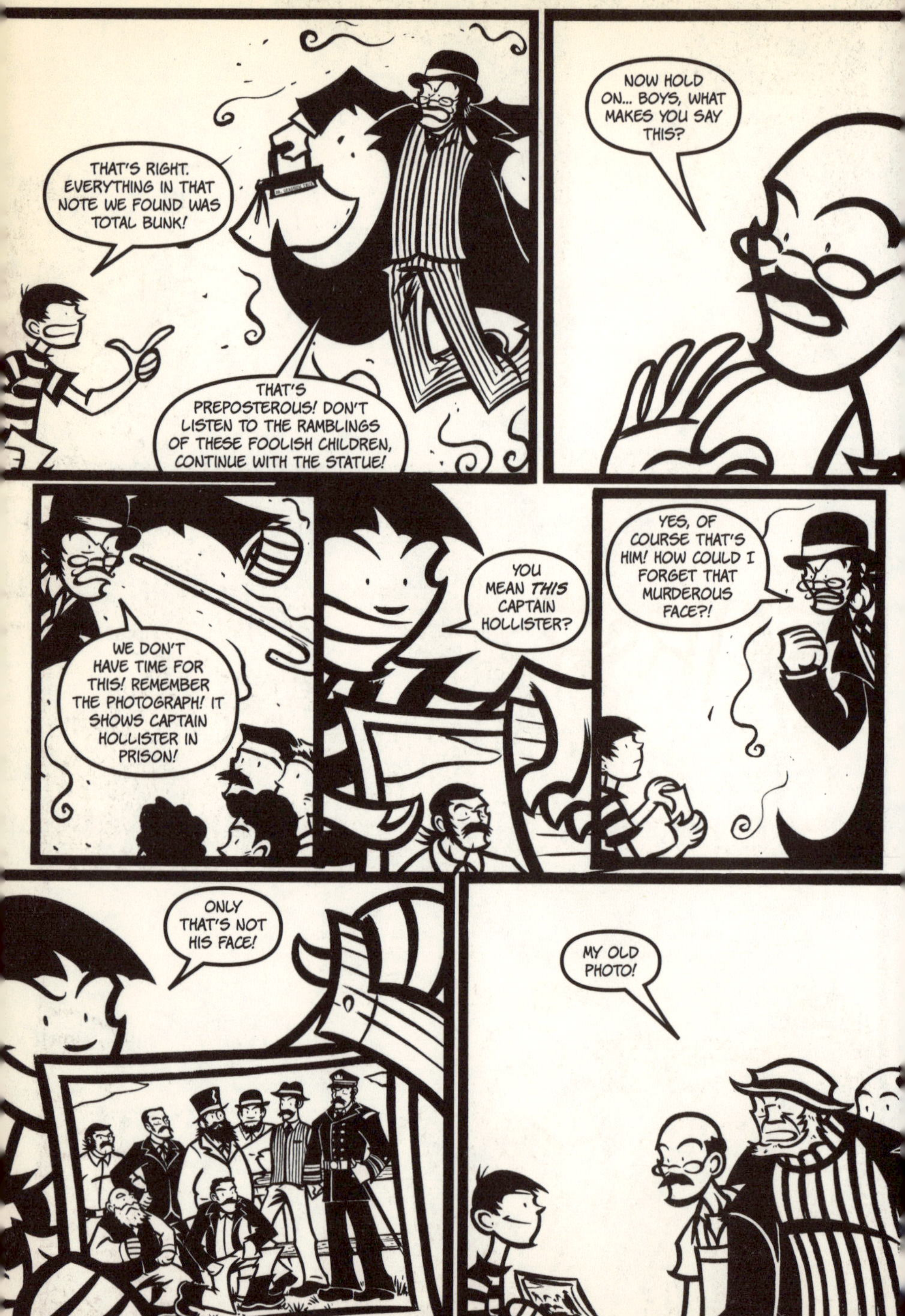
THAT'S RIGHT. EVERYTHING IN THAT NOTE WE FOUND WAS TOTAL BUNK!
THAT'S PREPOSTEROUS! DON'T LISTEN TO THE RAMBLINGS OF THESE FOOLISH CHILDREN, CONTINUE WITH THE STATUE!
NOW HOLD ON... BOYS, WHAT MAKES YOU SAY THIS?
WE DON'T HAVE TIME FOR THIS! REMEMBER THE PHOTOGRAPH! IT SHOWS CAPTAIN HOLLISTER IN PRISON!
YOU MEAN *THIS* CAPTAIN HOLLISTER?
YES, OF COURSE THAT'S HIM! HOW COULD I FORGET THAT MURDEROUS FACE?!
ONLY THAT'S NOT HIS FACE!
MY OLD PHOTO!

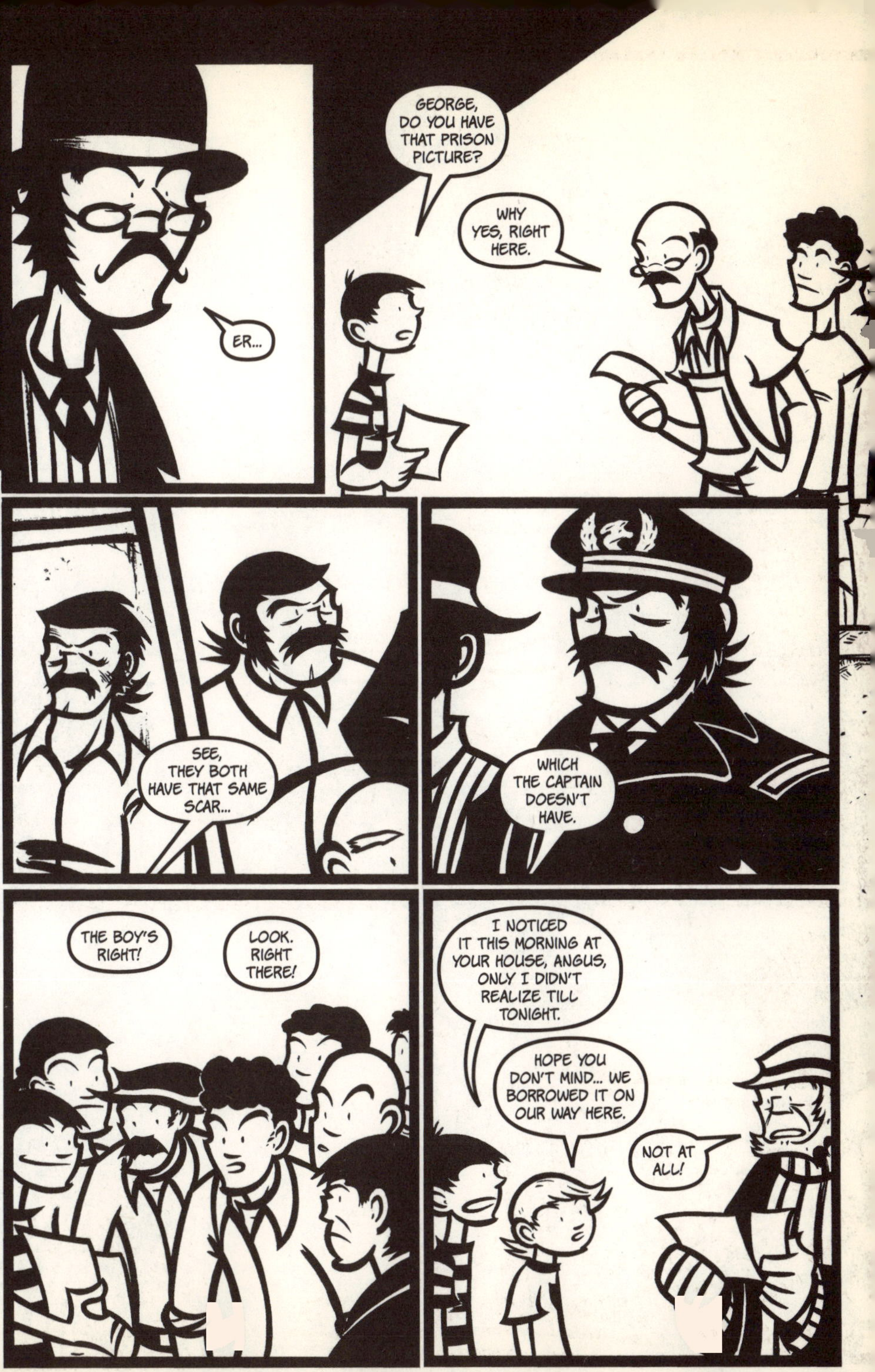
GEORGE, DO YOU HAVE THAT PRISON PICTURE?
ER...
WHY YES, RIGHT HERE.
SEE, THEY BOTH HAVE THAT SAME SCAR...
WHICH THE CAPTAIN DOESN'T HAVE.
THE BOY'S RIGHT!
LOOK. RIGHT THERE!
I NOTICED IT THIS MORNING AT YOUR HOUSE, ANGUS, ONLY I DIDN'T REALIZE TILL TONIGHT.
HOPE YOU DON'T MIND... WE BORROWED IT ON OUR WAY HERE.
NOT AT ALL!

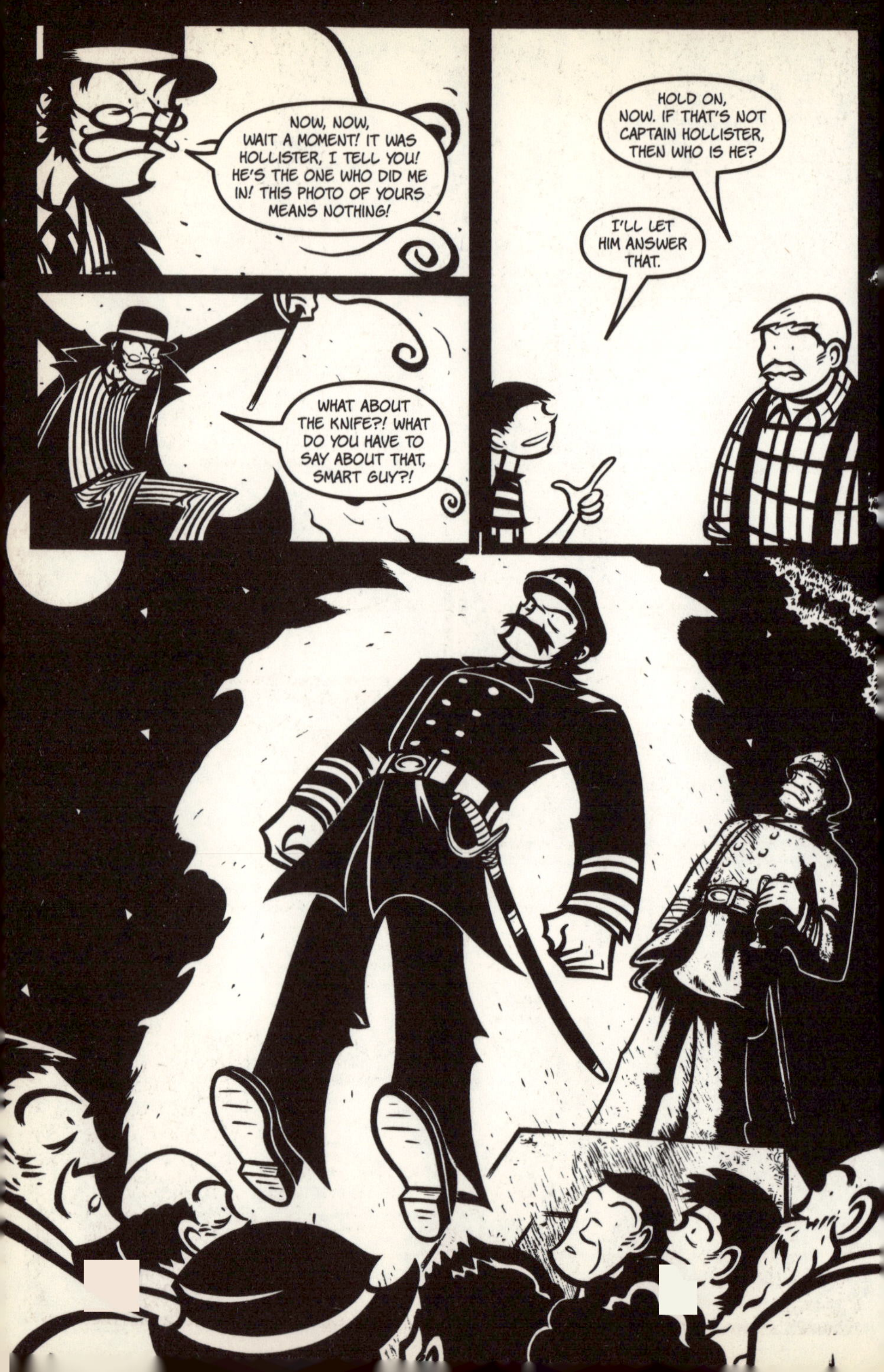
NOW, NOW, WAIT A MOMENT! IT WAS HOLLISTER, I TELL YOU! HE'S THE ONE WHO DID ME IN! THIS PHOTO OF YOURS MEANS NOTHING!
WHAT ABOUT THE KNIFE?! WHAT DO YOU HAVE TO SAY ABOUT THAT, SMART GUY?!
HOLD ON, NOW. IF THAT'S NOT CAPTAIN HOLLISTER, THEN WHO IS HE?
I'LL LET HIM ANSWER THAT.

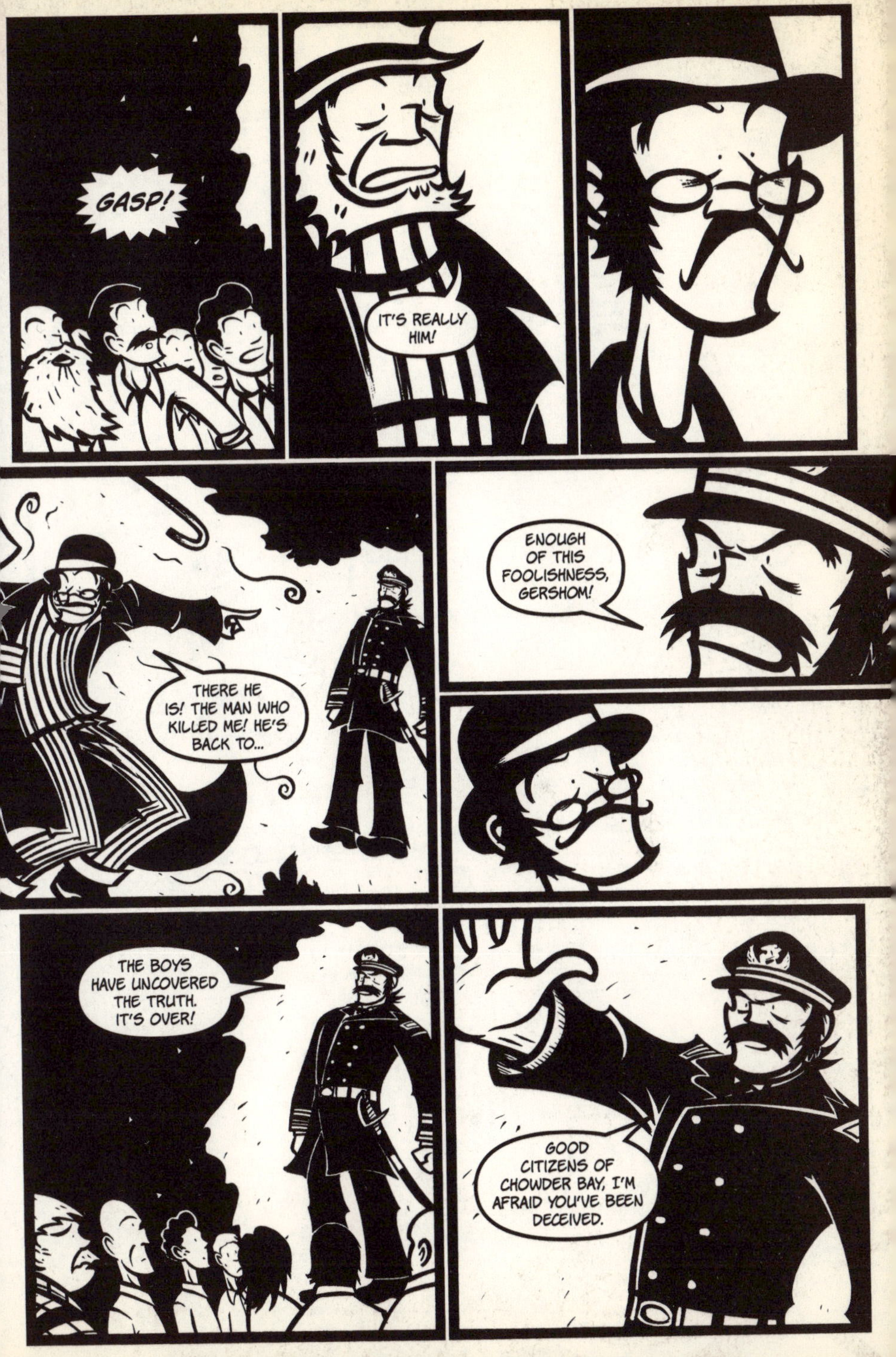
GASP!
IT'S REALLY HIM!
THERE HE IS! THE MAN WHO KILLED ME! HE'S BACK TO...
ENOUGH OF THIS FOOLISHNESS, GERSHOM!
THE BOYS HAVE UNCOVERED THE TRUTH. IT'S OVER!
GOOD CITIZENS OF CHOWDER BAY, I'M AFRAID YOU'VE BEEN DECEIVED.

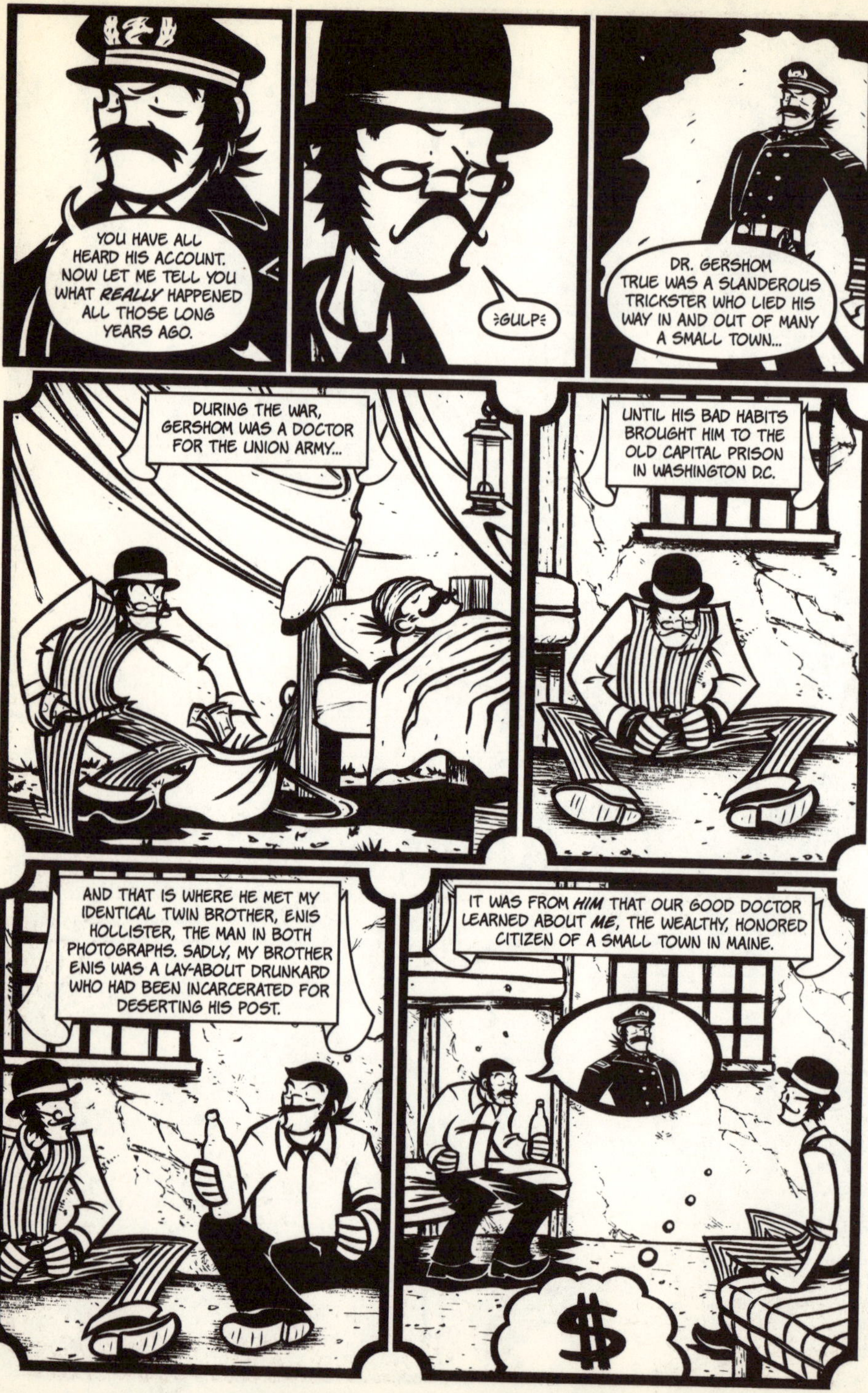
YOU HAVE ALL HEARD HIS ACCOUNT. NOW LET ME TELL YOU WHAT *REALLY* HAPPENED ALL THOSE LONG YEARS AGO.
GULP
DR. GERSHOM TRUE WAS A SLANDEROUS TRICKSTER WHO LIED HIS WAY IN AND OUT OF MANY A SMALL TOWN...
DURING THE WAR, GERSHOM WAS A DOCTOR FOR THE UNION ARMY...
UNTIL HIS BAD HABITS BROUGHT HIM TO THE OLD CAPITAL PRISON IN WASHINGTON D.C.
AND THAT IS WHERE HE MET MY IDENTICAL TWIN BROTHER, ENIS HOLLISTER, THE MAN IN BOTH PHOTOGRAPHS. SADLY, MY BROTHER ENIS WAS A LAY-ABOUT DRUNKARD WHO HAD BEEN INCARCERATED FOR DESERTING HIS POST.
IT WAS FROM *HIM* THAT OUR GOOD DOCTOR LEARNED ABOUT *ME*, THE WEALTHY, HONORED CITIZEN OF A SMALL TOWN IN MAINE.
$

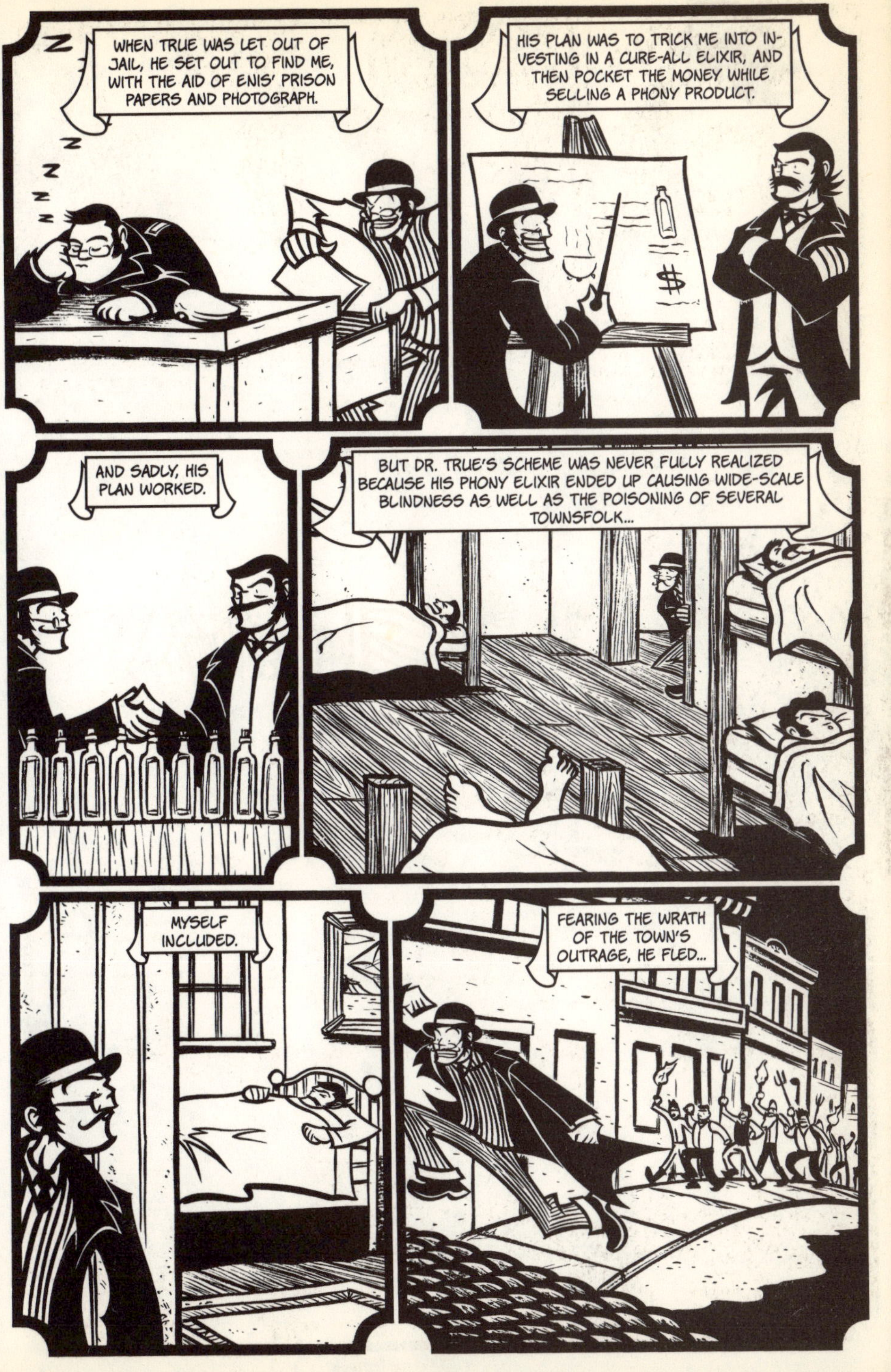
Z
Z
Z
Z
Z
WHEN TRUE WAS LET OUT OF JAIL, HE SET OUT TO FIND ME, WITH THE AID OF ENIS' PRISON PAPERS AND PHOTOGRAPH.
HIS PLAN WAS TO TRICK ME INTO INVESTING IN A CURE-ALL ELIXIR, AND THEN POCKET THE MONEY WHILE SELLING A PHONY PRODUCT.
$
AND SADLY, HIS PLAN WORKED.
BUT DR. TRUE'S SCHEME WAS NEVER FULLY REALIZED BECAUSE HIS PHONY ELIXIR ENDED UP CAUSING WIDE-SCALE BLINDNESS AS WELL AS THE POISONING OF SEVERAL TOWNSFOLK...
MYSELF INCLUDED.
FEARING THE WRATH OF THE TOWN'S OUTRAGE, HE FLED...

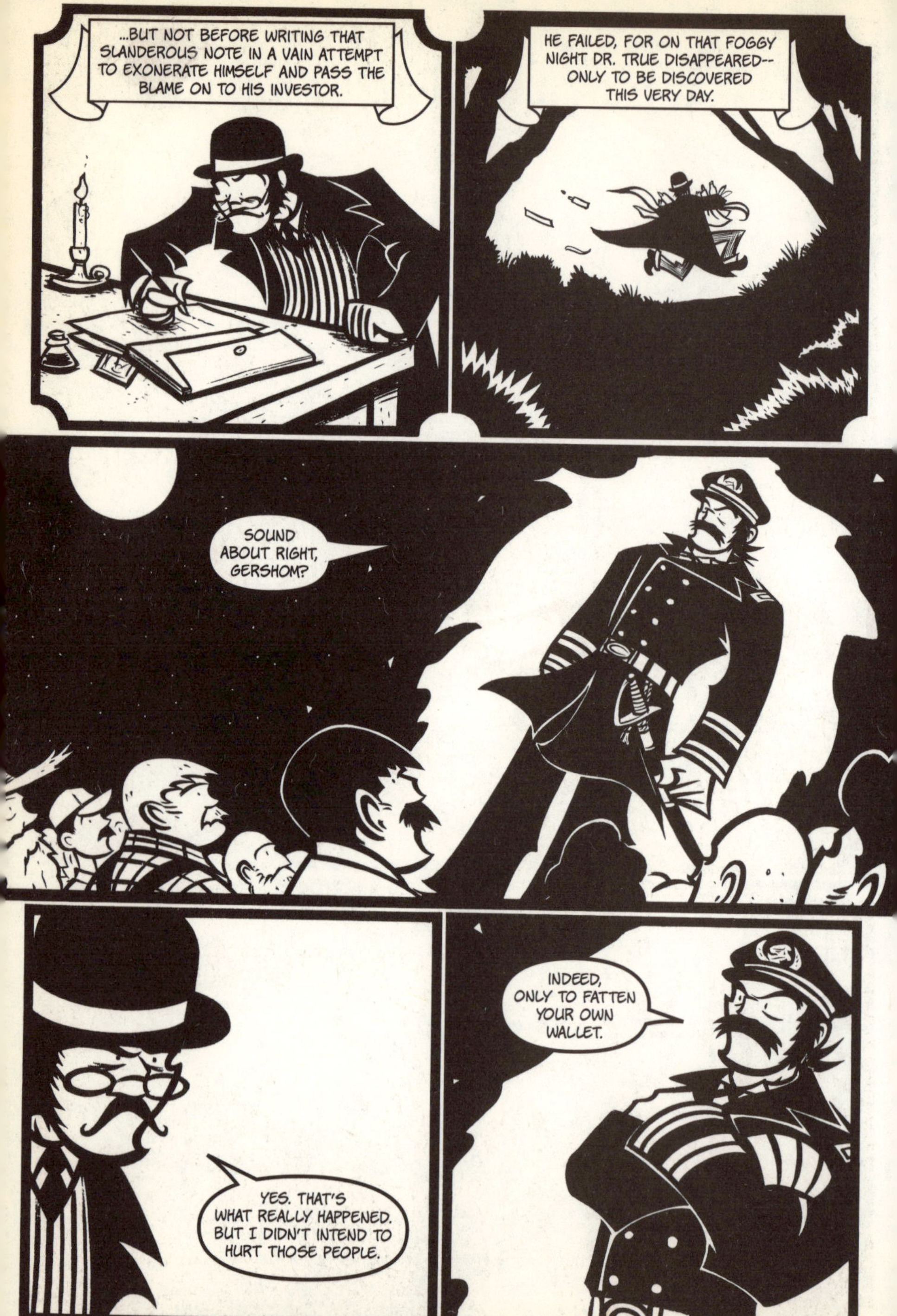
...BUT NOT BEFORE WRITING THAT SLANDEROUS NOTE IN A VAIN ATTEMPT TO EXONERATE HIMSELF AND PASS THE BLAME ON TO HIS INVESTOR.
HE FAILED, FOR ON THAT FOGGY NIGHT DR. TRUE DISAPPEARED-- ONLY TO BE DISCOVERED THIS VERY DAY.
SOUND ABOUT RIGHT, GERSHOM?
YES. THAT'S WHAT REALLY HAPPENED. BUT I DIDN'T INTEND TO HURT THOSE PEOPLE.
INDEED, ONLY TO FATTEN YOUR OWN WALLET.

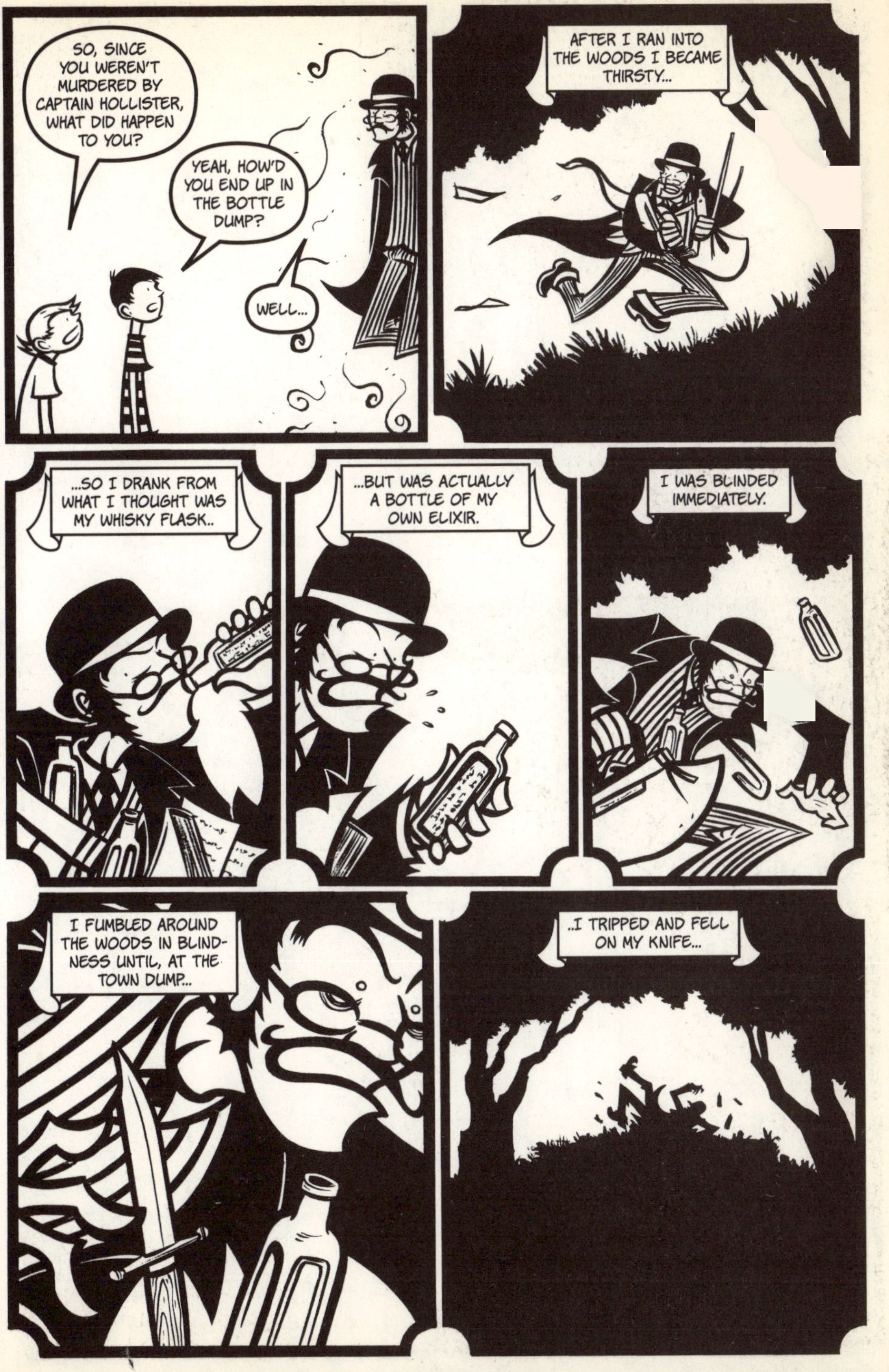
SO, SINCE YOU WEREN'T MURDERED BY CAPTAIN HOLLISTER, WHAT DID HAPPEN TO YOU?
YEAH, HOW'D YOU END UP IN THE BOTTLE DUMP?
WELL...
AFTER I RAN INTO THE WOODS I BECAME THIRSTY...
...SO I DRANK FROM WHAT I THOUGHT WAS MY WHISKY FLASK..
...BUT WAS ACTUALLY A BOTTLE OF MY OWN ELIXIR.
I WAS BLINDED IMMEDIATELY.
I FUMBLED AROUND THE WOODS IN BLINDNESS UNTIL, AT THE TOWN DUMP...
..I TRIPPED AND FELL ON MY KNIFE...

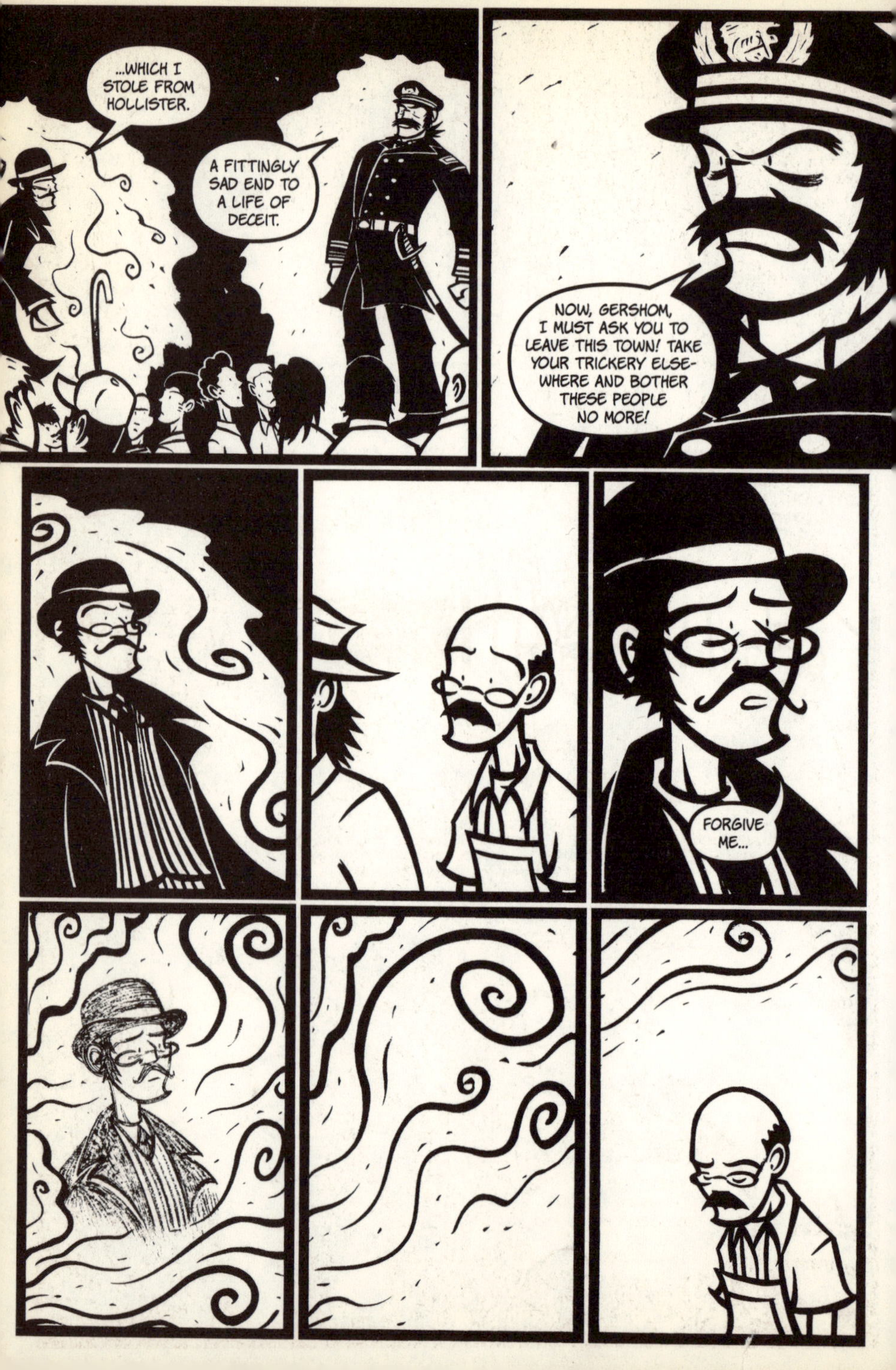
...WHICH I STOLE FROM HOLLISTER.
A FITTINGLY SAD END TO A LIFE OF DECEIT.
NOW, GERSHOM, I MUST ASK YOU TO LEAVE THIS TOWN! TAKE YOUR TRICKERY ELSE-WHERE AND BOTHER THESE PEOPLE NO MORE!
FORGIVE ME...

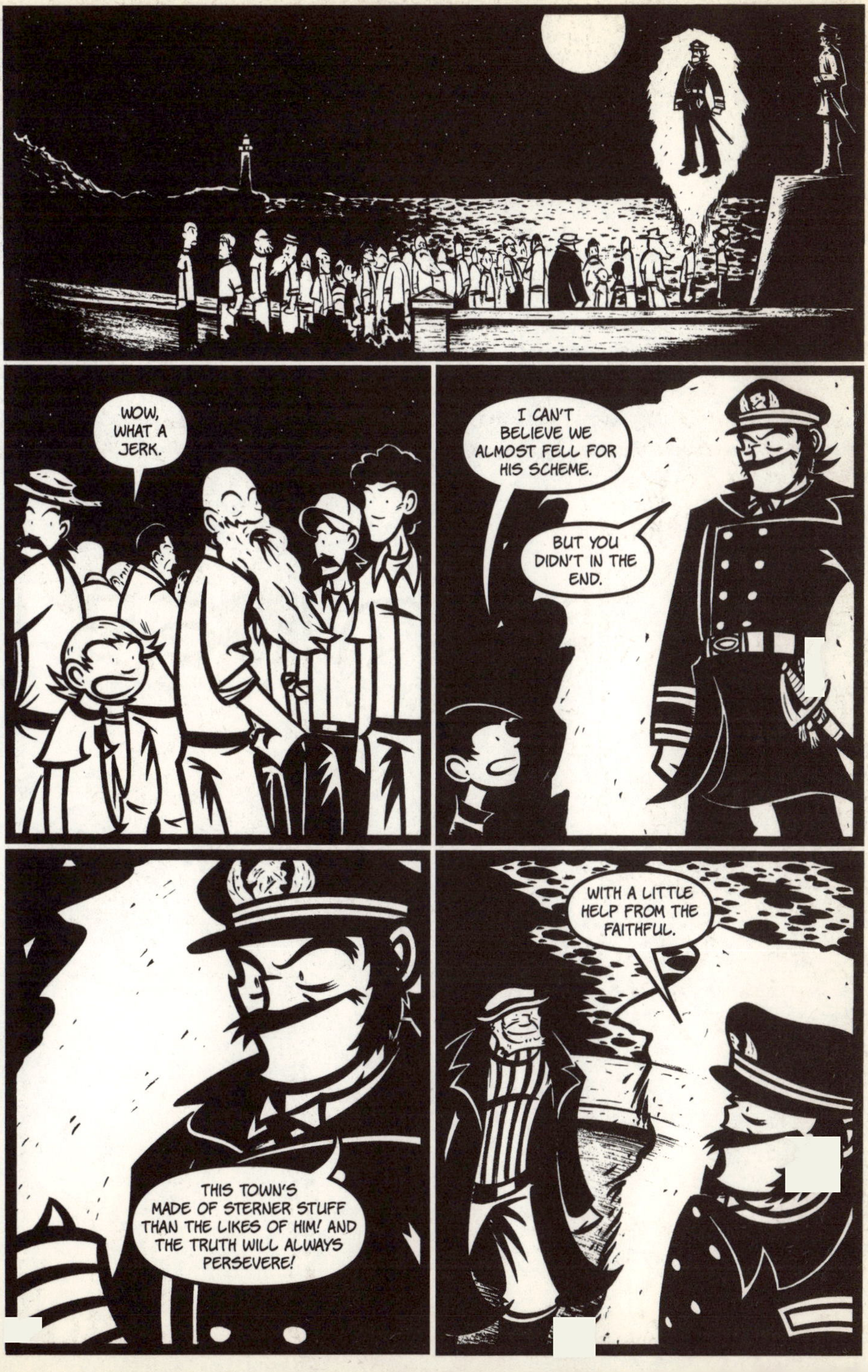
WOW, WHAT A JERK.
I CAN'T BELIEVE WE ALMOST FELL FOR HIS SCHEME.
BUT YOU DIDN'T IN THE END.
THIS TOWN'S MADE OF STERNER STUFF THAN THE LIKES OF HIM! AND THE TRUTH WILL ALWAYS PERSEVERE!
WITH A LITTLE HELP FROM THE FAITHFUL.

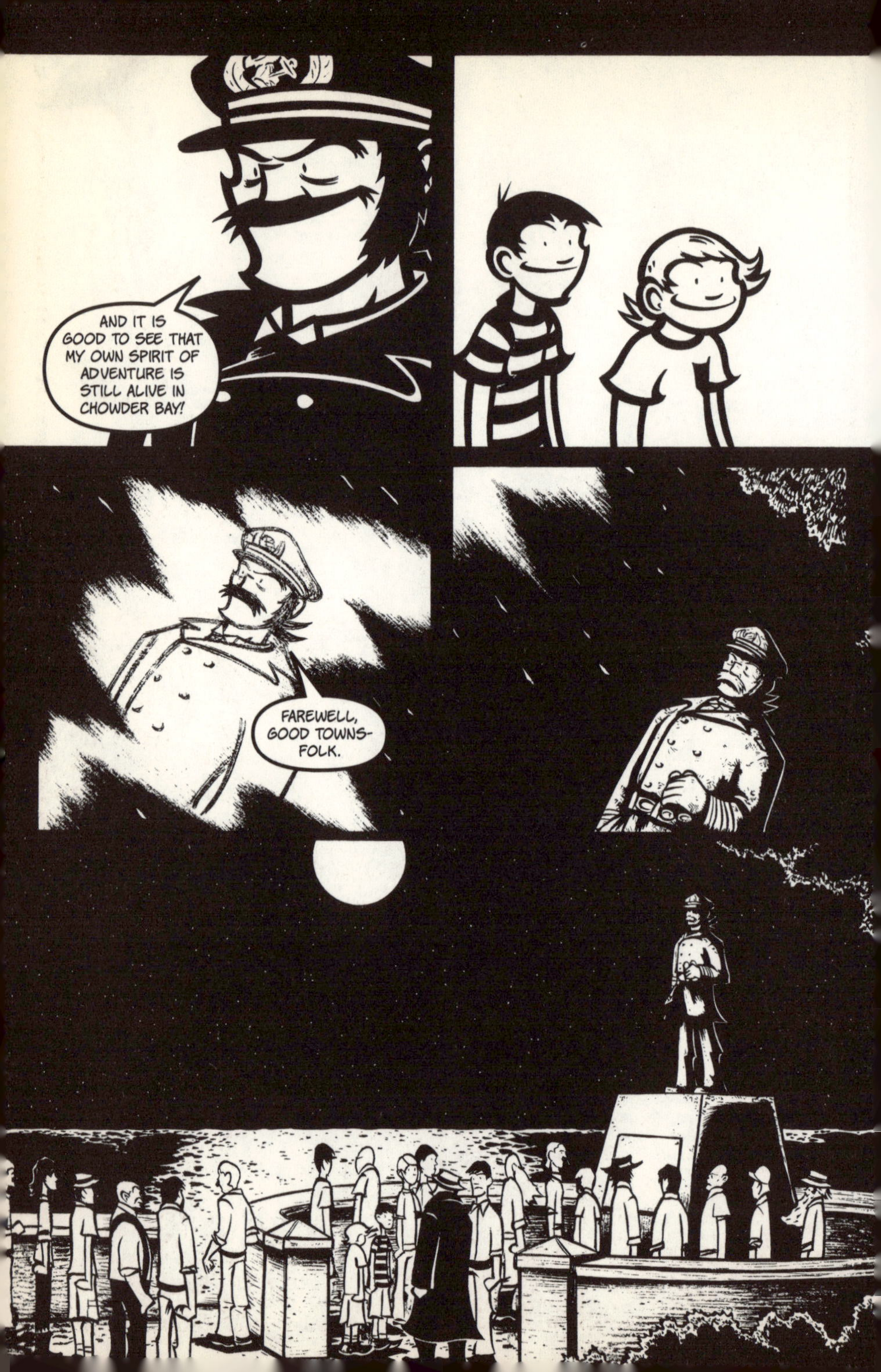
AND IT IS GOOD TO SEE THAT MY OWN SPIRIT OF ADVENTURE IS STILL ALIVE IN CHOWDER BAY!
FAREWELL, GOOD TOWNS-FOLK.

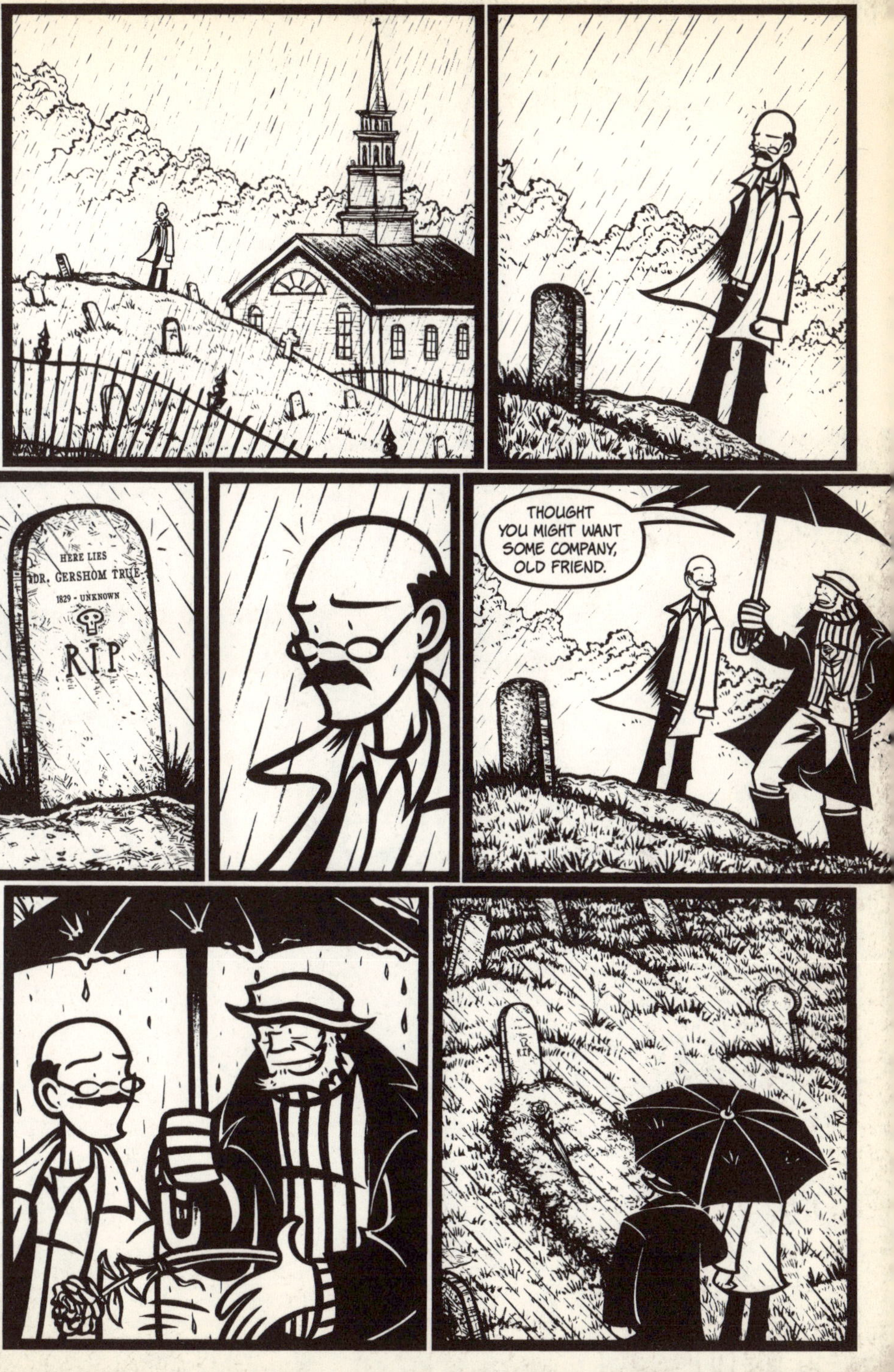
HERE LIES
DR. GERSHOM TRUE
1829 - UNKNOWN
RIP
THOUGHT YOU MIGHT WANT SOME COMPANY, OLD FRIEND.

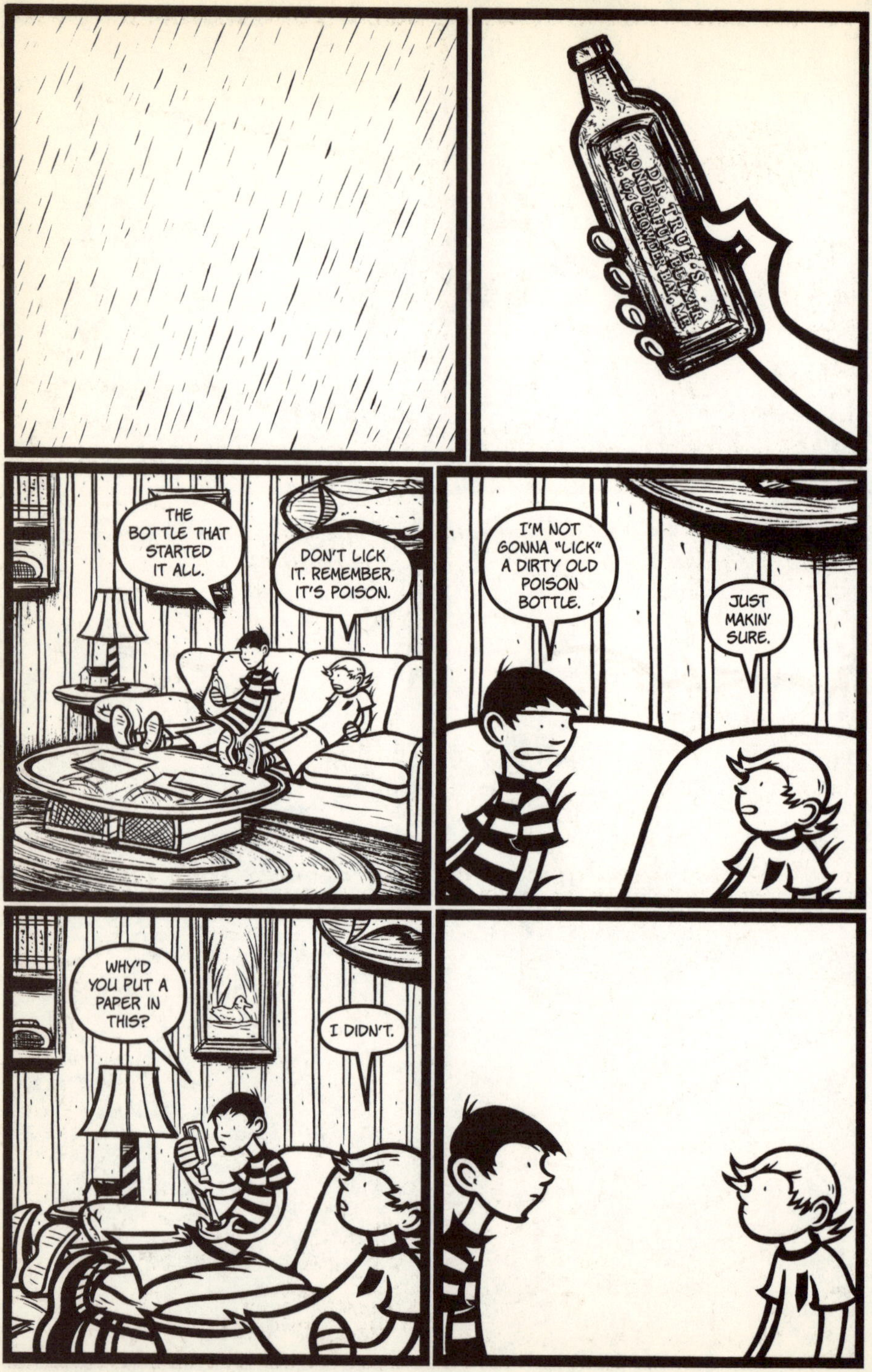
DR. TRUE'S
WONDERFUL ELIXIR
EST. 1876 CHOWDER BAY, ME
THE BOTTLE THAT STARTED IT ALL.
DON'T LICK IT. REMEMBER, IT'S POISON.
I'M NOT GONNA "LICK" A DIRTY OLD POISON BOTTLE.
JUST MAKIN' SURE.
WHY'D YOU PUT A PAPER IN THIS?
I DIDN'T.

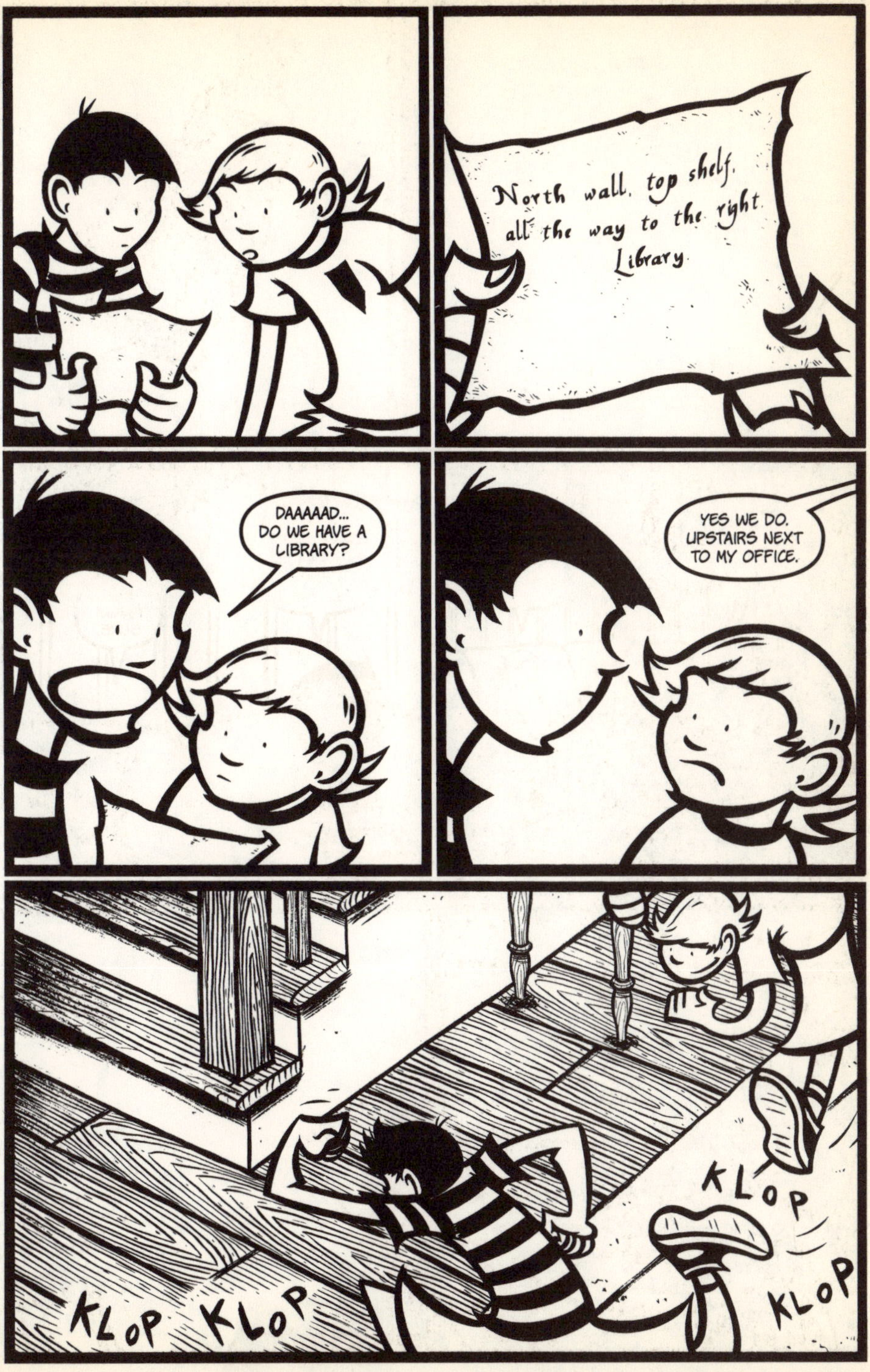
North wall, top shelf, all the way to the right. Library.
DAAAAAD... DO WE HAVE A LIBRARY?
YES WE DO. UPSTAIRS NEXT TO MY OFFICE.
KLOP KLOP
KLOP KLOP

WOAH!

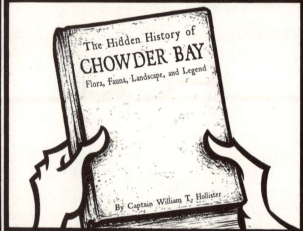

The Hidden History of
CHOWDER BAY
Flora, Fauna, Landscape, and Legend

By Captain William T. Hollister

May this book aid you
in all of your adventures.

Captain Hollister

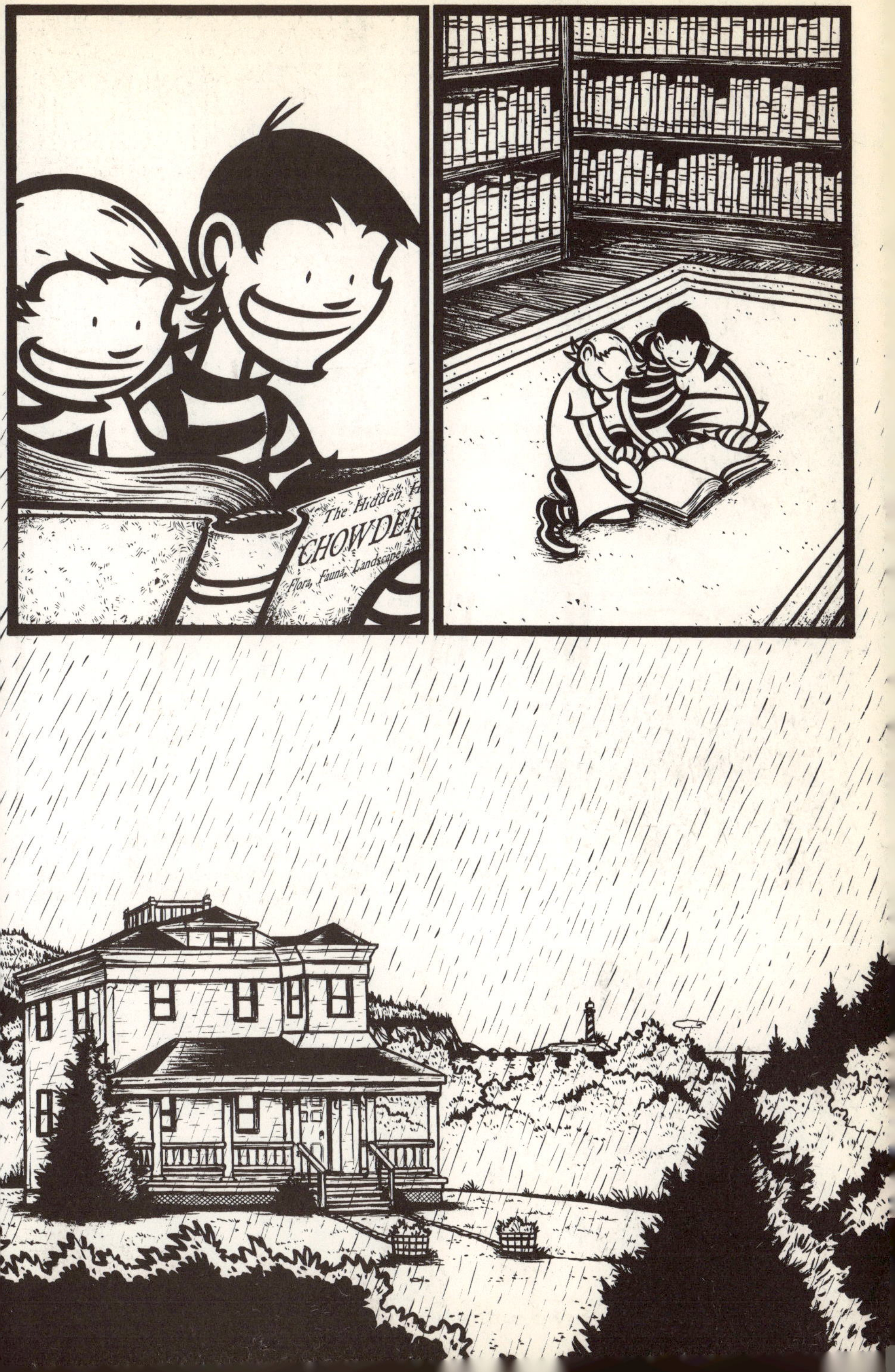
The Hidden
CHOWDER
Flora, Fauna,

Dedicated to Dan Loux

OTHER BOOKS FROM MATTHEW LOUX...

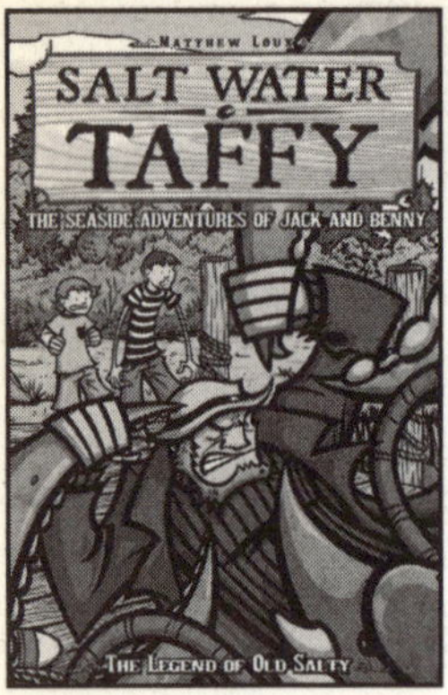

MATTHEW LOUX
SALT WATER TAFFY
THE SEASIDE ADVENTURES OF JACK AND BENNY
THE LEGEND OF OLD SALTY

SALT WATER TAFFY, THE SEASIDE ADVENTURES OF JACK AND BENNY, VOL. 1: "THE LEGEND OF OLD SALTY"

Written & Illustrated by Matthew Loux

96 pages, $5.95 US

ISBN: 978-1-932664-94-2

SALT WATER TAFFY, THE SEASIDE ADVENTURES OF JACK AND BENNY, VOL. 2: "A CLIMB UP MT. BARNABAS"

Written & Illustrated by Matthew Loux

96 pages, $5.95 US

ISBN: 978-1-934964-03-3

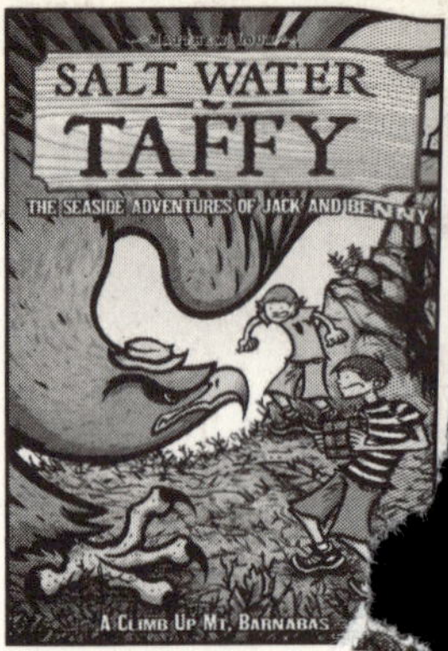

SALT WATER TAFFY
THE SEASIDE ADVENTURES OF JACK AND BENNY
A CLIMB UP MT. BARNABAS

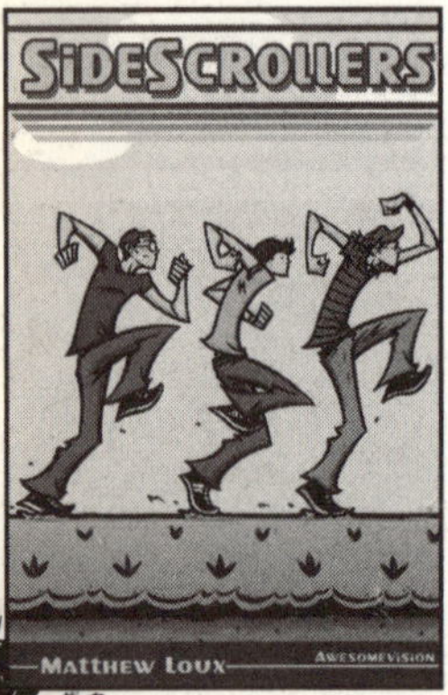

SIDESCROLLERS
MATTHEW LOUX
AWESOMEVISION

SIDESCROLLERS

Written & Illustrated by Matthew Loux

216 pages, $11.95 US

ISBN: 978-1-932664-50-8

F-STOP

Written by Antony Johnston

& Illustrated by Matthew Loux

168 pages, $14.95 US

ISBN: 978-1-932664-09-6

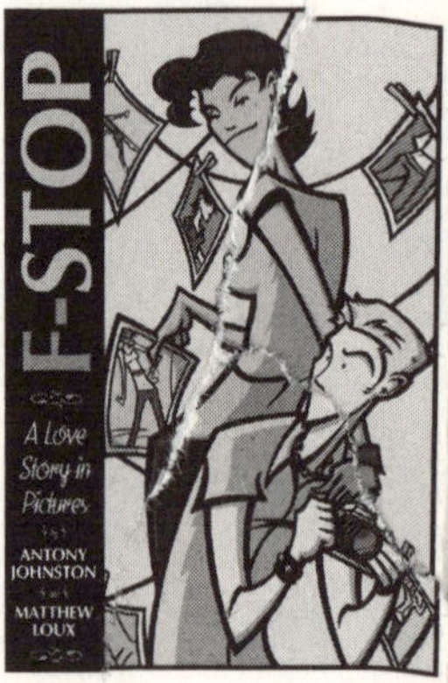

F-STOP
A Love Story in Pictures
ANTONY JOHNSTON
MATTHEW LOUX

Available at finer comics shops everywhere. For a comics store near you, call 1-888-COMIC-BOOK or visit www.comicshops.us.

For more Oni Press titles and information visit www.onipress.com.

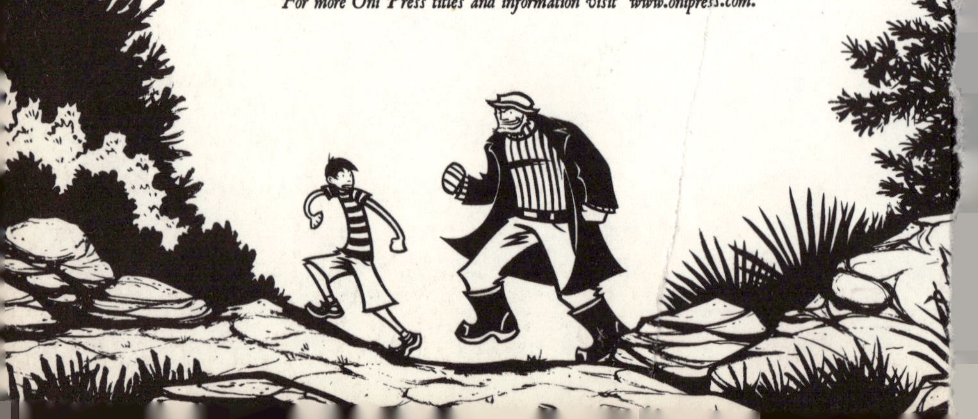